American Literature in Context

1865-1900

Andrew Hook

Routledge
Taylor & Francis Group
ROUTLEDGE REVIVALS

First published in 1983
by Methuen & Co Ltd

This edition first published in 2016 by Routledge
2 Park Square, Milton Park, Abingdon, Oxon, OX14 4RN
and by Routledge
711 Third Avenue, New York, NY 10017

Routledge is an imprint of the Taylor & Francis Group, an informa business

Publisher's Note
The publisher has gone to great lengths to ensure the quality of this reprint but points out that some imperfections in the original copies may be apparent.

Disclaimer
The publisher has made every effort to trace copyright holders and welcomes correspondence from those they have been unable to contact.

A Library of Congress record exists under LC control number: 81022302

ISBN 13: 978-1-138-69118-6 (hbk)
ISBN 13: 978-1-315-53581-4 (ebk)
ISBN 13: 978-1-138-69121-6 (pbk)
ISBN 13: 978-1-138-69132-2 (set hbk)
ISBN 13: 978-1-315-53545-6 (set ebk)

AMERICAN LITERATURE IN CONTEXT, III

1865–1900

ANDREW HOOK

METHUEN
LONDON AND NEW YORK

First published in 1983 by
Methuen & Co. Ltd
11 New Fetter Lane, London EC4P 4EE
Published in the USA by
Methuen & Co.
in association with Methuen, Inc.
733 Third Avenue, New York, NY 10017

Typeset by Scarborough Typesetting Services
Printed in Great Britain by
Richard Clay (The Chaucer Press) Ltd
Bungay, Suffolk

British Library Cataloguing in Publication Data

American literature in context.
3: 1865–1900
1. American literature—History and criticism
I. Hook, Andrew
810.9 PS88

ISBN 0–416–73680–7

Library of Congress Cataloging in Publication Data

(Revised for volume 3)
Main entry under title:
American literature in context.
Includes bibliographies and indexes.
Contents: —v. 3. 1865–1900 / Andrew Hook
—v. 4. 1900–1930 / Ann Massa.
1. American literature—History and criticism—
Addresses, essays, lectures. I. Goldman, Arnold.
II. Hook, Andrew. III. Massa, Ann.
PS92.A425 1982 810'.9 81–22302

ISBN 0–416–73920–2 (v. 4)
ISBN 0–416–73930–X (pbk.: v. 4)

Routledge Revivals

American Literature in Context

First published between 1982 and 1983, this series examines the peculiarly American cultural context out of which the nation's literature has developed.

Covering the years from 1865 to 1900, this third volume of *American Literature in Context* focuses on the struggles of American writers to make sense of their rapidly changing world. In addition to such major figures as Walt Whitman, Henry James, Emily Dickinson and Mark Twain, it analyses the writings of an unorthodox economist (Henry George), a Utopian reformer (Edward Bellamy) and a critical sociologist (Thorstein Veblen). Particular attention is paid to the challenge to conventional literary and cultural values represented by writers such as William Dean Howell who pursued a new form of scientific, democratic realism in American writing.

This book will be of interest to those studying American literature and American studies.

Contents

	General Editor's Preface	ix
	Introduction	1
1	Walt Whitman	10
2	Henry George	24
3	Henry James	38
4	Emily Dickinson	56
5	Mark Twain	69
6	William Dean Howells	84
7	Edward Bellamy	100
8	Hamlin Garland	115
9	Stephen Crane	129
10	Harold Frederic	143
11	Frank Norris	154
12	Kate Chopin	165
13	Thorstein Veblen	178
14	Theodore Dreiser	191
	Index	204

For Sarah, Caspar and Nathaniel

*And with special thanks to Miss Irene Elsey,
an invaluable typist.*

General Editor's Preface

The object of the *American Literature in Context* series is to offer students of the literature and culture of the United States a coherent, consecutive and comprehensive sequence of interpretations of major American texts – fiction and non-fiction, poetry and drama.

Each chapter is prefaced by an extract from the chosen text which serves as a springboard for wider discussion and analysis. The intention of each analysis is to demonstrate how students can move into and then from the pages of literature in front of them to a consideration of the whole text from which the extract is taken, and thence to an understanding of the author's *oeuvre* and of the cultural moment in which he or she lived and wrote. The extract and its interpretation *ground* the wider interpretation: students need not just take the critic's overall view on trust, but can test it against the extract from the primary text.

The selection of texts is intended to represent the critic's choice from the variety, quality and interest of important American writing in the period. In these essays students can see how a literary and cultural critic responds to the page of writing before him or her, and how sustained critical response to particular passages can be linked to broader analyses of texts, authors, culture and society. With this integrated format, students can better see how background material relates to the text and *vice versa*. While the chapters are not precisely intended as models for students to imitate, those who are learning to write about literature are encouraged to treat extracts of their own choosing in a comparable manner, relating the particular response to wider matters.

Arnold Goldman

Introduction

The period from the American Civil War to the opening of the twentieth century has on the face of it an obvious unity. From every point of view the Civil War marked a turning-point in American history. From the earliest days of the new republic, foreign observers of the American scene, many of them of course hostile to the very existence of a free and democratic United States, had been predicting that the existence of slavery in the Southern states would in the end bring about the total collapse of this republican society and its institutions. That collapse had seemed to occur, but the victory of the North in the Civil War ensured the survival of the United States in a manner that could be seen as a vindication of its original principles. But five years of bitter and bloody war inevitably produced changes. One era in America's life was over, a new one about to begin. Equally clearly 1900 strikes us as a new beginning: 'Nation Greets Century's Dawn,' as John Dos Passos's first 'Newsreel' in *USA* has it. A new century demands a sense of both of endings and of beginnings.

But however clearly 1865–1900 may appear to define a "period" in American history, the years between these dates were in no way characterized by cohesion, coherence, or unity of any kind. Their essence rather was rapid, sweeping, and violent change. Here in these years are to be found the roots of the conventional stereotype of American society as dynamic, fast-moving, constantly altering, rootless and restless. Here in these years the brawling, sprawling, powerful, but self-contradictory giant of America – the America that we still recognize today – was born. Yet the birth-pangs of this new America occurred in the context of an older world that did not disappear overnight. Despite the Civil War and its aftermath, the America of the earlier nineteenth century is in no absolute sense cut off from the America of the 1860s, 1870s, and beyond. In different areas of American life the currents of history flowed at quite different speeds.

America's literary culture, for example, was slow to register the scale and scope of the radical changes transforming so many aspects of American society after the Civil War. Even as late as 1900 there were powerful, conservative forces in America's cultural life reluctant to admit that old, ante-bellum America, with its traditional attitudes, values, and structures of thought and feeling, had finally passed away. Of course a nostalgia for an older, lost America remained a potent force in American culture in the 1920s and 1930s, and one may doubt whether it has entirely lost its power even today, but in 1900 representatives of that older tradition still exercised considerable authority within many of America's cultural institutions and within many areas of America's cultural experience. The entire social, economic, and political bases of American life may have been rapidly changing, but for many it was imperative that American culture should continue to enshrine the values of the traditional past.

Such an attempt to resist the movement of history could not be finally successful. And indeed it is a basic assumption of the series of books of which this volume is part that the literature and culture of a society cannot be understood in isolation from the wider social, economic, political, religious, and other forces, be they conservative or revolutionary, at work within that society. America's literary culture between 1865 and 1900 is then inevitably involved in the pattern of radical social change occurring between these dates. But within this period, as within others, the links between literature and society are not always immediately obvious; the literature and the society are not mere reflections of each other. Thus it took time for America's writers to begin to recognize the kinds of change in their society which had been occurring with often bewildering speed since the close of the Civil War. By 1900, however, not even the most conservative of Americans could deny that since 1865 their country had been undergoing the most massive and alarming transformation.

*

Just how massive can be indicated by a few statistics. In 1860 the population of America was under 40 million; by 1900 that figure had doubled. This population explosion was partly caused by a vast, new wave of immigration reaching America's shores: around 1900 immigration was running at a level of almost one million a year. In 1860, 60 per cent of the working population of America worked on farms,

26 per cent in industry and transport; in 1900 only 37 per cent worked on farms, while 46 per cent worked in industry and transport. Again, between 1860 and 1900 the towns and cities of America grew at twice the speed of the nation as a whole. By 1900 a third of Americans lived in towns or cities, while New York, Philadelphia, and Chicago all had more than a million inhabitants. Before the Civil War America had contained very few really rich men – John Jacob Astor, who left 20 million dollars in 1848, was an exceptional figure. Not much more than a generation later, Andrew Carnegie enjoyed an *annual* income of 25 million dollars; when he retired, Carnegie sold out his business interests for 450 million dollars. By 1900 a whole new order of wealth had been created in America, however inequitably it was distributed.

All of these developments were themselves the consequence of one basic factor: the scope and speed of economic growth in post-Civil War America. From about 1870 the United States experienced the most rapid rate of industrialization that the world had ever known. As one historian puts it: 'Overnight, it seemed, this nation of farmers and horse traders had mastered the intricate mysteries of a technical civilization.'* Thus in 1918 Gertrude Stein could explain to the French that America was the oldest country in the world because it had entered the twentieth century in the 1880s. Certainly by then the US was becoming the pacemaker among the world's industrial nations, and by 1900 she had emerged as the most advanced industrial power in the world: not only did she lead the world in the production of raw materials and foodstuffs, but by then she had overtaken both Britain and Germany in manufacturing as well. This startling economic growth was the springboard creating all the other profound changes which were transforming America. Now more than ever, it was the prospect of a better life in material terms that persuaded millions of Europeans to try their luck in the New World. These immigrants in turn helped to swell the rapidly-growing towns and cities of America, and to provide labour for her booming industries. The accelerating pace of economic life led to the drive for the completion of the transcontinental railroads and so to the closing of the moving frontier, so long a crucial factor in the American experience. Better communications made possible a faster exploitation of natural resources – oil, coal, timber, wheat, copper – and ensured the emergence of huge commercial corporations taking over the best farming, mining, forest and range land. Big business, monopolies, trusts – long before 1900 these had become the dominant powers in

* Frank Thistlethwaite, *The Great Experiment*, Cambridge, 1961, p. 213.

American society. By 1900, that is, the old Jeffersonian dream of an agrarian America populated by self-reliant, independent farmers had disappeared for ever. Indeed farmers and farming had become early victims of the new America of business trusts and corporations. Whatever contemporaries may have believed, hoped, or preferred, by the end of the nineteenth century the rhythms of American life had become not those of seasonal growth and change, but the pounding rhythms of the railroad and the industrial machine.

*

How did American culture respond to these changes? For a surprising number of years it broadly refused to acknowledge them. Thus in the early post-Civil War decades the role of what might be called "establishment" American culture was largely to reassure society that in the crucial areas of personal values, morality, and beliefs, nothing had changed. More surprisingly, perhaps, a similar complacency was shown towards the new power structures which the transformation of America's economic and business life was producing. For most of the period 1865–1900 capitalist America could rely on approval rather than criticism from the cultural standard-bearers of its society.

On the face of it this is astonishing. There were so many problems, so much that seemed obviously wrong: the pace of urbanization, business and political corruption, immense inequalities in the distribution of the country's new wealth, and the irresponsible use of riches by the few who possessed them. None the less, the truth is that for much of the period after 1865, protest was muted. The essential explanation, perhaps, is that traditional American values could be seen as authenticating what was taking place. America after all was the land of opportunity; the American was the self-reliant, self-made man; America offered every man the opportunity to succeed, to improve his lot by his own hard work. Such ideas were part and parcel of the American Dream. So entrenched were they that in the 1860s, 1870s, and 1880s, America's business and industrial leaders hardly needed to make any kind of defence of their activities.

While traditional American values seemed to ratify current practices, contemporary American religion and philosophy were equally ready to rally to the defence of the *status quo*. As early as 1862 the president of Williams College was ready to defend the acquisitive impulse as socially beneficial: 'As men now are, it is far better that they should be employed in accumulating property honestly, to be spent reasonably, if not nobly, than that there should be encouraged any sentimentalism about the worthlessness of property, or any tendency to a merely contemplative and quietistic life, which has so often been either the result or the cause of inefficiency or idleness.' Others were soon prepared to express similar views more forcibly. According to J. G. Holland, 'There always will be rich men and there always ought to be rich men.' In 1877, Henry Ward Beecher, one of the most popular of American clergymen of the period, declared that 'God has intended the great to be great and the little to be little.' But the extraordinary alliance between religion and big business is perhaps best illustrated by the career of the Baptist clergyman Russell Conwell. In a public lecture called 'Acres of Diamonds' Conwell argued that since money was essential to the doing of good then all good Christians should endeavour to get rich: 'I say get rich, get rich!' By delivering this lecture six thousand times Conwell himself did – and went on to found Temple University in Philadelphia.

American philosophy came equally to the defence of the new capitalism. For much of the nineteenth century, mainstream American philosophy – what was taught in colleges, universities, seminaries – was a naturalized version of the old Scottish "common-sense" philosophy, with its basically reassuring message of the soundness of traditional notions of morality and religious faith. One of the strengths of this philosophical mode had always been its capacity to unite traditional values with more modern concepts of rationality. In the decades preceding the Civil War the more exciting theories of Transcendentalism had captured the minds and hearts of a younger generation of Americans. But the optimistic, visionary tone of Transcendentalism hardly survived the turmoil of the Civil War. In succeeding decades American philosophy reverted to its essentially conservative social role. For a time, in America as elsewhere, the ideas of Darwin and his followers seemed to create problems for upholders of traditional Christian beliefs, but the work of John Fiske and others soon persuaded most Americans that there was no serious collision between the notion of evolution and a progressive Christianity. When, towards the end of the 1865–1900 period, protests at last began to grow over the unrestrained activities of the business interest in America, American philosophy was ready to play a conciliatory role.

Crucial in this connexion proved to be the ideas of the English philosopher Herbert Spencer. Spencer took over Darwin's evolutionary principles and applied them to the study of human society. His views made little impact in Britain but in America they were widely influential. That the doctrine of 'the survival of the fittest' could be appropriately applied to contemporary human society was inevitably music in the ears of all upholders of the *laissez-faire* principle of American capitalism. Spencer seemed to place the mark of intellectual respectability, and philosophical approval, on their activities. Philosophy then, like Christianity, offered convenient endorsement of what was going on in American society rather than presenting any kind of challenge to it.

*

By and large, America's literary culture for most of the period 1865–1900 was equally reluctant to confront what was happening within the country. In terms of popular appeal the books that did best were books of a sentimental, romantic, idealizing kind which offered no vestige of a threat to existing social attitudes, convention, or structures. Indeed it has been argued that the general level of America's literary taste in this period was bad – and getting worse. Of the fifty-three most popular books between 1877 and 1893, eleven were the work of authors of literary merit (five were by Mark Twain, two by Thomas Hardy, two by Leo Tolstoy, one each by Edward Bellamy and Henry George). Of the seventy-three most popular books between 1898 and 1914, only three were of literary merit. According to a different system of computation, best-sellers in the decade 1880–9 included two books by Twain, one by Tolstoy, and one by Bellamy. The twenty-one best-sellers for the decade 1900–9 included no works of literary worth.

But perhaps these figures are misleading. As we have seen, the America of the 1870s, 1880s and 1890s, was a very different place, peopled by a different kind of American, than the old America of the early nineteenth century. Perhaps it should be no surprise to discover that the general level of literary taste was not particularly high. Given the nature and speed of the changes transforming American society in the post-Civil War period, perhaps the real surprise is not a sense of cultural decline but evidence of cultural vitality and progress. Museums, art galleries, libraries, and symphony orchestras were established; illiteracy declined from 17 per cent in 1880, to 13 per cent in 1890, to 11 per cent in 1900; Dickens sold better in the 1880s than in the 1860s; literary and popular magazines developed and expanded at an enormous rate. In 1865, some 700 of such magazines were published in America, by 1885 the figure was 3300. Their readership had also soared: by 1885 *Harper's Monthly* had a sale of

100,000 copies, while *The Century* (formerly *Scribner's Monthly*) achieved a circulation figure of 200,000.

Yet is is true that these flourishing magazines, powerful and influential as they were, were anything but revolutionary documents. Rather they were upholders of a respectable, genteel culture, and of a general conservatism of attitudes and values untouched by what was happening in the world surrounding them. What they promulgated were the values of old, established, middle-class America, and their overriding aim was to ensure that theirs were the cultural attitudes and assumptions that would remain the norm for America as a whole.

In the decades immediately following the Civil War, American literature was dominated by writers who had made their names before it: Emerson, Longfellow, Oliver Wendell Holmes, J. G. Whittier, James Russell Lowell, Charles Eliot Norton. All were New Englanders and the respect in which they were held reflected the continuing cultural dominance exercised by New England over the rest of the country. But at a deeper level these writers remained the dominating figures because they reassured Americans that nothing had changed. The war was over, and the old world survived unscathed. It was not until the 1880s and 1890s that these writers finally passed from the scene.

By then new voices were at last making themselves heard. But it is as late as this – the 1880s and 1890s – before American literature can be said to have moved decisively into a new phase of development. Admittedly there had been earlier signs of change. Not long after the end of the Civil War a new concept entered America's literary culture which quickly became the rallying-cry of all those writers who in however modest a fashion felt the need to modify the existing conventions of American writing. That concept was realism. Realism became identified with the way forward for American writing. But it is important to note that the new realism was less a protest against the conservative New England establishment – though it is true that the new school of realist writing tended to be identified with the Middle West or frontier America – than against the contemporary, popular sentimental mode in American fiction. As we have noted, popular American fiction in the post-Civil War decades was of a highly romantic, idealizing nature. The enormously popular novels of such writers as Mrs E. D. E. N. Southworth, Susan Warner, and Elizabeth Ward reflected not life as it was, but life as its readers would have liked it to be. It was above all against this idealizing tendency that realism initially took its stand.

In the realist crusade, William Dean Howells quickly became the central figure. With the emergence of Howellsian realism – a realism committed to the faithful rendering of the ordinary, unexceptional, everyday realities of American life, American literature had clearly begun to move in a new direction. But the realism of Howells, however important as a new departure, was limited in its nature. Compared with the popular, sentimental tradition of novel-writing, it could fairly claim to be more democratic (because it was concerned with the lives of ordinary Americans) and more scientific (it had evolved as a natural response to the changed circumstances of American life). But at least in its early phase, the realism pioneered by Howells was no more able to cope with the massive issues and problems facing American society in the post-bellum decades than any other literary mode. In time, however, American realism gained in authority and power. As the scale and scope of America's social problems became increasingly obvious, and as disquiet over them became increasingly widespread, a new generation of realist writers emerged whose aim was to shape and form an imaginative response to the troubled America in which they lived. Thus it was that in the 1880s and 1890s a literature of protest at last began to make itself heard in America. And so prevalent did this movement become that by 1900 serious American literature had redefined itself as a literature of social protest and reform, with realism in some form as its dominant mode of expression.

The relative slowness with which realism developed in the period 1865–1900 explains why so large a proportion of the texts examined in this volume date from the second half of the period. It is broadly true to say that in its first half, American literature was marking time. The massive changes that were going to re-make American life and society were picking up speed from the earliest years of the period; but American writing was slow to register them. Realism emerged, like so many other new forms of aesthetic expression, as a gamble on the future; but it took time for that gamble to prove a winner. Quite suddenly in the 1880s and 1890s it happens: a new literature in a new mode defining new realities is everywhere in evidence as American authors struggle to make sense of the world around them.

In the structuralist and post-structuralist criticism of today, realism is conventionally seen as the expressive mode most closely linked to the ideology of industrial capitalism. The story that this volume tells hardly supports that view. In the literary culture of nineteenth-century America, realism, whatever its origins, became the chosen mode of those writers least willing to accept the social and economic order of the capitalist America of their time. And by 1900 just such a repudiation of the economic arrangements of the society that sustained them was the almost unanimous response of America's major writers. No doubt there are ways other than this of reading the story of American literature between 1865 and 1900, other contexts in which it can be seen. But the socio-economic one, inextricably linked in terms of literary form to the rise of realism, unquestionably meshes in with the aims and attitudes of the authors themselves, and the criticial cultural debates in which they were centrally involved.

The period 1865–1900 contained no single decade as imaginatively creative as the 1850s or 1920s in America. And it is significant that the greatest writer of the period, Henry James, chose to spend most of his life in Europe. But the age that saw the birth of the America we recognize today did finally produce a significant body of literature with its own new and distinctive features. What we find in the literature of the 1880s and 1890s is above all a powerful sense of individual and social crisis, of intense moral and spiritual insecurity, of doubt and pessimism over the direction in which American society is moving, even of a loss of faith in the future of liberal, democratic culture. What we read, that is, is a literature which struggles to reflect and understand the turbulence and tension of the years between 1865 and 1900.

Further reading

Ray Ginger, *The Age of Excess, The United States from 1877 to 1914*, New York and London, 1965.

H. Wayne Morgan (ed.), *The Gilded Age, A Reappraisal*, Syracuse, NY, 1963.

John Tomsich, *A Genteel Endeavour, American Culture and Politics in the Gilded Age*, Stanford, 1971.

I

Walt Whitman (1819–92)

Passing the visions, passing the night,
Passing, unloosing the hold of my comrades' hands,
Passing the song of the hermit bird and the tallying song of
  my soul,
Victorious song, death's outlet song, yet varying
  ever-altering song,
As low and wailing, yet clear the notes, rising and falling,
  flooding the night,
Sadly sinking and fainting, as warning and warning, and yet
  again bursting with joy,
Covering the earth and filling the spread of the heaven,
As that powerful psalm in the night I heard from recesses,
Passing, I leave thee lilac with heart-shaped leaves,
I leave thee there in the door-yard, blooming, returning
  with spring.

I cease from my song for thee,
From my gaze on thee in the west, fronting the west,
  communing with thee,
O comrade lustrous with silver face in the night.

Yet each to keep and all, retrievements out of the night,
The song, the wondrous chant of the gray-brown bird,
And the tallying chant, the echo arous'd in my soul,
With the lustrous and drooping star with the countenance
  full of woe,
With the holders holding my hand nearing the call of the
  bird,
Comrades mine and I in the midst, and their memory ever
  to keep, for the dead I loved so well,

For the sweetest, wisest soul of all my days and lands –
and this for his dear sake,
Lilac and star and bird twined with the chant of my soul,
There in the fragrant pines and the cedars dusk and dim.

From 'When Lilacs Last in the Dooryard Bloom'd',
16th and concluding section (1865)[1]

* * *

In these concluding stanzas Whitman is reluctantly relinquishing his hold on his poem, releasing its central images of lilac, star, and bird from the visionary process that has woven them together in mournful and rapturous memorialization of the death of President Lincoln. Yet releasing them, he is also retaining them – 'each to keep and all, retrievements out of the night' – because, through the unfolding process of the poem, these images have been moulded into a permanent memorial of 'the sweetest, wisest soul of all my days and lands.' So, at the last, the poem dedicates itself to Lincoln – 'and this for his dear sake' – rehearsing and reiterating its own constituent parts, its central, recurring images (lilac, star, and bird) 'twined' within the creative process itself – 'the chant of my soul' – and set, as throughout, in the sensuous richness of 'fragrant pines' and 'cedars dusk and dim.' In its sense of a simultaneous releasing and retaining, of a process continuing and stilled, of a parting requiem in which the parting retains a sense of vitality, even urgency, so that retention, stillness, requiem, seem long drawn-out, not quite at rest, this ending sums up more than the central qualities of 'When Lilacs Last in the Dooryard Bloom'd'. It also suggests how Whitman, at his best, can achieve the authority and poise, the *gravitas*, of the great poet.

*

All of Whitman's poetry went to make up *Leaves of Grass* which had been first published in 1855. After 1855, *Leaves of Grass* went through a continuous process of development and expansion paralleling the growth of Whitman's creative life. In the years that followed, new groups or collections of poems were separately published, but at different points all of these were incorporated within *Leaves of Grass*. In its pattern of growth and development, *Leaves of Grass* thus enacts the notion of the poetic process central to Whitman's idea of poetry.

Whitman never lost a transcendental sense of the unity of all things; all of life and experience, reality itself, were process, a ceaseless, continuing, all-embracing flow. This is the fundamental principle that underlies and explains Whitman's rejection of the traditional forms and structures of nineteenth-century poetry; such forms and structures are at odds with the notion of poetry as process; they impose rigidity and completeness upon the reality which is in fact constantly unfolding. And this in turn explains how Whitman could describe *Leaves of Grass* as 'a passage way to something rather than a thing in itself concluded'.[2] There can be no conclusion to the poem that is reality itself. The somewhat modernist aesthetic principle involved here is not one entirely alien to the American literary tradition. In *Moby Dick*, for example, at the end of Chapter 32, Herman Melville announces that his system of whale classification has to be left unfinished 'even as the great Cathedral of Cologne was left, with the crane still standing upon the top of the uncompleted tower'. 'God keep me', he goes on, 'from completing anything.' Endings, conclusions, it is implied, falsify or distort; openness, incompleteness better suggest the nature of reality. It is this sense of an ending that is not an ending that is present in the concluding stanzas of 'When Lilacs Last in the Dooryard Bloom'd'. The bird's song, the lilac, and the star are neither transcended nor brought to a finish. They continue, and not merely in the sense that they are preserved, like the images on Keats's Grecian urn, by their permanent presence in the poem. The poet ceases his song by turning away from them; they are still there, left behind, not simply objects that have been used up by the poem. Bird, lilac and star, growing in meaning, compose the unfolding process of the poem, making it what it is. Whitman ends by simply letting them go, ever-returning, spring-like as they are, while at the same time creating a satisfying sense of a finished achievement by the formal leave he takes of the images which have in fact allowed the poem to come into being.

'When Lilacs Last in the Dooryard Bloom'd' originally appeared in a group of poems added to *Drum-Taps*, which was Whitman's first collection of Civil War poems, published in May 1865, only a month after Lincoln's assassination on 14 April 1865. When *Drum-Taps* appeared Whitman was already at work on the elegy, and the poem was published as the first of eighteen new poems bound in with the second issue of *Drum-Taps* in the autumn of 1865. *Drum-Taps* itself, Whitman subsequently saw as contributing significantly to the 'passionate song', identity and homogeneity of *Leaves of Grass*. Partly in question was

Whitman's view of what he called the Secession War: he saw the war as an heroic episode in the national epic of America, which is embodied in *Leaves of Grass*. On a more personal level, Whitman's experiences among the wounded in Washington hospitals gave the theme of death, already a preoccupation of his poetry, particular prominence among the poems in *Drum-Taps*, and so in *Leaves of Grass* as a whole.

That one particular death – that of President Lincoln – should have compelled from Whitman some form of elegiac poetic celebration was more or less inevitable. Whitman had always been a devotee of Lincoln, whom he regarded as an archetype of the representative democratic man; he had of course voted for him in the crucial presidential election of 1860. Central elements in 'When Lilacs Last in the Dooryard Bloom'd' arose out of the personal associations with which, for Whitman, the death of Lincoln came to be linked. In later years, Whitman gave two memorial lectures on Lincoln's death in which he recalled seeing him on the occasion of his second inaugural address as president. He noted the marks of fatigue and worry – this was 1864, when the Civil War was far from over – on 'the dark brown face' which still showed 'all the old goodness, tenderness, sadness, and canny shrewdness'. Just before the president spoke, a violent storm ceased, and the day became exceptionally clear so that the stars appeared 'long, long before they were due'. In the weeks before, Whitman said, the weather had been characterized by dramatic changes, and some nights had been superbly beautiful: 'the western star, Venus, in the earlier hours of evening, has never been so large, so clear; it seems as if it told something, as if it held rapport indulgent with humanity, with us Americans.'[3] In *Specimen Days* (1882), Whitman provides further evidence of how the western star, Venus, came to be associated in his mind with Lincoln and his death. He describes the setting of Venus on 18 March, 1879:

> Venus nearly down in the west, of a size and lustre as if trying to outshow itself, before departing. Teeming, maternal orb – I take you again to myself. I am reminded of that spring preceding Abraham Lincoln's murder, when I, restlessly haunting the Potomac banks, around Washington city, watch'd you, off there, aloof, moody as myself.

Just as clear as the associational link between Lincoln and the western star is that between the lilac and the time of Lincoln's death. In the Lincoln lectures, Whitman said of the 14 April on which the president was shot: 'I remember where I was stopping at the time, the season being advanced, there were many lilacs in full bloom. By one of those caprices that enter and give tinge to events without being at all a part of them, I find myself always reminded of the great tragedy of that day by the sight and odor of these blossoms.' In fact Whitman may also have learned that lilacs were blooming around the house in Washington where Lincoln lay dying after the assassination attack. Julia Taft, a friend of Whitman's children, and brother of Colonel Charles S. Taft, the surgeon who attended Lincoln throughout the night of 14–15 April, reports: 'The yard of the house . . . was full of blossoming lilacs, and as long as Charlie Taft lived the scent of lilacs . . . brought back the black horror of that dreadful night.'

The poem's third key image – the hermit thrush and its song – originates, appropriately enough, in Whitman's art, rather than his life. The poet did, however, make some enquiries about the bird while composing the poem. In September 1865, John Burroughs, the naturalist, wrote to a friend about Whitman's interest: 'He is deeply interested in what I tell him of the Hermit Thrush, and says he has used largely the information I have given him in one of his principal poems.' But it is in the earlier poem 'Out of the Cradle Endlessly Rocking', first published in 1859, that the bird image makes its decisive appearance. Lilac and stars are also present in the poem, but it is the bird and its song that are central. The bird sings to its lost mate, and the child who is listening becomes a figure of the poet's own persona; as he hears the bird's lament, the boy is transformed into 'the outsetting bard'. Most significant of all, in relation to 'When Lilacs Last in the Dooryard Bloom'd', is the nature of the message communicated through the song of the bird and the whispering of the waves in the sea:

> The word final, superior to all,
> Subtle, sent up – what is it? – I listen;
> Are you whispering it, and have been all the time, you
> sea-waves?
> Is that it from your liquid rims and wet sands?
>
> Whereto answering, the sea,
> Delaying not, hurrying not,
> Whisper'd me through the night, and very plainly before
> daybreak,
> Lisp'd to me the low and delicious word death,
> And again death, death, death, death,

Hissing melodious, neither like the bird nor like my arous'd
child's heart,
But edging near as privately for me rustling at my feet,
Creeping thence steadily up to my ears and laving me softly
all over,
Death, death, death, death, death.

In 'When Lilacs Last in the Dooryard Bloom'd' it is the song of the bird, rather than the whisper of the sea, that announces the omnipresence and vitality of death, and celebrates its egalitarian, all-encompassing supremacy. None the less, in the later poem too, it is (in section 14) the ocean that provides the definitive image of death, the 'Dark mother always gliding near with soft feet'. Hence at the end of that section, the universality of the thrush's carol in praise of death is imaged in terms of the sea:

Over the tree-tops I float thee a song,
Over the rising and sinking waves, over the myriad fields
and the prairies wide,
Over the dense-pack'd cities all and the teeming wharves
and ways,
I float this carol with joy, with joy to thee O death.

What is clear is that, in 'When Lilacs Last in the Dooryard Bloom'd', the death of Lincoln provides a new, more specific and individual basis for images and ideas that 'Out of the Cradle Endlessly Rocking' had already helped to set in motion.

*

The first stanza of section 16 is one long sentence. The sense of movement, long-drawn-out, is enforced by the massive use of repetitive participles: 'passing', 'unloosing', 'using', 'falling', 'flooding', 'sinking', 'fainting' (here made to mean 'growing faint'), etc., etc. What is suggested above all is the process of leaving, the movement or motion of parting. Any metrical or even rhythmical regularity is absent. Yet the repetition of words and phrases – 'passing', 'I leave thee' – and the constant use of participle endings, create a strong sense of a chanting voice, varying its rhythm and line-length according to semantic need. The 'visions' of the first line of the extract are those of the previous section of the poem in which the poet had witnessed a series of images of the violence and destruction of the Civil War battle-fields, the 'battle-corpses' and the 'debris of all the slain soldiers of the war'. But these visions had unfolded after the carolling song of the hermit thrush in praise of death and its universality, hence they become visions, not of pain and suffering, but of rest. The 'night' is the night in which the bird sings, and the poet's comrades, whose lands are unloosed, rather than the Civil War soldiers, are 'the knowledge of death' and 'the thought of death' which, in the previous section, are described as walking on either side of the poet. The song of the bird, which by this stage in the poem has also become the poet's song – 'the tallying song of my soul' – is the ultimate agent of reconciliation to Lincoln's death. The lines that follow, describing its continuing but ever-changing song, flood across the page just as the song itself fills the night and the whole expanse of heaven and earth. The bird's 'powerful psalm' in praise of death had entered the poem as early as section 4, but in the following sections, the poet had held back from, or resisted, the meaning of its song. Now the song is 'victorious'; it is 'death's outlet song' – the phrase had occurred in 4, though there it is 'death's outlet song of life', suggesting perhaps that the song, in its acceptance of death, provides a mystical release (outlet) into a fuller understanding of life.

What had held the poet back from a positive and reconciling recognition of death's place in the fullness of life was his overwhelming grief at Lincoln's death. In section 9, the poet simultaneously recognizes and rejects (for the moment) the meaning of the bird's song:

> Sing on there in the swamp,
> O singer bashful and tender, I hear your notes, I hear your
> call,
> I hear, I come presently, I understand you,
> But a moment I linger, for the lustrous star has detain'd
> me,
> The star my departing comrade holds and detains me.

And in 13 he articulates again the conflict he experiences between the chant of the bird and the emotional appeal of the poem's counter images:

> O liquid and free and tender!
> O wild and loose to my soul – O wondrous singer!
> You only I hear – yet the star holds me, (but will soon
> depart,)
> Yet the lilac with mastering odor holds me.

The star, that is, which is Lincoln, and the lilac, which is the poet's overpowering love for the president, for a time compel his mourning, his rendering his powerful sense of grief and loss, even though it already coexists with the reconciling, harmonizing knowledge which the song of the hermit thrush means. The poem then renders both grief and the transcendence of grief. Certainly the experience of the poem, as we read it, is in no way one solely of the overcoming and transcending of grief; among its most powerful sections are those (5 and 6) which chart the dark progress of Lincoln's coffin, on its journey by rail through the springtime landscapes, the fields and cities of America, to its resting-place in Illinois. This sombre procession the poet salutes:

> Here, coffin that slowly passes,
> I give you my sprig of lilac.

The sprig of lilac, however, is only one of the gifts that the poet offers the dead Lincoln. His song is another, and the images and pictures it evokes also 'perfume the grave of him I love'. Through the particular 'pictures' of the marvellous sections 11 and 12, Whitman contrives to identify Lincoln with all the grandeur, all the natural fertility, all the crowded, active life of America's land and cities. Lincoln, that is, becomes:

> . . . this land,
> My own Manhattan with spires, and the sparkling and hurrying tides, and the ships,
> The varied and ample land, the South and the North in the light, Ohio's shores and flashing Missouri,
> And ever the far-spreading prairies cover'd with grass and corn.

The United States themselves are essentially, Whitman once affirmed, the greatest poem, and these sections of 'When Lilacs Last in the Door-yard Bloom'd' show how the poem which is reality may become part of the poem which is the poet's imaginative creation. It is America itself that hangs on the walls of 'the burial-house of him I love', it is America itself that shares Lincoln's grave. It seems as though there can be no end to the grief and sadness of the poet, because the scale of his loss is the scale of the entire nation:

> Falling upon them all and among them all, enveloping me with the rest,

> Appear'd the cloud, appear'd the long black trail,
> And I knew death . . .

Hence it is appropriately now that the poet seeks refuge in 'the hiding receiving night' among 'the solemn shadowy cedars and ghostly pines so still', where the 'gray-brown bird' pours out its song of acceptance and reconciliation, its 'carol of death' which will soothe and temper the poet's sadness and grief.

The forward movement of the first stanza of section 16, which we have already looked at, ends with the poet's farewell to the lilac, its heart-shaped leaves the image of love. The lilac blooming had appeared in the very first line of the poem, which now circles back to this, and its other central images, as though confirming the notion of cyclical movement and rebirth inherent in the 'ever-returning spring' of line three. The song of the bird, the lilac, the western star – in the second line of the poem 'the great star early droop'd in the western sky in the night' – all of these opening images of the poem are returned to in its close, perhaps with the suggestion that all of them at this point share in the 'victoriousness' of the bird's song, purified of any remaining sense of grief or loss.

So, as has been suggested, the movement of the first half of 16 is one of passing, releasing, leaving behind: the poet's leave-taking of the images which have created his poem. Yet Whitman cannot leave the poem there. In one last inclusive sentence he pulls it back, retains it a moment longer. Just as Milton begins *Lycidas*, his great elegy, by appealing 'Yet once more' to the symbols of poetic fame and inspiration, so Whitman ends his great elegy by arresting its fading, recessional movement – 'Yet each to keep and all, retrievements out of the night' – reiterating once again its central images, though this time re-including his woe at Lincoln's death. The 'wondrous chant' of the bird, the 'echo arous'd' in the poet's soul, the 'lustrous and drooping star', all are to be kept, preserved, as memorials of Lincoln 'for his dear sake'. So, its images simultaneously released and held back, the elegy in its final two lines, which are now the entire poem, marvellously blends process and movement (release), with permanence and stasis (retention):

> Lilac and star and bird twined with the chant of my soul,
> There in the fragrant pines and the cedars dusk and dim.

*

Whitman's is the most authentic American poetic voice of the nineteenth century. It is only with Whitman, at mid-century, that American poetry frees itself from the domination of the English poetic tradition. Whitman is the new poet of the New World. As he wrote in the autobiographical *A Backward Glance O'er Travel'd Roads* (1889), 'the time had come to reflect all themes and things, old and new, in the lights thrown on them by the advent of America and democracy – to chant those themes through the utterance of one, not only the grateful and reverent legatee of the past, but the born child of the New World.' Whitman believed he recognized the New World's need for 'poems of realities and science and of the democratic average and basic equality', and set about the creation of a new poetic language and new poetic forms which would adequately articulate the new American poetry he aimed to write: 'For all these new and evolutionary facts, meanings, purposes, new poetic messages, new forms and expressions, are inevitable.'[4] In so far as he succeeded in creating new messages, new forms and expressions, it is Whitman who provides America with its distinctive, poetic voice. As Ezra Pound saw, Whitman *is* America.[5]

To say all this, however, is to suggest how far Whitman is to be identified with the old, democratic America that both proved and destroyed itself on the bloody battle-fields of the Civil War. *Leaves of Grass* first appeared in 1855: hence Whitman is very much part of what F. L. Matthiessen has persuaded us to see as the American renaissance of the 1850s. Whitman, that is, belongs to the cultural world which produced *The Scarlet Letter*, *Moby-Dick*, *Walden*, and Emerson's *Representative Men*. Indeed his distinctiveness is at least in part a question of the unequivocal enthusiasm with which, unlike the sceptical Melville and Hawthorne, he celebrated the visionary hopes and dreams and optimisms of the new, democratic American republic. Whitman's response to life and experience was unflinchingly positive and affirmative. The aim of his poetry was to communicate a belief 'in the wisdom, health, mystery, beauty of every process, every concrete object, every human or other existence' (*A Backward Glance*).[6] For Whitman there were no limits to what the self, particularly the American self, could achieve; every American was potentially an epic hero, and every hero has a song of himself to sing parallel to Whitman's own, definitive 'Song of Myself', the poem which made up more than half of the first edition of *Leaves of Grass*. Whitman is above all the poet of that powerful Adamic and transcendental vision of America and the American, present in American culture from the earliest settlements, but given massive reinforcement by the triumphant conclusion of the American Revolution and the establishment of a new nation dedicated to the life, liberty and pursuit of happiness, of its inhabitants. It is the democratic idealism of this enduring tradition that Whitman centrally embodies and celebrates.

Because this is so, Whitman is hardly to be seen as the poet of post-Civil War America. *Leaves of Grass* went on evolving in the decades after the war, but its essential notes had been sounded in the ante-bellum world. Whitman saw in the Civil War, and the victory of the Union, a triumphant reaffirmation of America's oldest and best ideals, and as we have seen, he subsequently insisted that the experience of the war was crucial to the final creation of *Leaves of Grass*. What Whitman did not see so clearly was that the war, and still more ironically, the death of Lincoln, marked the end of American idealism, or rather, the beginning of an epoch in which the gap between the principles of American democratic idealism, and the social and economic realities of American life, was destined to grow increasingly wide.

In the decades after the 1860s, Whitman tended increasingly to take on the role of a national spokesman, an American poet-prophet. Public themes are certainly much in evidence in the poems he wrote in these years. *Passage to India* (1871), for example, takes as occasions for its rhapsodic celebration of human progress the opening of the Suez Canal, the completion of the East-West railway link in America, and the laying of the Atlantic cable. In his earlier work, one would agree, Whitman's idealistic, democratic fervour had coexisted with a recognition of individual weakness and frailty. *Crossing Brooklyn Ferry* (1856), one of his finest poems, includes, for example, the following:

> I am he who knew what it was to be evil,
> I too knitted the old knot of contrariety,
> Blabb'd, blush'd, resented, lied, stole, grudg'd,
> Had guile, anger, lust, hot wishes I dared not speak,
> Was wayward, vain, greedy, shallow, sly, cowardly,
> malignant,
> The wolf, the snake, the hog, not wanting in me,
> The cheating look, the frivolous word, the adulterous wish,
> not wanting,
> Refusals, hates, postponements, meanness, laziness, none of
> these wanting. . . .

In the post-bellum period, however, Whitman seems to have been unwilling or unable to translate this recognition of personal weakness into an equally searching analysis of the swiftly growing social evils which were becoming disturbingly characteristic of American life. It is true that in the early pages of *Democratic Vistas* (1871), the poet does acknowledge the deficiencies of American government under the presidency of Ulysses S. Grant, and seems also to recognize the growing social and political anarchy of the so-called Gilded Age, the growth of corruption, bribery and falsehood in public and political life, and 'the depravity of the business classes'. *Democratic Vistas*, however, though Richard Chase has described it as an American version of Matthew Arnold's *Culture and Anarchy*, does not sustain and develop its analysis of contemporary social and political realities. Whitman's democratic hopes and dreams soon reassert themselves; the old Jeffersonian-Jacksonian principles are reaffirmed; the ideals of individualism and comradeship are insisted upon. How these principles and ideals are to survive in face of the new and immensely powerful forces of economic and commercial materialism and exploitation is a problem that is not faced or recognized. Despite the fact that he lived until 1892, Whitman essentially remained the poet of the America which, in the period 1865–1900, rapidly became a golden, mythical past.

What Whitman elegiacally celebrates in 'When Lilacs Last in the Dooryard Bloom'd', then, is more than the death of Abraham Lincoln. The poem clearly marks the end of an era in American history, but it may also be seen as heralding a major shift in the direction of American literature. After this, the Party of Hope, as R. W. B. Lewis called it in *The American Adam* (1959), will but rarely be heard; simply because, with the Civil War and the death of Lincoln, the idealism which had inspired it became increasingly difficult to sustain. Perhaps the poem, splendid and moving as it is, marks even more: the death not only of Lincoln, but of Whitman's own, essential, imaginative life. The 1867 edition of *Leaves of Grass* contained 236 poems; Whitman would subsequently add over a hundred more, but it is none the less possible to regard the writing of 'When Lilacs Last in the Dooryard Bloom'd' as the last occasion on which, blending as in all his best work his public role with private feeling, he produced a truly great poem. Certainly it is tempting to see the Lincoln elegy as marking the end of the tradition of optimism and idealism which had formed so important a part of ante-bellum American writing. It is significant that, near the end of his life, Whitman admitted in 'American National Literature' (1891) that

America had failed to produce the kind of national poetry he had hoped and expected it would.

Whitman's own failure – and it is a failure only in terms of the supremely high standards he had set for himself in 'When Lilacs Last in the Dooryard Bloom'd' – was a failure to grasp the true scope and nature of the changes occurring within American society, largely as a result of economic developments, even though he lived through the decades in which these basic changes were taking place. It is a powerful irony that Lincoln, dying in 1864, had a much clearer perception of what the future had in store for the United States. Just as Jefferson had foreseen the inevitability of the Civil War in the situation which produced the Missouri Compromise of 1819, so Lincoln saw in the economic consequences of the Civil War a new and major threat to the survival of the Union:

> I see in the near future a crisis arising that unnerves me and causes me to tremble for the safety of my country. By a result of the war, corporations have been enthroned, and an era of corruption in high places will follow, and the money power of the country will endeavour to prolong its reign by working upon the prejudices of the people, until all wealth is aggregated in a few hands and the Republic is destroyed. I feel, at this point, more anxiety for the safety of my country than ever before, even in the midst of war.[7]

Lincoln's prescience here is astonishing. The future he envisaged came all too fully into being. If the Republic was not destroyed, its survival at different times frequently seemed to observers to be in the balance. But this was a future which the poetry of Whitman, despite its central commitment to consciously American and democratic themes, was hardly capable of confronting. Lincoln had told his fellow-Americans that they could not escape history, but for Whitman the truth of America remained the truth of 1776; the notion of historical change, and the degree and scope of the actual changes occurring in post-bellum America, were never for him possible poetic themes. It was to be left to younger writers, novelists rather than poets, for whom pre-Civil War America was a distant past, to try to come to terms imaginatively with that future whose coming Abraham Lincoln had so clearly foreseen.

Notes

1 The text is that of Harold W. Blodgett and Sculley Bradley (eds), *Walt Whitman, Leaves of Grass, Comprehensive Reader's Edition*, New York, 1965.

2 Quoted by Charles Feidelson, 'Whitman as Symbolist', in Roy Harvey Pearce (ed.), *Whitman, A Collection of Critical Essays*, Englewood Cliffs, NJ, 1962, p. 86.
3 This and subsequent references to the sources of the poem can be found in Richard Chase, *Walt Whitman Reconsidered*, London, 1955, pp. 139–45, and in the notes to the poem in the Blodgett and Sculley edition.
4 Blodgett and Sculley, op. cit., pp. 565, 566, 568.
5 See Pearce, op. cit., p. 8.
6 Blodgett and Sculley, op. cit., p. 573.
7 Letter to W. R. Ellis, quoted by Sylvia Bowman, *The Year 2000, A Critical Biography of Edward Bellamy*, New York, 1958, p. 74.

Further reading

Gay Wilson Allen, *The New Walt Whitman Handbook*, New York, 1975.
Richard V. Chase, *Walt Whitman Reconsidered*, London, 1955.

2

Henry George (1839-97)

In the very centers of our civilization to-day are want and suffering enough to make sick at heart whoever does not close his eyes and steel his nerves. Dare we turn to the Creator and ask Him to relieve it? Supposing the prayer were heard, and at the behest with which the universe sprang into being there should glow in the sun a greater power; new virtue fill the air; fresh vigor the soil; that for every blade of grass that now grows two should spring up, and the seed that now increases fifty fold should increase a hundred fold! Would poverty be abated or want relieved? Manifestly no! Whatever benefit would accrue would be but temporary. The new powers streaming through the material universe could only be utilized through land. And land, being private property, the classes that now monopolize the bounty of the Creator would monopolize all the new bounty. Land owners would alone be benefited. Rents would increase, but wages would still tend to the starvation point!

This is not merely a deduction of political economy; it is a fact of experience. We know it because we have seen it. Within our own times, under our very eyes, that Power which is above all, and in all, and through all; that Power of which the whole universe is but the manifestation; that Power which maketh all things, and without which is not anything made that is made, has increased the bounty which men may enjoy, as truly as though the fertility of nature had been increased. Into the mind of one came the thought that harnessed steam for the service of mankind. To the inner ear of another was whispered the secret that compels the lightning to bear a message round the globe. In every direction have the laws of matter been revealed; in every department of industry have arisen arms of iron and fingers of steel, whose effect upon the production of wealth has been precisely the same as an increase in the fertility of nature. What has been the result? Simply that land owners get all the gain. The wonderful discoveries and inventions of our century have neither increased wages nor lightened toil. The effect has simply been to make the few richer; the many more helpless!

Can it be that the gifts of the Creator may be thus misappropriated with impunity? Is it a light thing that labor should be robbed of its earnings while greed rolls in wealth – that the many should want while the few are surfeited? Turn to history, and on every page may be read the lesson that such wrong never goes unpunished; that the Nemesis that follows injustice never falters nor sleeps! Look around to-day. Can this state of things continue? May we even say, 'After us the deluge!' Nay; the pillars of the state are trembling even now, and the very foundations of society begin to quiver with pent-up forces that glow underneath. The struggle that must either revivify, or convulse in ruin, is near at hand, if it be not already begun.

The fiat has gone forth! With steam and electricity, and the new powers born of progress, forces have entered the world that will either compel us to a higher plane or overwhelm us, as nation after nation, as civilization after civilization, have been overwhelmed before. It is the delusion which precedes destruction that sees in the popular unrest with which the civilized world is feverishly pulsing, only the passing effect of ephemeral causes. Between democratic ideas and the aristocratic adjustments of society there is an irreconcilable conflict. Here in the United States, as there in Europe, it may be seen arising. We cannot go on permitting men to vote and forcing them to tramp. We cannot go on educating boys and girls in our public schools and then refusing them the right to earn an honest living. We cannot go on prating of the inalienable rights of man and then denying the inalienable right to the bounty of the Creator. Even now, in old bottles the new wine begins to ferment, and elemental forces gather for the strife!

But if, while there is yet time, we turn to Justice and obey her, if we trust Liberty and follow her, the dangers that now threaten must disappear, the forces that now menace will turn to agencies of elevation. Think of the powers now wasted; of the infinite fields of knowledge yet to be explored; of the possibilities of which the wondrous inventions of this century give us but a hint. With want destroyed; with greed changed to noble passions; with the fraternity that is born of equality taking the place of the jealousy and fear that now array men against each other; with mental power loosed by conditions that give to the humblest comfort and leisure; and who shall measure the heights to which our civilization may soar? Words fail the thought! It is the Golden Age of which poets have sung and high-raised seers have told in metaphor! It is the glorious vision which has always haunted man with gleams of fitful splendor. It is what he saw whose eyes at Patmos were closed in a trance. It is the culmination of Christianity – the City of God on earth, with its walls of jasper and its gates of pearl! It is the reign of the Prince of Peace!

Progress and Poverty (1880)[1]

* * *

Progress and Poverty, which these paragraphs of passionate rhetoric effectively bring to an end, is not a work of imaginative literature. However surprisingly, given the expressive eloquence of this extract, its genre is that of 'the dismal science' of economics. None the less, the place of *Progress and Poverty* in America's literary culture in the period 1865–1900 is of the utmost significance. Essentially an unorthodox, radical, anti-establishment work, no single book did more to focus for masses of American readers in the later 1880s and 1890s their growing discontent over what was being done to American society and American life by the economic developments characteristic of the post-Civil War period. Begun in September 1877, and completed in March 1879, *Progress and Poverty* was offered for publication to D. Appleton and Company. It was rejected in the following terms: the work 'has the merit of being written with great clearness and force, but it is very aggressive. There is very little to encourage the publication of any such work at this time and we feel we must decline it.'[2] This was the book destined to appear in over one hundred editions, to be translated into almost every European language and, by 1906, to be read by some six million men and women.

Throughout the extract, George writes with the kind of emotional fervour and conviction that converts logical analysis into apocalyptic vision. Each paragraph unit rises to its own climax, but the units build together to produce an exhilarating and visionary climax to the whole book. Such a degree of rhetorical drama is not characteristic of the book in general; long chapters are given over to extremely sober and unemotional economic argument and analysis. Yet *Progress and Poverty* is consistently aimed at a general reader with no specialized knowledge, and is thus entirely free of jargon of any kind. If its general tone is somewhat dry, its prose is frequently illumined by lively illustration or example, as well as by a constant, underlying emotional conviction which makes its statement direct, lucid, hard-hitting. Dryness, of course, is not much in evidence here. Rather, George uses a range of rhetorical devices to compel our agreement, to make us share his vision. In doing so, he summarizes his major themes.

The opening paragraph insists on George's initial, crucial insight concerning progress and poverty. 'Civilization' coexists with 'want and suffering' on an enormous scale. The thrust of the rest of the paragraph is an enforcing of the view that the responsibility for this situation rests entirely with man, and the economic arrangements he accedes to. There is no divine necessity that things should be the way they are. In fact an increase in divine benevolence towards mankind would produce no alleviation of the current human condition. All that would happen would be that 'the classes that now monopolize the bounty of the Creator would monopolize all the new bounty'. George now uses the opportunity he has created to underline the central tenet of his economic theory: that the absolutely critical economic fact is the private ownership of land. Increases in fertility would simply lead to increases in land values and rents; wages would remain unaffected.

These observations are developed and illustrated in the second paragraph. Highly significant is George's readiness to attribute to divine power the immense developments in material progress which have characterized the nineteenth century. The biblical language and tone employed here may well be relevant to George's tremendous popularity; a great many readers must have been reassured to find that his economic analysis existed within the framework of an apparently conventional Christian understanding. The conclusion that the paragraph draws, however, is identical with that of the previous one. George insists once again on the point that Shelley was perhaps the first of many nineteenth-century figures to register: the 'wonderful discoveries and inventions of our century have neither increased wages nor lightened toil'. Shelley in 'The Defence of Poetry' makes the point by asking why it is 'that the discoveries which should have lightened, have added a weight to the curse imposed on Adam?' John Stuart Mill's formulation – 'hitherto it is questionable if all the mechanical inventions yet made have lightened the day's toil of any human being!' – was sufficiently striking for Thorstein Veblen to pick up and quote in his own radical analysis of American social and economic values, *The Theory of the Leisure Class* (1899). George agrees that the mass of the people have gained nothing from the century's enormous strides in scientific and industrial development. Only landowners have benefited.

'The effect has simply been to make the few richer; the many more helpless!'

In paragraph three, George, like so many other Victorian sages, assumes a prophetic voice. If the *status quo* is maintained, if injustice is left to flourish, the outcome will be violence and disruption. Here in the 1870s, George is expressing a view that, as the 1880s go on, will become increasingly widely and loudly stated: American society is under such pressure that, unless it is relieved by some kind of responsive change, a revolutionary explosion in some form is inevitable. In George's view 'the pillars of the state are trembling even now, and the very foundations of society begin to quiver with pent-up forces that glow underneath'. The 'pent-up forces' that he has in mind are above all those latent in America's industrial working class which, during the 1870s, had already erupted into dangerous violence. In 1874–5, among the mining communities of Pennsylvania, there had been industrial unrest and violence which had been repressed with equal violence. But, in the later 1870s, times were hard for all of America's 4.5 million industrial workers. The order of the day was long hours – seventy-two hours a week or even more – low pay, brutalizing conditions, and the constant threat of lay-offs or wage cuts whenever the market took a downward turn. The vast majority of workers and their families existed on or near the poverty line. These were the kinds of condition that produced the great strikes of 1877. In the summer of that year strikes broke out on the railways in different sections of the United States. In West Virginia, a 10 per cent wage reduction caused a strike; the railway company recruited strikebreakers; as a result, trains were stopped by force, and the strikers were fired on by state militia called out to protect the strikebreakers. Federal troops had to be sent in to maintain law and order. In Maryland the situation was worse. The state militia was fired on by a hostile crowd in Baltimore. The streets of the city were reduced to a state of civil war, and again Federal troops had to be sent in. In Pennsylvania a similar pattern of events occurred. The state militia fired on a mob in Pittsburgh, killing at least ten men. The result was a total descent into anarchy. Railway engines and wagons were derailed and set on fire; looting and rioting were widespread throughout the city; the main railway station burned down. Soon afterwards, the strike spread into the Middle West, and there were riots in Chicago and St Louis. When George began the writing of *Progress and Poverty* these events must have been fresh in his mind. They give point to his fear that, unless changes are made, American society will disintegrate in violent conflict and bloodshed.

Paragraph four develops and extends the central perception of the previous one. Progress is inevitable. But the benefits of that progress cannot go on being denied to the mass of the people. Skilfully George capitalizes on the orthodox acceptance of the unstoppable, inevitable, nature of evolutionary progress; democracy and the rights of man are aligned with the powers born of evolutionary progress; 'aristocratic' resistance to democratic progress can produce only 'irreconcilable conflict'. Readers are reminded of the promises contained within the American Constitution itself – 'the inalienable rights of man' – and exhorted to agree that it is time for the promises to be fulfilled. America's political history is thus harnessed to the doctrine of the inevitability of evolutionary social progress to produce a powerful, forceful demand for immediate change, if elemental strife is to be avoided.

Characteristically, however, Henry George ends on a note of optimism and hope. The great promises of America and of universal progress can be achieved. Progress admits of no limitations, and if its benefits were everywhere shared, then the ideal society of the American Dream could at last be born. When a spirit of fraternity and co-operation replaces the competitive conflict inherent in the present social and economic system, civilization can soar to new heights. In *Progress and Poverty*, George believes he has shown the way. He has identified the problem, indicated its cause; and shows how it could be solved. The utopian fervour of this final paragraph helps us to understand why, towards the end of the nineteenth century, for countless readers in America and the world beyond, *Progress and Poverty* was an inspiriting and inspiring book.

*

Henry George's interest in the problem of poverty increasing in the midst of affluence originated in his early life. In 1855 he had sailed as a ship's boy to Calcutta, a city where the contrast between extremes of wealth and poverty was legendary. His own early manhood was spent around San Francisco, and his concern over economic problems grew in part out of the personal difficulties he experienced there. However it was in 1869, when he visited New York City, that his interest in economic issues was transformed into a burning determination to do something about them. Subsequently he wrote: 'Years ago I came to this city from the West, unknown, knowing nobody, and I saw and recognized for the first time the shocking contrast between monstrous wealth and debasing want, and here I made a vow from which I have never faltered, to seek out and remedy, if I could, the cause that condemned little children to lead such a life as you know them to lead in the squalid districts.'[3]

It was in fact not long after this visit to New York that George gained possession of what he regarded for the rest of his life as the key to understanding how it came about that economic progress seemed to increase, rather than dissipate, poverty. Travelling through a land-boom area in California, he asked a passing teamster what land was worth in the area. The teamster 'pointed to some cows grazing off so far that they looked like mice, and said: "I don't know exactly, but there is a man over there who will sell some land for a thousand dollars an acre." Like a flash it came upon me that there was the reason of advancing poverty with advancing wealth. With the growth of population, land grows in value, and the men who must work it must pay more for the privilege. I turned back, amidst quiet thought, to the perception that then came to me and has been with me ever since.'[4] So Henry George was convinced that the explanation of the paradox of poverty and progress lay in traditional assumptions about the ownership and valuation of land. It was the ever-increasing value of land, and thus the ever-increasing wealth in the form of rental value accruing to those who owned land, that produced the constantly growing gap between the rich and the poor. Having recognized the problem, and identified its cause, all that remained for George was to come up with a solution. This he did in Chapter 5 of *Our Land and Land Policy, National and State*, published in 1871: the answer was 'a tax upon the value of land'. In time this became the 'single tax' policy with which Henry George's name was to be above all identified. Soaring rents, because of the soaring value of land, were the source of America's – and other countries' – economic problems. The answer lay in the benefits for all of a tax on land values.

Progress and Poverty is a detailed exposition of George's theories. Much of it is written in a mode of cool and rational analysis. In particular, when he is setting out his fundamental objections to classical economic theory – from Adam Smith, through Malthus and Ricardo, down to John Stuart Mill – George's tone remains that of conventional academic discourse and debate. The issues in question, however, were anything but conventional. Classical economic doctrines were seen as justifying the *laissez-faire* capitalism of post-Civil War America. Classical economic theory was regarded as confirming the 'there is no alternative' approach to America's social and economic problems. Smith's *Wealth of Nations* was a symbolically revered text, and on 12 December, 1876, a hundred leading American intellectuals attended a dinner at New York's famous Delmonico's restaurant to celebrate the centenary of its publication. Afterwards Appleton's *Popular Science Monthly*, a magazine which promoted the doctrines of the English thinkers Charles Darwin and Herbert Spencer more enthusiastically than any other American journal, announced that *The Wealth of Nations* was 'probably the most important book in its influence upon the politics of states and the economical welfare of mankind that was ever written'.[5] Smith and his economist successors were therefore important in post-bellum America; they could be appealed to in order to provide intellectual cover for what the business interest was doing to American society. For George to attack classical economic theory was to signal his total rejection of contemporary American capitalism.

In fact George's careful, academic arguments occur in a context of burning moral and ethical fervour. For George, the failure of orthodox economic thinking is in the end a moral failure. The way things are, justice and liberty are everywhere being trampled underfoot. What is needed is a return to the principles enshrined in the American Constitution; the only alternative, he warns – as the extract indicates – is a descent into anarchy or revolutionary violence. At the end of the day though, as we have seen, George still belongs to the old Party of Hope: he is a visionary, still persuaded that the American Dream can be achieved. Whatever the views of the men of power who assembled at Delmonico's in 1876, for George 1776 remains the year, not of *The Wealth of Nations*, but of the Declaration of Independence.

What is needed, in George's view, for the reinstatement of America's old and best ideals, is a transformation of the economic basis of society. This is why *Progress and Poverty* is a major work of social reconstruction, meriting comparison with Karl Marx's *Das Kapital*. Its overriding aim is to place society's economic arrangements on a wholly new footing. And its argument is carried forward with overwhelming certainty and conviction. One should not be misled by the apparent naivety of George's own remarks about the squalid districts of New York and mice-like cattle grazing in the distance. What is remarkable about *Progress and Poverty*, and an explanation of its popularity, is the cogency of its analysis of the deficiencies and limitations of orthodox economic thinking, and its sweeping confirmation of the feeling of an increasing number of George's contemporaries that what was happening in the economically expanding countries of the world involved unnecessary exploitation, suffering, and poverty; and this in the context of a clear and simple explanation of the root causes of all such problems.

Clarity and cogency of argument, allied to moral and ethical fervour, help to explain *Progress and Poverty*'s popularity. An additional factor perhaps counted even more. *Progress and Poverty* appealed because it rejected the doctrines of all those who argued that the sufferings and injustices of the present were inevitable and immutable. Just as he rejected the pessimism of Malthus's theory of over-population, so George rejected the Social Darwinism of Herbert Spencer and his American followers. Crucial here is the point that Spencer was a key figure in the intellectual world of post-bellum America. Indeed it was peculiarly in America that the English thinker's views on the relevance of Darwin's theories of evolution and natural selection to the study of human society had been widely welcomed as basically sanctioning the unchecked operation of a capitalist economic system. George, however, refused to agree that social evolution was a slow and blind process with which man should not interfere. E. L. Youmans, one of Herbert Spencer's leading American disciples, told George that in five thousand years social evolution would have solved the kinds of problem he had seen in New York City. George, and his supporters, were not prepared to wait. If action was not forthcoming, society would collapse into ruin and anarchy. By countless readers, then, *Progress and Poverty* was welcomed and revered as a mighty and revolutionary book because it amounted to a comprehensive, philosophical rejection of the whole superstructure of ideas, broadly Social Darwinist in nature, that had come to underpin the post-bellum *status quo* in America's social and economic life.

In these circumstances it is hardly surprising that Herbert Spencer himself should have dismissed George's book as 'trash'. The alternative was to concede that his own work was based on a fundamental misconception – that evolution occurred within human society just as it did in the natural world. In fact George's dissent from Spencer's postulates was absolute. He rejected utterly the whole theory that the 'progress of civilization' depended upon a development or evolution which itself proceeded according to the laws appropriate to the genesis of a species: laws, that is, 'of the survival of the fittest and the hereditary transmission of acquired qualities'. The 'hopeful fatalism' of such a 'vulgar explanation of progress', George set aside in favour of the view that society develops and men improve 'as they become civilized, or learn to co-operate in society'.[6] Such an observation was immensely significant. What it means is that George, like Edward Bellamy a few years later, was prepared to argue that society progressed essentially through *peaceful* association; such association was immensely more productive than the impulse towards competitive conflict. Such a view ran counter to one of the fundamental tenets of the ideology of contemporary capitalism, which Social Darwinism had readily endorsed: the idea that competition, and the conflict that competition produced, were essential to desirable social development. George was equally unsympathetic to another of Social Darwinism's fundamental assumptions: the primacy of heredity in influencing the nature and behaviour of the individual. George rejected nature in favour of nurture:

> each society, small or great, necessarily weaves for itself a web of knowledge, beliefs, customs, language, tastes, institutions, and laws. Into this web . . . the individual is received at birth and continues until his death. This is the matrix in which mind unfolds and from which it takes its stamp. This is the way in which customs, and religions, and prejudices, and tastes, and languages, grow up and are perpetuated.[7]

George, that is, unlike Marx (who incidentally dismissed *Progress and Poverty* as 'the capitalists' last ditch'), did not regard the means of production as the single factor which determined the life of the individual, but rather, like Antonio Gramsci and other twentieth-century Marxists, saw the individual as the product of a configuration of forces, including a superstructure of ideas and assumptions and world-views, which jointly work upon him.

Herbert Spencer and his Social Darwinist followers, however, not Karl Marx, were the key opponents Henry George had in mind in writing *Progress and Poverty*. This is why, in terms of the social, economic, and intellectual orthodoxies of post-bellum America, it was above all a radical, subversive, challenging and influential book. As George's voice became only one among many challenging the Darwinist world-view, as that had been interpreted by defenders of late nineteenth-century American capitalism, so the impact and significance of his book continued to grow.

*

When he learned that Appleton's, who happened to be Herbert Spencer's American publishers, had decided not to publish his book, and after Harper's and Scribner's had also shown no interest, George decided to go ahead and produce a private edition of his work. Hence *Progress and Poverty* first appeared in an Author's Edition of 500 copies late in 1879. Among those who received complimentary copies were Gladstone and Herbert Spencer. At this point, however, Appleton and Company had second thoughts and agreed to publish the book, making use of the author's own plates. As a result, the first commercial edition of one thousand copies appeared in January 1880. By March the thousand copies had been sold, and an additional 500 were printed. From this point on the pace began to quicken. *Progress and Poverty* was serialized in various New York and Chicago newspapers, and a series of cheap editions followed. In 1881, Kegan Paul brought out an English edition, and translation into French, German, Italian, Swedish and Norwegian soon followed. The book's early reception was, as one would have expected given its unorthodoxy and hostility to accepted attitudes, considerably less than enthusiastic. But George was in no way surprised or dismayed. He was confident that what he had written was a great book.[8]

As the 1880s passed, the ideas propounded in *Progress and Poverty* were received and taken up by an ever-increasing audience. In Great Britain – and in Australia and New Zealand – George's ideas were soon circulating with the same electrifying effect they were producing in the United States. *Progress and Poverty* became in fact a key work in the development of British working-class politics. According to Beatrice and Sidney Webb, the rise to dominance of the Labour Party in the Trades Union Congress of 1893 was largely due to 'the wide circulation in Britain of Henry George's *Progress and Poverty*'. 'The optimistic and aggressive tone' of the book, they believed, 'sounded the dominant note alike of the new unionism and of the British Socialist movement'.[9] It is hardly surprising, given this degree of interest, that George should have visited the British Isles five times in the course of the 1880s, speaking at public meetings in places as diverse as London, Manchester, Liverpool, Oxford, Belfast, Glasgow, Edinburgh, Dundee, Aberdeen, Paisley, and the Isle of Skye. Among his British converts was George Bernard Shaw. Shaw's attention, we are told, 'was first drawn to political economy as the science of social salvation by Henry George's eloquence, and by his *Progress and Poverty*, which . . . had more to do with the Socialist revival of that period in England than any other book'.[10] And through Shaw, George's theories passed into the thinking of the Fabian Society. The Christian Socialist movement represents yet another group who proved highly responsive to George's ideas, while Philip Snowden and Keir Hardie were other future leaders of the British Left who fell under George's powerful influence. William Morris once reported that when he asked a group of Socialists what had given them their political convictions they all spoke of reading *Progress and Poverty*. Even Liberals – like Joseph Chamberlain – found George's arguments hard to resist.

In America the increasing impact of *Progress and Poverty* made its author into a figure of considerable political eminence and significance. George ran twice for the office of Mayor of New York. On his return from his 1882 British tour, he was welcomed by a grand dinner at Delmonico's attended by 170 guests. (This dinner-party was perhaps a response to that at which Herbert Spencer was welcomed by his American admirers during his tour of the United States in the same year.) On American writers, George's impact was substantial. William Dean Howells who, as we shall see, became increasingly aware in the 1880s of the cruelties and injustices permeating American society and its economic system, was powerfully drawn by George's 'solution of the riddle of the painful earth'. (Elizabeth Peabody, a social reformer and educationalist, had written to George on the appearance of *Progress and Poverty* congratulating him on having solved 'the tremendous conundrum of progress and poverty'.) Hamlin Garland, another major figure in the school of American realism, became an active campaigner in Boston in the 1880s on behalf of George and his theories. One of the most popular of all of Garland's stories – 'Under the Lion's Paw' – was no more than a direct expression in dramatic form of George's view of the massive injustice involved in allowing landlords to raise the rental value of land improved by the toil of others. James Herne, an actor friend of Garland, later a friend and correspondent of George's own, gave successful public readings of this story around the Boston area.

Progress and Poverty showed American writers how their society could be looked at critically. It articulated an increasingly pervasive sense of discontent with considerable intellectual rigorousness. It showed that there was an alternative. It made scepticism about the present, and about current attitudes and philosophies designed to sustain the present, respectable. For a younger generation of thinkers and writers *Progress and Poverty* became a classic anti-establishment statement. It was almost inevitable that someone like Thorstein Veblen, while still an undergraduate at Carleton College in Minnesota in 1880, should have taken up the book and praised it at a time when established academic economists and philosophers were only too anxious to dismiss it. Orthodox academic opinion is represented by Francis A. Walker, President of Massachusetts Institute of Technology, and author of the period's standard economics textbook for colleges and universities. Henry George and his single tax theory are dismissed as immoral: 'I will not insult my readers by discussing a project so steeped in infamy.'[11] The young Veblen, on the other hand, as soon as *Progress and Poverty* appeared, 'did not hesitate to let it be known that he supported it.'[12]

Progress and Poverty is thus a critical work in establishing a tradition that runs on through Edward Bellamy's *Looking Backward* (1888), through the works of realists and naturalists in the later 1880s and 1890s, and into the so-called 'muckraking' activities of the investigative writers and journalists who around the end of the century were prepared to expose the scandals and corruptions of the American capitalist system. *Progress and Poverty*, that is, was a crucial, pioneering expression of that radical critique of America's social and economic life which a new movement in American literature, originating in the 1870s and developing through the 1880s and 1890s, would go on to articulate in imaginative terms. Like *Looking Backward*, published some eight years later, another radical analysis of the social and economic ills of America, *Progress and Poverty* contributed massively to the creation of an intellectual climate in which a new kind of American writing could develop. Newness, in the literary battle that was fought between the literary and cultural establishment and the emergent school of writers, came to be identified with the mode of its expression – realism initially, naturalism a little later – but what the new writing mode increasingly registered was a deepening discontent with the harsh realities of life in post-Civil War America as these were experienced by the great mass of the country's population. What *Progress and Poverty* did was to establish a position, argue a case, that gave intellectual credibility and respectability to such feelings of discontent. Caught up and absorbed in the ferment of ideas and emotions provoked by the increasingly widely-held view in the 1880s and 1890s that American society, as Lincoln had predicted, was in danger of disintegration and collapse, the book also offered a message of hope, pointed a way forward.[13] Social and economic inequalities and injustices, however massive, could, it suggested, be corrected.

From 1880 on, *Progress and Poverty*, at once symbol and creator of change, was a kind of time-bomb ticking away beneath the dominant orthodoxies of American social and economic thinking. All that was needed for the book to explode into massive popularity was for the unease, the dissatisfaction, the outrage, over what was being done to America by the business interest, registered by George in the 1870s, to become much more general. In the mid-1880s, and through the 1890s, it happened. As a result, *Progress and Poverty* became one of the great best-sellers of American literature.

Notes

1 Henry George, *Progress and Poverty: An Inquiry into the Cause of Industrial Depressions, and of Increase of Want with Increase of Wealth. The Remedy*, London, 1883. All page references are to this edition.
2 See Charles Albro Barker, *Henry George*, New York, 1955, pp. 312–13.
3 See Elwood P. Lawrence, *Henry George in the British Isles*, East Lansing, 1957, p. 4.
4 ibid., pp. 4–5.
5 Quoted by Paul F. Boller, Jr, *American Thought in Transition*, Chicago, 1969, p. 71.
6 *Progress and Poverty*, pp. 429–31.
7 ibid., p. 453.
8 In a letter to his father, George wrote: 'It will not be recognized at first, maybe not for some time – but it will ultimately be considered a great book, will be published in both hemispheres, and will be translated into different languages.' See Barker, op. cit., pp. 313–14.
9 Lawrence, op. cit., p. 3.
10 Quoted by Lawrence, op. cit., pp. 75–6.
11 See Joseph Dorfman, *Thorstein Veblen and His America*, London, 1935, p. 63.
12 ibid., p. 32.
13 For Lincoln's prediction, see p. 18;
14 Barker, op. cit., p. 598.

Further reading

Charles Albro Barker, *Henry George*, New York, 1955.
Elwood P. Lawrence, *Henry George in the British Isles*, East Lansing, 1957.

3

Henry James (1843-1916)

Hadn't he all the appearance of a man living in the open air of the world, indifferent to small considerations, caring only for truth and knowledge and believing that two intelligent people ought to look for them together and, whether they found them or not, find at least some happiness in the search? He had told her he loved the conventional; but there was a sense in which this seemed a noble declaration. In that sense, that of the love of harmony and order and decency and of all the stately offices of life, she went with him freely, and his warning had contained nothing ominous. But when, as the months had elapsed, she had followed him further and he had led her into the mansion of his own habitation, then, *then* she had seen where she really was.

She could live it over again, the incredulous terror with which she had taken the measure of her dwelling. Between those four walls she had lived ever since; they were to surround her for the rest of her life. It was the house of darkness, the house of dumbness, the house of suffocation. Osmond's beautiful mind gave it neither light nor air; Osmond's beautiful mind indeed seemed to peep down from a small high window and mock at her. Of course it had not been physical suffering; for physical suffering there might have been a remedy. She could come and go; she had her liberty; her husband was perfectly polite. He took himself so seriously; it was something appalling. Under all his culture, his cleverness, his amenity, under his good-nature, his facility, his knowledge of life, his egotism lay hidden like a serpent in a bank of flowers. She had taken him seriously, but she had not taken him so seriously as that. How could she – especially when she had known him better? She was to think of him as he thought of himself – as the first gentleman in Europe. So it was that she had thought of him at first, and that indeed was the reason she had married him. But when she began to see what it implied she drew back; there was more in the bond than she had meant to put her name to. It implied a sovereign contempt for everyone but some three or four very exalted people whom he envied, and for everything in the world but half a dozen ideas of his own. That was very well; she would have gone with him even there a long distance; for he pointed out to her so much of the baseness and shabbiness of life, opened her eyes so wide to the stupidity, the depravity, the ignorance of mankind, that she had been properly impressed with the infinite vulgarity of things and of the virtue of keeping one's self unspotted by it. But this base, ignoble world, it appeared, was after all what one was to live for; one was to keep it for ever in one's eye, in order not to enlighten or convert or redeem it, but to extract from it some recognition of one's own superiority. On the one hand it was despicable, but on the other it afforded a standard. Osmond had talked to Isabel about his renunciation, his indifference, the ease with which he dispensed with the usual aids to success; and all this had seemed to her admirable. She had thought it a grand indifference, an exquisite independence. But indifference was really the last of his qualities; she had never seen any one who thought so much of others. For herself, avowedly, the world had always interested her and the study of her fellow creatures been her constant passion. She would have been willing, however, to renounce all her curiosities and sympathies for the sake of a personal life, if the person concerned had only been able to make her believe it was a gain! This at least was her present conviction; and the thing certainly would have been easier than to care for society as Osmond cared for it.

He was unable to live without it, and she saw that he had never really done so; he had looked at it out of his window even when he appeared to be most detached from it. He had his ideal, just as she had tried to have hers; only it was strange that people should seek for justice in such different quarters. His ideal was a conception of high prosperity and propriety, of the aristocratic life, which she now saw that he deemed himself always, in essence at least, to have led. He had never lapsed from it for an hour; he would never have recovered from the shame of doing so. That again was very well; here too she would have agreed; but they attached such different ideas, such different associations and desires, to the same formulas. Her notion of the aristocratic life was simply the union of great knowledge with great liberty; the knowledge would give one a sense of duty and the liberty a sense of enjoyment. But for Osmond it was altogether a thing of forms, a conscious, calculated attitude.

The Portrait of a Lady (1881)[1]

* * *

This extract is taken from the most famous chapter in one of the finest novels of the nineteenth century. When writing the new Prefaces for the novels to be included in the great New York edition of his fiction of 1907–9, James referred to this chapter as 'obviously the best thing in the book'.[2] His appreciation is significant. Chapter 42 of *The Portrait of a Lady* heralds the major development in James's art of fiction that would determine much of the form and content of his future novels. The passage, like the chapter from which it is taken, registers nothing except the movement of a consciousness. Isabel Archer sits alone in the Palazzo Roccanera in Rome until far into the night; she does nothing but think, about herself, her husband, and their life together. Action and event exist only in her response to them. For James, the rendering of a consciousness, so responding, was increasingly becoming the overriding objective of the novelist's art. Only through such a focus on an inner consciousness, an intelligence, could what might be called 'the story of a story' be told. That is the phrase James used to describe the 1907 Prefaces, but it is capable of wider application and can be seen as pointing towards James's contribution to a profounder realism than any of his contemporaries were able to achieve. The story is simply what happens – action and event – but the real story lies in the way the consciousnesses of those involved in what happens, perceive, respond to, and understand, such action and event. This is why the plots of James's novels come rarely to stray beyond relatively commonplace areas of personal relationships, and the problems, failures, treacheries and betrayals, that so often characterize them. In themselves, such plots amount to very little; what transmutes them into art is James's focus on the moving, expanding, exploring consciousnesses of those involved in them. It was the psychologist William James, Henry's brother, who first used the phrase the 'stream of consciousness' – destined to be taken up by twentieth-century novelists to describe what they saw as a new literary technique of psychological realism – but Henry James had long before arrived at the view that it was indeed the movement of consciousness that should provide the essential form and content of the art of fiction. The narrative form of a novel, that is, James came to believe, is determined by the need to register, with increasing exclusiveness and refinement, nothing but the perceiving consciousness; the novel's content is what such consciousnesses are capable of perceiving.

Isabel Archer's 'extraordinary meditative vigil', as James called it in 1907, thus signals the direction in which James's art was moving. In one sense nothing happens. Isabel sits alone, motionless. There are no interruptions, no alarms or excursions, no excitement of any kind. Yet the occasion is a dramatic crisis, a turning-point in the novel. That the chapter successfully conveys as much is the reason James took such delight in it in 1907. As he wrote then, the scene 'throws the action further forward than twenty "incidents" might have done'. What it does is enact the very process by which Isabel Archer comes to recognize the precise situation in which she finds herself. The chapter traces the developing consciousness, brilliantly intertwining the movement itself with the growth in understanding which that movement brings about. Isabel's expanding consciousness is both subject and form. The drama and excitement are exclusively internal, heightened, even, by the stasis of the character and her setting. As James describes it, the chapter 'was designed to have all the vivacity of incident and all the economy of picture'. Its life is the life of the mind; its economy is produced by the transformations that growing awareness is inevitably effecting within the character. James's final summarizing comment in 1907 was that the chapter was 'a representation simply of [Isabel's] motionlessly *seeing*, and an attempt withal to make the mere still lucidity of her act as "interesting" as the surprise of a caravan or the identification of a pirate'. Caravans and pirates belong to a mode of novel-writing remote from James's; but he is unwilling to allow that mode to pre-empt all forms of excitement and surprise. There is drama to be found in the emerging consciousness; as Isabel Archer sees more and more clearly the precise realities of her position, that drama is played out. His continuing commitment to the drama of the consciousness, achieved here in Chapter 42 of *The Portrait*, is central to an understanding of James's subsequent refinements of technique, and to the imaginative achievement of the great novels that were to follow.

*

Vital as the passage is as a revelation of Isabel's developing consciousness, its movement and style remain James's own. In James's hands, the stream of consciousness is never in any danger of becoming a naturalistic device. It is James's own presence in the passage that assures its coherence, its progressive development, its poetic expansion of image and symbol. His control is such that the passage does exactly what he wants it to do. So careful and constructed is it, that it almost refuses explication or explanation. What it does require, however, is a sense of what has gone before. It is the novel's past that invades and enriches the passage. For its fullest impact, the stage in Isabel's development enacted here depends upon the whole prior movement of the novel that has brought the protagonist to the situation in which we discover her. This cumulative assimilation of what has gone before adds immensely to the rich density of the passage.

Like the chapter from which it is taken, and to a considerable degree like *The Portrait of a Lady* as a whole, the passage is centrally concerned with the collision between the bright beauty of freedom and spontaneity on the one hand, and the darkness and evil of restriction and imprisonment on the other. Even Isabel Archer's situation, sitting alone in her candle-lit drawing-room far into the night, becomes part of the meaning, the truth, that is slowly unfolded in Chapter 42. Isabel is indeed alone; she is immured; she is surrounded by darkness. The Palazzo Roccanera is well-named, and James has already skilfully exploited its sinister connotations. The palace of black rock, we learn, is situated 'in the very heart of Rome' (II, 87): throughout *The Portrait of a Lady* James consistently uses the Roman Catholic church as an image of restriction and control; it is an institution associated with power, in particular with the power to limit and constrain individual freedom. If such a view appears to suggest an attitude more characteristic of Hawthorne than of James, it is true that the description of the Palazzo Roccanera reminds us forcibly of the Hawthorne of *The Marble Faun*. Subtler than Hawthorne, however, whose New England conscience is perhaps too obviously dismayed by the Gothic antiquity of the capital of Christendom, James is prepared to mediate his first account of the palace through the consciousness of Edward Rosier, a young American in love with Isabel's step-daughter. The palace is 'a dark and massive structure' and to Rosier's 'apprehensive mind' – he is doubtful if he can win Pansy's hand in face of her father's suspected opposition – it appeared more like a 'dungeon' than a palace. To his eye, it seems that Pansy is 'immured in a kind of domestic fortress', 'a pile which bore a stern old Roman name, which smelt of historic deeds, of crime and craft and violence'. And he is 'haunted by the conviction that at picturesque periods young girls had been shut up there to keep them from their true loves, and then, under the threat of being thrown into convents, had been forced into unholy marriages' (II, 88). James of course implies that it is Rosier's particular circumstances that make him see a fine example of a Roman renaissance palace in such a light; had things been different, he would have better appreciated 'the love of local color' (II, 88) that had persuaded Mr and Mrs Osmond to settle here. None the less,

Rosier's account releases into the novel a set of distinctly ominous suggestions surrounding the Palazzo Roccanera, which subsequent events will confirm rather than dispel. Even the high Gothic of the 'picturesque periods', and the shut up young girls, will prove not so wide of the mark: Pansy is in fact fated to be shut up in a covent until she is ready to give up Rosier.

What Chapter 42 unfolds is Isabel's conscious admission of the prison she is in. Hence the appropriateness of the Palazzo Roccanera as the setting within which, at night, alone, this realization comes in full. At last Isabel is allowing her mind to flow freely; she is reviewing her life with her husband, Osmond, fully, without inhibition. But what her consciousness is revealing is that only her mind is free – free to recognize and understand that she has allowed herself to be trapped. Even that irony, however, is dwarfed by a greater one: she has sacrificed her freedom in the belief that she was discovering it. Her marriage, as we shall see, had been her declaration of independence; but declaring her independence, she had in fact been surrendering her freedom. Hence in the passage the constant redefinitions of the forms of freedom, openness, independence, spontaneity, and their opposites: narrowness, restraint, limitation, confinement, imprisonment.

As the passage begins, Isabel is thinking of the impression made upon her by her husband. She is trying to justify to herself the enormity of the mistake she has made. Osmond had had 'all the appearance' of a man 'living in the open air of the world'. But 'appearance' proved to be all it was. The reality of Osmond had no connexion with notions of freshness and freedom and openness. This initial sentence itself, with its series of related clauses, suggests movement, progress, a life perhaps of meaningful journeying, as Isabel romantically conceives it. 'Indifferent to small considerations', and 'caring only for truth and knowledge' suggest largeness, an expansive view, but it is the narrowness of the 'small considerations' that really characterizes Osmond. He had, she admits, warned her that he loved the conventional. She is recalling a conversation before their marriage. In response to his declaration that he worshipped propriety, Isabel had asked: 'You're not conventional?' Osmond had responded: 'I like the way you utter that word! No, I'm not conventional: I'm convention itself' (II, 19). Characteristically, Isabel had refused to accept the literal meaning of this. She had interpreted Osmond's words in accordance with her romantically idealistic vision of his character. Into 'convention' she had read that notion of tradition which she, like James himself, prizes: that sense 'of the love of harmony and order and decency and of all the stately offices of life'. Hence his words had become for her a 'noble declaration'. In fact, 'I'm convention itself' was a revelation both of Osmond's monstrous egotism and of his devotion to all the emptiest formalities of social existence. That Isabel had been deaf to the warning implicit in Osmond's remark was no more than part of her inability to see him as in fact he was. The Osmond she had married had been a phantasy of her own creation. As she had just admitted a paragraph or two earlier, 'she had imagined a world of things that had no substance.' 'She had had a more wondrous vision of him, fed through charmed senses and oh such a stirred fancy! – she had not read him right.' As she finally admits, she had seen in Gilbert Osmond a suitable recipient for the wealth she had inherited. The money had been left her to make her independent, so that she could pursue the opportunities of life she had seemed so intent on, untrammelled by economic needs. Ironically, she had decided it was Osmond who needed to be free. This American dilettante, of such delicate good taste, had seemed a poor, lonely, yet noble figure. 'She would', romantically, 'launch his boat for him.' This was the 'factitious theory' on which she had married him. And this was the theory for which she now was suffering.

Because marriage to Osmond did not lead outward to a fuller life, an enhanced freedom. It led only inward, inward to the confines of Osmond's requirements and expectations. Marriage to Osmond had meant a withdrawal from the open air of the world into the mansion of Osmond's own habitation, a mansion composed less of bricks and stones than of attitudes and assumptions erected into a system as inflexible and rigid as the walls of the Palazzo Roccanera. This is the house of Osmond into which she has been lured, and it is the lineaments of such a house she has been compelled to recognize.

The Portrait of a Lady is a book full of houses, which are developed by James into one of his novel's central metaphors. But none of these houses, not even the Palazzo Roccanera, is as dark and sinister as the structure Osmond has built to keep the world at bay, and which it has become Isabel's fate to share. Houses can be places of romantic freedom shutting out the vulgar realities of the world outside – like the house in Albany, New York, which Isabel had left to come to Europe with her rich aunt; or places of high culture and civilization, in which freedom coexists with the forms of manners and tradition – like Gardencourt in England, where Isabel initially arrives after crossing the Atlantic; or places of apartness from, and superiority to, the everyday world – like

Osmond's hill-top villa outside Florence; or prisons – like the Palazzo Roccanera. But, to repeat, none of the houses in *The Portrait* are as negative and life-denying as the 'house' whose inner reality is Osmond himself. The 'terror' with which Isabel had finally recognized this – Chapter 42 succeeds in making such a Gothic term much more than melodramatic – had been 'incredulous' because she still could not believe the depth of her error, the immensity of her mistake. But Osmond's measure was now her measure; his walls closed her around – and for life. From 'the house of darkness, the house of dumbness, the house of suffocation', there was to be no escape. Before their marriage, Isabel had thought she had seen in Osmond 'an indefinable beauty' – 'in his situation, in his mind, in his face' (II, 168). What she has had to learn is that for her Osmond's 'beautiful mind' has created only dumbness and suffocation: in the image of that beautiful mind seeming to 'peep down' from a small high window, James captures the essential pettiness of Osmond perfectly. Osmond looks down on everyone and everything.

Osmond's love of the conventional, as we have seen, indicates less a concern for the formalities of harmony and order than a mere submission to the outward proprieties of social decorum. Such a pusillanimous submission circumscribes freedom. But Osmond's case is worse. His deference to society conceals the fact that in the end he defers only to himself. His is the only measure that really counts. The prison in which Isabel is immured is not the Palazzo Roccanera – she is free to come and go – but the prison of Osmond's egotism. It is his egotism – 'I'm convention itself' – which finally prevents Osmond's culture and knowledge from creating more than the appearance of a man 'living in the open air of the world'. For James, culture and knowledge and the rest are indeed, in terms of another central set of images in *The Portrait of a Lady*, flowers, capable of growth; but in Osmond's case, they are flowers concealing the 'serpent' of egotism. And the poison of that egotism is capable of blighting and withering flowers of every kind.

Osmond's egotism is such that he believes that only his views and opinions have the right to exist. Soon after their marriage her husband had told Isabel 'that she had too many ideas and that she must get rid of them' (II, 170). What was required was her acceptance of him at his own self-evaluation 'as the first gentleman in Europe'. Ironically, she had been prepared to believe that that was indeed what he was. In fact, in Osmond's sense of it, the phrase points to nothing more than his belief in his own superiority, his condescension, and contempt for humanity at large. Once, Osmond had told Isabel of the few men he envied: the Emperor of Russia, the Sultan of Turkey, and the Pope. The tyranny he wishes to exercise over Isabel and Pansy leads one to believe that he had only been half joking.

Isabel admits that she had been prepared to go very far towards accepting Osmond's opinions, however vain. Caring only for the 'truth and knowledge' they could discover together, she had been prepared to go along with him, to see with his eyes the baseness and shabbiness, the stupidity and depravity, the ignorance, the 'infinite vulgarity' of so much of mankind. What she cannot accept is that such a recognition should be made only as a way of insisting upon one's own superiority. For Isabel, the recognition of such things is only justifiable if it is conjoined with a need to 'enlighten or convert or redeem' such a world. In the end it will be Isabel's fate to recognize herself as supremely the victim of all the baseness that Osmond sees in the world. What she chooses to do in that situation – her decision to return to her husband, to renounce any avenue of escape – perhaps involves an acting out of the attitude she articulates here. At this point in Chapter 42 her understanding is focused upon another aspect of Osmond's falsity: his 'renunciation' and 'indifference' are but hollow things. He is the slave of the society he affects to despise. But just as earlier she had admitted she had been prepared to go a long way towards accepting Osmond's attitudes, so now she accepts an element of similarity in their positions. She too had been interested in 'the study of her fellow creatures' – the phrase hints at too great a degree of detachment for comfort. There is within Isabel an impulse towards withdrawal from, rather than engagement with, life. Her ideal of happiness, of the 'personal life' for which she would have been prepared to settle, is of 'high places', 'from which the world would seem to lie below one, so that one could look down with a sense of exaltation and advantage, and judge and choose and pity . . .' (II, 166). The language here, like the basic metaphor, is dangerously close to that used in relation to Osmond himself. This is why, in the final section of the extract, James allows his heroine once again to see things almost with Osmond's eyes.

Isabel recognizes Osmond's ideal to be his conception of the aristocratic life, a life of 'high prosperity and propriety'. She understands his desire to sustain such an ideal, never to fall away from it. She understands because she shares such an ideal: 'that again was very well; here too she would have agreed.' What Isabel is agreeing to is the supreme value of the aristocratic life. But the crucial difference that splits Isabel and Osmond apart is in the area of definition. For Isabel, the aristocratic life means 'the union of great knowledge with great liberty'; for Osmond, it was 'altogether a thing of forms'. For Osmond, aristocratic values enshrine traditions and conventions, but in such a way as to empty them of the human decencies they are designed to preserve. For him they compose a system, a posture, a set of prescriptions of what is and is not allowed. It is just this system that is constricting, limiting, suffocating Isabel; it is this that has destroyed her sense of liberty. Liberty, on the other hand, is precisely what she sees the aristocratic life as preserving: great liberty with great knowledge. It is a definition clearly dear to James's own heart. But it contains an element of paradox of which Isabel is scarcely aware: are great liberty and great knowledge wholly compatible? *The Portrait of a Lady* is in part at least an exploration of just that question.

*

To consider such a question is to move towards an understanding of how it is that Isabel Archer has arrived at the circumstance which Chapter 42 is concerned to reveal. In this chapter, James allows Isabel's consciousness to move to a full and unflinching acknowledgement of the folly of her marriage to Gilbert Osmond. James, however, does not allow Isabel full self-knowledge; the reasons that lie behind her decision to marry Osmond in the first place are, some of them, alluded to; others, though, are no more than implied. Unlike Laura Kennedy in Trollope's *Phineas Finn* – a novel which may have furthered James's interest in the theme of a woman imprisoned by a disastrous marriage – who makes a self-destructive marriage more or less aware that she is doing so, Isabel has simply mistaken her man. She is prepared to acknowledge that she has allowed her romantic imagination to transmute Osmond's reality. But Chapter 42 at times implies that there are other underlying links between Isabel and Osmond that help to explain their fateful marriage.

The portrait of Isabel Archer that James draws in the early sections of the novel is that of a young American girl, appealingly frank and vivacious, but with quite a high opinion of her own worth. Her pride and self-esteem, however, her 'meagre knowledge', her self-confidence, James persuades us, are more than compensated for by her 'fixed determination to regard the world as a place of brightness, of free expansion, of irresistible action' (I, 60). Isabel has 'a great desire for knowledge', 'an immense curiosity about life', and carries within herself 'a great fund of life' (I, 39). In all of James's fiction such phrases amount to great positives. In *The Ambassadors* (1903), one of the last and greatest of James's novels, the message Strether urges upon little Bilham is still 'live all you can'. To experience life to the full, to be open and receptive to the immensities of experience: such is the stance towards life that James's fiction endorses and promotes.

Despite her faults, all of them a consequence of her youthful inexperience or innocence, Isabel Archer arrives in Europe with just such attitudes and expectations. The novel's central concern is how such a world-view fares when confronted by the complexities which may exist within reality. Initially, Isabel demonstrates the seriousness of her determination to remain an independent, individual participant in life's variety and scope in the most obvious way open to the heroine of a nineteenth-century novel: she turns down two excellent offers of marriage. Lord Warburton, an English aristrocrat, active on the reform side in contemporary politics, is immensely appealing; still more 'immense' is his willingness to marry a young American girl. But, for Isabel, marriage to Lord Warburton would mean the acquisition of a fixed social role; her identity would be determined by the place in society she would occupy. She would no longer be free to be herself. Caspar Goodwood is an American, a man Isabel subsequently thinks she might well have married, had her aunt not carried her off to Europe. Goodwood is a powerful presence throughout *The Portrait of a Lady*, his importance much underrated in many accounts of the novel. His love for Isabel is permanent, unshakable, rock-like. At regularly phased intervals in the novel he confronts Isabel with his love (Chapters 16, 32, 48), and on each occasion she is shaken to the core of her being. Inevitably, in the closing pages, it is Goodwood who offers her an escape route from the path that will lead her back to Rome and Osmond. Overwhelmed by the 'white lightning' of his kiss, sinking in the sea of his passion and love, she once again barely preserves her independence of action (II, 381). Like Warburton, Goodwood is a threat to Isabel's freedom. His passion is always on the point of sweeping her away. Marriage to Goodwood would mean loss of self in physical fulfilment. Thus rejecting both sex and society, Isabel is marking out her sense of individual freedom and independence. That a young woman can so act, can so assert her determination to explore experience, to 'affront' her destiny – this is what fascinates Ralph, her cousin, and persuades him to arrange for the inheritance that will allow her the financial freedom to continue on her way.

In Isabel's rejections of Warburton and Goodwood, however, there is also a hint of an attitude towards experience of a more problematical kind. She denies to Ralph that she wishes 'to drain the cup of experience. "No [she tells him], I don't wish to touch the cup of experience. It's a poisoned drink! I only want to see for myself." "You want to see, but not to feel," Ralph remarked' (I, 188). The disengagement apparent here may help to explain the refusal of marriage, but it is clearly also a stance that carries its own dangers. Disengagement can easily harden into coldness and remoteness, a dehumanizing, non-involvement. When Osmond appears in the novel, Isabel meets a man whose air of cultured superiority to life conceals exactly these characteristics. What this means is that Isabel's marriage to Osmond comes about at least in part because of an apparent likeness between them. Osmond seems to offer Isabel exactly what she wants: an involvement with life which will somehow remain detached from it.

The point is an important one because it has often been argued that it is a weakness of the novel that Isabel stubbornly insists on marrying Osmond against the advice of all her friends. Ralph Touchett, for example, has no doubt whatsoever about Osmond's worth, and conveys his view to Isabel quite directly: Osmond is no more than 'a sterile dilettante' (II, 62). That he says so much, so directly, is a mark of Ralph's love for his cousin. He it is who has launched Isabel – just as she is now proposing to launch Osmond. So perhaps Ralph is guilty of a form of manipulation: making it possible for Isabel to be free so that he, inhibited by his ill-health from any more direct involvement, can at least enjoy the spectacle of observing what she does. The manipulation of one person by another is in James's fiction a capital crime: his version of Hawthorne's Unpardonable Sin. But there is a world of difference between Ralph's securing financial independence for Isabel, and the exploitative manipulation she will suffer at the hands of Osmond and Madame Merle, Osmond's former mistress. What is required is a finer discrimination. Isabel and Osmond may have some features in common, which helps to explain how Isabel, despite the warnings she receives, could fall into the trap devised for her by Madame Merle. But in the end husband and wife are fundamentally opposed to each other, as different as two people could be. Similarly with Ralph and Osmond. Both are connoisseurs, as Isabel appreciates. But for Ralph, as indeed for Rosier who is prepared to sell his superb collection of bibelots in the vain hope that Osmond will agree he is wealthy enough to marry Pansy, art and beauty are a part of life, not, as for Osmond, substitutes for it. It is

Isabel's failure to understand this – to appreciate Ralph's tone – a failure springing from her lack of knowledge and experience, that allows her to set aside his advice and be duped by Osmond.

Isabel is too young, too inexperienced, too unknowing – too American – not to be deceived by the devious complexity of the world in which she finds herself. Her qualities of vigour, frankness, openness, and spontaneity – admirable as they are – are not enough to save her. Just such a young American girl remained one of James's favourite characters, because through her he found an admirable way of articulating that international theme so central to his work. In the 1907 Preface, he agrees that when he was writing *The Portrait of a Lady* 'the "international" light lay, in those days, to my sense, thick and rich upon the scene'. What that 'international light' involved, however, was always more than a simple opposition between Europe and America; metaphysics are quite as important as geography, as the example of *The Portrait of a Lady* makes clear. That Isabel is American is of course important. Her origins are intended to make more explicable the attitudes she brings with her to Europe. And there is a sense in which James is interested in juxtaposing traditional notions of a New World's freshness and innocence against an Old World's more complex knowingness. But the fact that Osmond and Madame Merle, the novel's most devious characters, are American expatriates, underlines the fact that James's understanding of the international theme is more metaphorical than sociological.

James as artist cannot afford to dispense with either element of the international metaphor. He needs a kind of hospitality towards the variety and chances of life, he must retain a sense of openness to experience, a form of imaginative freedom; at the same time he has to be aware, to know what the world is like, of what it is capable. Freshness and spontaneity remained values to be prized. In a letter of 1889, on the art of fiction, he insisted that a concern for 'freedom' and 'life' – which 'is infinitely large, various and comprehensive' – is required of the novelist.[3] But in James's fiction life includes the knowledge and awareness that limit freedom. The early novels present us again and again with characters in search of experience; many of them, like James himself, come to Europe in the belief that it is there, rather than in America, that the full richness and diversity of life are to be found. But all too often what they find is that the experience they have advanced so eagerly towards injures or destroys them. In James's first novel, *Roderick Hudson* (1876), the pilgrim in search of experience in Europe is a young American artist. Ironically, the experience that was meant to enhance his art, destroys his life. In Europe Roderick discovers, as it were, too much of life; and his involvement with it proves to be at the expense of his art. Art and life, James implies, may be mutually destructive.

James's next voyager, the protagonist of *The American* (1877), fares little better than Roderick Hudson. Christopher Newman, whose name suggests both Christopher Columbus and the 'new man' the American was so frequently alleged to be, is clearly intended by James to be a representative American figure: he is successful, aggressive, determined, and his manners are free and easy in a decidedly democratic way. In the world of European high culture, however, he is an innocent abroad. In search of a wife, Newman lays siege to Europe; but he is repulsed. At the end of the novel, his honesty and moral integrity prove superior to those of his European antagonists; but his moral superiority does not save his life from impoverishment. *Daisy Miller* (1879), once again involves the defeat of (American) innocence by the complexities of (European) life. Daisy is a young American girl who flouts the conventions of European good manners; her frankness and naiveté, however, do not save her. Having seen the Coliseum in Rome by moonlight, in the company of a young Italian, she dies of a fever.

Roderick Hudson, Christopher Newman and Daisy Miller are all Americans who find themselves defeated by the order of experience they encounter in Europe. But *The Europeans* (1877) once again warns us against too simple a reading of the meaning of Europe and America in James's fiction. In *The Europeans* it is the un-American characters who see life as challenge, opportunity, freedom, the Americans – admittedly all from puritan New England – who see it in terms of narrowness, discipline, and duty.

The Portrait of a Lady thus emerges as a fuller examination of themes which had already established themselves as central to James's fiction. And however far James's method, his manner of writing and narrating, may have refined itself – in the direction heralded by Chapter 42 of *The Portrait* – such themes never ceased to fascinate him. Society and the individual, freedom and constraint, spontaneity and awareness, Europe and America, art and life, James constantly re-embarks on the imaginative exploration of these areas. Aware of the 'complex fate' of being an American, and satisfied to be neither just an English nor just an American artist, James sought above all for an art that would contain all such opposites, and in its pursuit he was prepared to sacrifice much.

Perhaps *The Portrait of a Lady* hints at his view of the necessary position of the artist. Gilbert Osmond is a portrait of the false artist: cold, remote, superior, despising life. Ralph Touchett, on the other hand, is a portrait of the true artist: detached, observing, but fascinated by, committed to, loving, understanding, life. Yet Ralph is unable to control the actions of those he observes. The artist can record and register, and make us understand, but nothing more. That is the price of his remaining detached.

In James's fiction the relationships between art, life, and morality in fact compose the ultimate figure in the carpet. To bring all these into aesthetic harmony is the ideal at which James's art of fiction is aimed. But any such resolution remains distinctly problematical. Over and over again, the endings of the novels suggest only a complex balancing of the three crucial elements. Art and morality both involve the ordering, patterning, arranging of life in some form. But life itself is fluid and resistant, unwilling to submit to the cage either of art or morality. Hence the sense of defeat, of something lost, of a price paid, which recurs in James's endings. Such a sense of loss is at the heart of James's tragic vision. In *The Portrait of a Lady* the ending involves Isabel's renunciation of freedom, a new life. The 'straight path' she chooses of return to Rome and Osmond may express a moral affirmation; but the triumph of morality, and perhaps of art, is gained, one feels, almost at the expense of life itself.

*

Henry James's decision to live most of his life in Europe underlines his belief that post-bellum American society could not provide him with adequate artistic sustenance. Like Cooper and Hawthorne before him, James was convinced that American society was too fluid, too new, too lacking in density and richness, too lacking in history, to provide the true novelist's imagination with material to be shaped and formed into art. He had made the point explicit in *Hawthorne* (1879), a short critical study of the American novelist which he had written not long before embarking on *The Portrait of a Lady*. James found much to admire in Hawthorne – his delicacy, purity, lightness – but argued that the lack of substance, of reality, in his fiction, was a consequence of the America in which he lived. Hawthorne's America lacked the social and cultural density which only an old, established civilization could provide. And in a famous passage, James went on to list 'the items of high civilization' present in English society, but absent from America: 'No State, in the European sense of the word, and indeed barely a specific national name. No sovereign, no court, no personal loyalty, no aristocracy, no church, no clergy, no army, no diplomatic service, no country gentlemen, no palaces, no castles, nor manors, nor old country-houses, nor parsonages, nor thatched cottages, nor ivied ruins; no cathedrals, nor abbeys, nor little Norman churches; no great Universities nor public schools – no Oxford, nor Eton, nor Harrow; no literature, no novels, no museums, no pictures, no political society, no sporting class – no Epsom nor Ascot!'[4] James of course is not arguing that America would be better off were it more like England; thinking as a novelist, he is suggesting that a society deprived of the forms and structures, the traditions and conventions which his list encapsulates, is one which under-nourishes the novelist's imagination. However, because it seemed to compare America unfavourably with England, *Hawthorne* sparked off a critical storm in America that dismayed James by its violence. Such a reaction, he felt, confirmed his view that America was still a provincial country. William Dean Howells refused to join in the attacks on James, and reviewed *Hawthorne* favourably. But Howells was in no way ready to agree with James about the inadequacy of American society as a subject for the novelist. He wrote to James expressing his disagreement. In his reply, James refused to budge:

> I sympathize even less with your protest against the idea that it takes an old civilization to set a novelist in motion – a proposition that seems to me so true as to be a truism. It is on manners, customs, usages, habits, forms, upon all things matured and established, that a novelist lives – they are the very stuff his work is made of. . . .

Howells had argued that James's list of items present in English life but lacking in America represented no more than 'dreary and worn-out paraphernalia' which the American novelist could well do without, since he had 'the whole of life' left to write about. But for James this was to beg the question: 'I should say we have just so much less of it [human life] as these same paraphernalia represent, and I think they represent an enormous quantity of it.'[5]

With our knowledge of what was about to occur in American fiction in the 1880s and 1890s – the emergence, under the leadership of William Dean Howells himself, of a new school of American writers dedicated to the realistic portrayal of the American scene – we are perhaps tempted to side here with Howells against James. If, more fairly, we set James's observations in the context of what was actually being written in America in the 1860s and the 1870s, then his views gain in weight. One literary historian has suggested that 'the literary life in the United States around 1880 was more soddenly parochial and unambitious than it had been for half a century', and it is difficult to disagree.[6] In such a situation, something did seem to be lacking in America's literary culture, and James's decision to seek richer literary sustenance in Europe is entirely understandable. As a result, by the time America's literary culture began to stir itself and think of moving in new directions – such as the new realism championed by William Dean Howells himself – James had already marked out his own international territory. But international is what it always remained. James never repudiated America. On the contrary; he was never other than fascinated by America and the American character. As *The Portrait of a Lady* shows, the idea of America, the challenge the New World represented to the Old, remained as creatively fruitful a concept for him, as it had been for Cooper and all the other classic American authors of the nineteenth century.

Taken as a whole, the writings of Henry James represent a literary achievement well beyond that attained by any other American writer in the period 1865–1900. The driving force of realism in the 1880s and 1890s inevitably turned American writing inwards: to the delineation of the American scene in all its social and geographical variety. For serious writers, living and writing in American society, it is hard to see how it could have been otherwise. But the school of realism, despite the occasional suggestion of European influence, did produce a degree of narrowness, even provincialism. It is James alone who remains in touch, not only with the classic American tradition of the novel, but with the English and European traditions as well. Whatever the reservations of some American critics, uneasy over James's expatriatism, one may doubt whether he would have achieved so much had he stayed at home. And while it is true that James seems to remain aloof from the social and economic issues increasingly preoccupying his contemporaries in America, it is worth emphasizing that in James there is no final rejection of American idealism, and that the values of freedom and spontaneity within society which his fiction celebrates, are precisely the values that the new American materialism, with its capitalist economic system and Social Darwinist philosophy, seemed primarily to threaten.

Notes

1 The text of the extract from Chapter 42 of *The Portrait of a Lady* is taken from the Macmillan two-volume edition, published in London in 1921.
2 This and subsequent quotations from James's Preface to *The Portrait of a Lady* are taken from Henry James, *The Art of the Novel, with an Introduction by Richard P. Blackmur*, New York, 1962, pp. 40–58.
3 See 'A Letter to the Deerfield Summer School', in Leon Edel (ed.), *Henry James, The Future of the Novel*, New York, 1956, p. 29.
4 Henry James, *Hawthorne*, London, 1879, p. 43.
5 For an account of the reception of *Hawthorne*, and of the exchange between James and Howells, see Leon Edel, *Henry James, The Conquest of London 1870–1883*, London, 1962, pp. 387–94.
6 Warner Berthoff, *The Ferment of Realism, American Literature, 1884–1919*, New York, 1965, p. 47.

Further reading

'Henry James' in Spiller, Thorp, Johnson and Canby, *Literary History of the United States*, 1948, 4th rev. edn 1974.
Richard Poirier, *The Comic Sense of Henry James*, 1960.
Tony Tanner (ed.), *Henry James: Modern Judgments*, 1968.

4

Emily Dickinson (1830–86)

As imperceptibly as Grief
The Summer lapsed away –
Too imperceptible at last
To seem like Perfidy –
A Quietness distilled
As Twilight long begun,
Or Nature spending with herself
Sequestered Afternoon –
The Dusk drew earlier in –
The Morning foreign shone –
A courteous, yet harrowing Grace,
As Guest, that would be gone –
And thus, without a Wing
Or service of a Keel
Our Summer made her light escape
Into the Beautiful.

(1882)[1]

* * *

On one obvious level, this untitled poem, numbered 1540 in Thomas H. Johnson's standard edition of Emily Dickinson's poems, is a nature poem. It is a poem about summer's end or ending; ending is preferable because it better suggests the sense of process, of gradual movement, of slow fading, or evanescence, of slipping away, central to the poem. The poem is delicately poised, like the moment in the seasonal cycle it elegizes. It makes no assertions, insists on nothing; it infiltrates the consciousness of the reader almost as unobtrusively as the fine perception, out of which it grows, has been registered by the poet. In the end it is the perception itself that becomes the poem; it gains in definition, grows more real, through the careful movement of the poem. The intangible fading away of summer becomes an experience that can be perceived and registered, through the suggestive, recreative power of the poem. The poem looks back to an experience that is already in the past; but, writing the poem, Emily Dickinson has arrested, preserved, even defeated, the dissolution that characterizes it. However imperceptible, however difficult to define, the poet's sensibility has perceived and registered, and therefore in a sense captured and redeemed, summer's ending. Summer has slipped away – but not unnoticed. Its escape attempt has failed, because the movement of the season's fading has been transformed into the delicate perception which is the poem. Summer has escaped only into the poem.

Is it only summer that is in question though? Re-reading the poem, one begins to feel that what it registers is not limited to regret at the passing of summer. What is transformed is the whole natural world; summer's ending becomes a metaphor for all change, perhaps most of all for the change that overtakes the emotion identified in the poem's first line: grief. Seasonal change becomes a metaphor for the transformation of grief into its own kind of beauty. Change, the poem says, does not always mean change for the worse.

1540 has usually been printed as though it were a four-stanza poem. However, the final manuscript version has no stanza divisions. Nevertheless, the poem does clearly fall into four four-line sections, a structure supported by the pattern of rhyme in the second and fourth line of each section. The rhymes themselves seem to register the poem's meaning; like the seasonal moment it focuses upon, they are delicate, almost imperceptible. 'Shone'/'gone' seems to be a full rhyme, but 'away'/'Perfidy', 'begun'/'Afternoon', and 'Keel'/'Beautiful', even if allowance is made for a New England pronunciation, are not. Rather they are off-rhymes, a conscious 'effect', part of the process of imperceptible lapsing or fading with which the poem is concerned.

In the first section, the processes by which summer passes into autumn, and grief loses its original sharpness, are so conflated that it is difficult to know which is the primary subject. Yet the linking is in no way random, in the sense that the lapsing of summer is naturally an occasion of regret and sorrow. It is the words 'imperceptibly' and 'imperceptible', however, that dominate and set the tone of the section. The motion, the movement, is so fine, so gradual, so minimal, as to be scarcely distinguishable. Grief and summer cease to be themselves by the most delicate of modulations. Hence no act of treachery is involved – no betrayal of the unfallen state and its value:

> Too imperceptible at last
> To seem like Perfidy –

Any perfidy would, however, have been illusory; grief's slow fading is as inevitable as the season's change. Such fading, at worst, might '*seem* like Perfidy'. Emily Dickinson takes too realistic a view of human experience to see so inevitable a progression as involving actual betrayal. In the three earlier manuscript versions this last line of the first section reads: 'To feel like Perfidy.' 'Feel' is finally rejected presumably because it goes too far towards implying that some element of perfidy is indeed involved in the pattern of such change. Yet at least a hint of just such a feeling remains. The gentle negation of the lines hardly effaces the impression created by a word as powerful as 'perfidy'; and the change from 'feel' to 'seem' is a move away from subjectivity towards a more objective statement. In the end the perfidy of the opening four lines is paradoxically, evenhandedly, both real and unreal.

The two following four-line sections define the indefinable. Summer's lapsing is perceived through a group of natural images. Sound and vision are conflated in such a way that each images the other:

> A Quietness distilled
> As Twilight long begun,

Summer's ending has produced a pure quiet, a stillness like that of twilight time. And twilight itself is beginning earlier – 'The Dusk drew earlier in.' The second two lines in this section:

> Or Nature spending with herself
> Sequestered Afternoon –

equally suggest quiet, stillness, withdrawal – even isolation. Nature has turned it upon itself as summer slips away, using itself up, 'spending' itself.

The third section of the poem contrasts the times of morning and evening. In the morning, summer, with its bright sunshine, still seems like summer. But such brightness already appears a trifle unnatural, 'foreign', out of place. In a wonderfully imaginative image, the sun becomes a polite guest who knows it is time for him to leave; his continued presence is a courtesy, but a rather disturbing one, almost as though he has overstayed his welcome.

On the basis of these perceptions the poet recognizes summer's ending, 'its light escape'. As an adjective, 'light' suggests the delicacy of movement, the barely perceptible quality of the seasonal change, while, as a noun, 'light' picks up the earlier suggestion of dusk and twilight's fading. The escape itself is associated with images of flight and movement, a bird and a ship. Summer, denied wing or keel, none the less becomes a migrant bird or sailing ship voyaging into new waters, escaping the world of seasonal change, becoming instead the entirely beautiful. Winters thinks that the last line 'verges ever so slightly on an easy prettiness of diction'.[2] But what is meant, perhaps, is that its very evanescence is what gives summer its final beauty.

Such an idea is certainly one that recurs in Emily Dickinson's poetry. It is Wallace Stevens who insists in 'Sunday Morning' that 'death is the mother of beauty', but Emily Dickinson would certainly have understood what he meant. In a letter of 1876 she wrote that 'going out of sight in itself has a peculiar charm',[3] and in poem 1714 she writes:

> By a departing light
> We see acuter, quite,
> Than by a wick that stays.
> There's something in the flight
> That clarifies the sight
> And decks the rays.

Poem 1540 is precisely full of 'departing light' and the kind of flight 'that clarifies the sight'. Summer's ending is perceived by just such a light, and it is that light that gives the poem its parting poignancy. Other poems which celebrate seasonal change, spring and winter and autumn, as well as summer, share a similar perspective. 1422, another summer poem, is closely linked to 1540 through the suggestion it contains that summer is made more real by being over:

> Summer has two Beginnings –
> Beginning once in June –
> Beginning in October
> Affectingly again –

– as though the recollected summer has a greater imaginative reality than the real thing. Or again, in the words of the poem:

> As finer is a going
> Than a remaining Face –

presumably, that is, because 'By a departing light / We see acuter. . . .'

These different poems, like 1540, remind us that the evanescence of season into season is itself only an index of a wider pattern of change, movement, dissolution, the passing away of things. A sense of loss, even of grief, at such inevitable change is common to them all. The grief of the first line of 1540 never disappears from the poem. In the lapsing of summer, in the quietness of twilight, in the sequestered afternoon, in the early dusk, and particularly in the 'harrowing Grace' of the problematical brightness of the morning sun, grief and evanescence are subtly intertwined. The linking is a natural one because the sense of loss, of passing away, involved in fading and evanescence, is in the end the same sense as is produced by the absolute of loss which is death. All of Emily Dickinson's poems involve an exploration of the circumferences of her consciousness, an imaginative leap towards the outer limits of her awareness. But death she recognizes as the final limit, the boundary of that consciousness and awareness. Death thus becomes inevitably a major preoccupation, and also the sharpest and most absolute intensifier of all human experience. It is in the light produced by the change which is death that we see life most sharply of all. The death at seven weeks old of an infant daughter of T. W. Higginson produced this extraordinary poem:

A Dimple in the Tomb
Makes that ferocious Room
A Home –

(1489)

as well as the slightly longer poem (1490) which begins:

The Face in evanescence lain
Is more distinct than our's –

It was apparently the sense of loss, of losing and fading away, above all, which vivified and expanded the circumference of Emily Dickinson's consciousness. The result was the creation of poems which, with extraordinary frequency, escape, like 1540, into the Beautiful.

*

Poem 1540 is dated 1882 because that is the year in which the last of the four manuscript copies of the poem was written out, and because it is that fourth copy which is reproduced here. However, the poem originated in 1865 when Emily Dickinson wrote what subsequently proved to be not a final draft of the poem. That this earliest surviving manuscript version should be regarded as only a preliminary draft is suggested by the fact that the two manuscript versions of 1866 – like the final 1882 one – agree in reducing the 1865 poem to half its original length by omitting four middle four-line stanzas.

Such a consideration of the manuscript versions of an Emily Dickinson poem is necessary because no more than seven of her poems exist in an authorized public version: almost none of her poems, that is, were published in her lifetime. In fact this particular poem is one of the few made available to nineteenth-century readers. In 1866, Emily Dickinson sent a copy of it, and three other poems, to the critic T. W. Higginson, and much later, in 1891, five years after her death, Higginson published the poem in *Atlantic Monthly*, in the course of an article about the poems and letters he had received from her. In the same year the poem also appeared in *Poems by Emily Dickinson*, the very first collection of her poems to be published, and one which printed no more than 116 out of the 1775 poems she wrote.

Emily Dickinson's publishing history is thus rather similar to that of Gerard Manley Hopkins. Both are nineteenth-century poets whose impact was delayed until well into the twentieth century. Such a circumstance makes Emily Dickinson a particular problem for a student concerned with the context, as well as the text, of American writing. Emily Dickinson's lack of interest in publication of her work during her lifetime seems to indicate an intensely personal poetic life, and an unconcern for the world outside, perhaps even a disinclination to be engaged with external, public realities. And it is true that her poems hardly ever allude directly to the society and history of the country in which she lived. Her period of greatest creative intensity occurred during the American Civil War; but that war hardly appears in her poems. Again, one of the greatest preoccupations of nineteenth-century American literature is with America itself: what it is, and what it means. For a poet like Whitman, who believed that 'the United States themselves' were 'the greatest poem', what it meant to be an American poet was an overriding question. Not so, however, for Emily Dickinson, who showed no interest in such issues. On the other hand, she cannot be seen as embodying an alternative, Anglo-American tradition; she is not a latter-day Washington Irving, nor even a precursor of James's internationalism. She never visited Europe, and apart from brief visits to Boston, Philadelphia and Washington, hardly travelled in the United States. All her life was passed in Amherst, Massachusetts, where she was born, and where she lived with her family and a small circle of acquaintances. In one poem she wrote 'I see – New Englandly' (285), but even her New England vision was largely limited to what she could see inside her house, in her garden, from her window, or in church.

It is facts such as these which helped to give rise to the myth of Emily Dickinson as the poet recluse, imprisoned in her Amherst house, victim either of a tyrannical father or of a frustrated love affair, the archetype of the writer as the isolated, alienated figure, finding in her art an escape from the barrenness of life. Recent biographical research has done much to challenge this picture. Emily Dickinson's friendships kept her well in touch with that wider world beyond Amherst, while her correspondence was more diverse and more extensive in range of subject than earlier commentators realized. About her reading, too, there was nothing narrow or limited or provincial; books were always among her best companions. Given the cultural traditions of the New England society in which she lived, it was inevitable that she should know the Bible, and psalm- and hymn-books well. She plundered all of them in her poems. Shakespeare she pondered deeply. 'After long disuse of her eyes,' Higginson said, 'she read Shakespeare and thought why is any other book needed.' She read all the familiar New England writers: Emerson, Lowell, Hawthorne, William Cullen Bryant. She admired the Brontës, and both Brownings; she read Dickens and George Eliot. But of Edgar Allan Poe she said, 'Of Poe, I know too little to think,' and poor Whitman fared even worse: 'You speak of Mr Whitman,' she wrote to Higginson, 'I never read his Book – but was told that he was disgraceful.' Her friends, her correspondents, her reading – all of these kept Emily Dickinson in contact with a wider world. Her father, too, was an eminent figure in public life: treasurer of Amherst College, twice a member of the state legislature, and once a Whig member of Congress. Emily Dickinson herself may not have had a devoted interest in American politics, but she was in a position to keep up with current events. And at the very least the Civil War meant the death of several young men from Amherst whom she had known.

On the basis of such evidence, the notion of Emily Dickinson as the poetic recluse, totally divorced from the life surrounding her, has clearly to be qualified. Yet revisionist criticism can only go so far. There is no way in which the poetry of Emily Dickinson can be seen as having much contact with the changing America in which she lived. In every sense of style and theme she *is* the poetic antithesis of Walt Whitman. For Whitman, private life and public life are one; his life is America's life.

For Emily Dickinson real life is private life; there is no other. Strangely, on one occasion she did write a poem about one of the crucial factors in the transformation of America occurring in her lifetime.

> I like to see it lap the Miles –
> And lick the Valleys up –
> And stop to feed itself at Tanks –
> And then – prodigious step
>
> Around a Pile of Mountains –
> And supercilious peer
> In Shanties – by the sides of Roads –
> And then a Quarry pare
>
> To fit its sides
> And crawl between
> Complaining all the while
> In horrid – hooting stanza –
> Then chase itself down Hill –
>
> And neigh like Boanerges –
> Then – prompter than a Star
> Stop – docile and omnipotent
> At its own stable door –
>
> (585)

This poem about a railway engine Yvor Winters regarded as 'abominable', marked by that 'quality of silly playfulness' which he saw as frequently disfiguring the author's poems.[4] Other critics, inevitably, have found the poem admirable. What is true is that the poem makes the engine seem decently quaint, a fiery horse much more docile than omnipotent. Like the railway that passes Thoreau's Walden Pond, or the train on which Clifford and Hepzibah Pyncheon travel in Hawthorne's *House of the Seven Gables*, it is an echo of a new world that remains finally distant.

In any event, a poem about a railway engine is exceptional in the canon of Emily Dickinson's poetry. Normally her poetic interests never stray very far away from the great perennial themes which are defined in such abstractions as love, death, time, desire, pain, God. Reality in the sense of an immediately observed world of action and activity rarely obtrudes directly; and when it does, it is usually left behind in the course of the poem or even, as in the case of 1540, at the moment when the poem begins. As Denis Donoghue puts it, 'Reading her poems, one is surprised to find that they have any base in reality or fact, since a base in that element is what they seem least to need.'[5] What this means is that, to an unusual degree, Emily Dickinson's poems are flights of fancy or the imagination. And perhaps that old distinction is as good a way as one can find of distinguishing between her greater and lesser achievements. Some of her poems are the result of a play of fancy rather than of any greater imaginative intensity:

> Who is the East?
> The Yellow Man
> Who may be Purple if He can
> That carries in the Sun
>
> Who is the West?
> The Purple Man
> Who may be Yellow if He can
> That lets Him out again.
>
> (1032)

But of course there are many occasions when language and imagination combine to catch a stronger fire than this; when the poetic sensibility transforms experience, however meagre it may seem, into something new and strange. Emily Dickinson may not have 'lived' much in James's sense, but her sensibility seems not to have suffered; what Amherst could bring her was more than enough to work on. In her case, the landscapes of the imagination proved more than rich enough to supply the absences of active life.

Yet Emily Dickinson's imagination, like that of any other artist, did not come into being in a vacuum. It was the product of a New England culture which, in the period 1865–1900, was gradually losing the hegemony it had previously exercised over America's intellectual and cultural life. Thus there is a sense in which Emily Dickinson, like Whitman, belongs more to pre-Civil-War America than to the new nation brought to birth in the war's aftermath. If, for example, her exact religious position is difficult to define – at different times she appears as believer, sceptic, agnostic, or heretic – her poetry is none the less haunted by religious language, religious metaphors, and religious themes, which the Puritan poets of colonial America would have recognized. In terms of the cast of her imagination and its sources, Emily Dickinson's creative life seems to look backwards rather than forwards: back to Emerson and the Transcendentalists, back to Hawthorne and Melville, back to the Puritan poets of New England, back even to the religious poetry of Donne and Herbert in seventeenth-century England. There is irony, therefore, in the fact that her impact as a poet was to be made in the future, in the twentieth century when she came to be seen as possessing the only poetic voice, apart from Whitman's, worth attending to in nineteenth-century America. So entrenched is this view that all of twentieth-century American poetry has frequently been seen as deriving ultimately either from the antithetical Whitman or Dickinson strains in the American poetic tradition. The deeper irony is that it was during her own lifetime, and in the period 1865–1900, that Emily Dickinson mattered least. Her day in one sense was already over; in another, it was yet to come.

*

American literature between 1865 and 1900 is not distinguished by the strength of its poetic voice. It is as though, amid the clamour and stress of economic transformation and rapid social change, the voice of poetry is drowned out. In fact, large numbers of poets continued to write and publish. When E. C. Stedman, himself a minor New York poet, published his *An American Anthology* in 1901 (Emily Dickinson was included), he represented the period after 1865 by some 150 poets. But rarely if ever do many of these poets write in a manner that demands they be listened to. Whether they represent the New York school, like Stedman himself, Bayard Taylor, Richard Stoddard, Thomas Bailey Aldrich, and George Boker, or the Harvard group, William Vaughn Moody, George Cabot Lodge or Trumbull Stickney, or even if they belong to the older, pre-Civil War generation like J. R. Lowell, O. W. Holmes, or J. G. Whittier, their poetry remains resolutely minor. For most of them, poetry was a wholly genteel activity, conventional in mode of expression and quality of feeling. Above all, poetry was a retreat, an escape from the harsher realities of America's crude and bustling life. Stedman himself, when he was compiling his anthology, was quite explicit on the point. Surveying American poetry in 1900, he asked the question, 'What do we have?' and the answer he gave was, 'We have . . . minor voices and their tentative modes and tones.'[6] Even more interestingly, Stedman observed that the decline of American poetry, particularly in the previous twenty-five years, was related to the growing prestige of the realistic novel: the favoured mode of those American writers who were struggling above all to cope with the socially divided, the problematical and violent world in which they lived. Probably it is only with the short lyrics of Stephen Crane's two small volumes of poetry – *The Black Riders* (1895) and *War is Kind* (1899) – and Edgar Arlington Robinson's early narrative volumes at the end of the 1890s, that a distinctive new note begins to emerge in American poetry.

Nevertheless, through the 1860s and 1870s, in a small town in New England, Emily Dickinson was at work. Clearly, as we have seen, and it is a problem that demands acknowledgement, it cannot be argued that her poetry took any more account of the new American society being created around her than did the great majority of Stedman's anthology poets. How, then, does one explain her success as a poet as opposed to their relative failure – particularly in the context of Stedman's own recognition of the way in which the new realistic novel, gaining in prestige, had come to displace poetry as a serious aesthetic activity? In the first place, one should not over-state either the degree or nature of Emily Dickinson's success. There is often an element of deliberate quaintness about her poems which, initially at least, makes them seem to belong to an older, remoter world, an Amherst of the past. Such an impression does not survive closer attention, but it remains part of the poetic effect. Then, as once again in the poetry of Hopkins, there is in Emily Dickinson's poems an overwhelming preoccupation with nature and the natural world. The fact that this material is often used for strikingly original purposes does not wholly, in Dickinson's case any more than in Hopkins's, redeem it from that sense of limitation and narrowness of focus characteristic of so much nineteenth-century romantic poetry; as though what was happening in Boston and New York and Philadelphia had nothing to do with the cycle of life in Amherst, Massachusetts.

These, however, are minor points. The fact is that Emily Dickinson's poetry is of a quite different level of achievement from that of her minor contemporaries. What that poetry reveals is a capacity to bypass immediate social realities without any consequent dissolution into genteel sentimentalities or thoughtless nostalgia. The result is the production of work of startling originality and permanent value: originality and value beyond the range of most of those novelists, realists or naturalists, who did try to understand what was going on in Boston and New York and Philadelphia, who did struggle to come to terms imaginatively with the immense pressures and strains building up in American society throughout the 1865–1900 period. None the less, in terms of America's literary culture between 1865 and 1900, Emily Dickinson is an eccentric, exceptional figure. It took the passage of time for her quality to be recognized and understood. For that to happen, what was needed was the emergence of what might be called a literary world-view much like her own. With the development of the modern movement in twentieth-century literature precisely that occurred; reality was seen for a time in individual and existential rather than social terms, and certainly all notions of a stable social reality were dissolved in favour of the view that reality was opaque, fluid, indeterminate, contingent. Such a view in turn helps to explain the critical prestige accorded to modes of writing of an ironic, ambiguous, paradoxical nature: modes much in evidence in the poetry of Emily Dickinson.

To recognize a modernist dimension to the poetry of Emily Dickinson – and it should be borne in mind that it is now something of a commonplace to suggest that all of the major American writers of the pre-Civil War period have a flavour of modernism about them – is in no way to suggest that the mainstream American writers of the post-Civil War period, as opposed to her, were complacently unaware of all metaphysical and epistemological issues. Despite their widespread commitment to the forms of realism or naturalism, none of them envisaged an entirely stable or wholly coherent reality. But the problems of change, of the disappearance of traditional attitudes and values, of doubt and uncertainty about the meaning of existence – doubts and uncertainties they shared with Emily Dickinson – were in their case largely conceived of in terms of social and economic relationships; the new reality they confronted defined itself in terms of the relationship between society and the individual, of the role of the individual in capitalist-organized, industrial society, and of the role of man in the post-Darwinian biological universe. Such concerns simultaneously stretched the imaginative capabilities of writers in America, in the period 1865–1900, and tied them to their own, immediate world, because it was there that the new and often frightening reality was best exhibited. Confronting the metaphysical, rather than social or economic, circumferences of a similar chaos from Amherst – or anywhere – Emily Dickinson floated freer, her voice more muted. In the century to come, however, that voice was destined to be listened to with the avidity and care shown only to great poets.

Notes

1 The text is taken from Thomas H. Johnson (ed.), *The Poems of Emily Dickinson*, Cambridge, Mass., 1955. All subsequent references to the text and number of individual poems refer to this edition.
2 See Yvor Winters, 'Emily Dickinson and the Limits of Judgment', in R. B. Sewall (ed.), *Emily Dickinson: A Collection of Critical Essays*, Englewood Cliffs, NJ, 1963, p. 38.
3 Denis Donoghue, *Emily Dickinson*, Minneapolis, 1969, p. 26.
4 Winters, op. cit., p. 29.
5 Quoted by Donoghue, op. cit., p. 20.
6 See Bernard Duffey, *Poetry in America*, Durham, NC, 1978, p. 142.

Further reading

Richard B. Sewall, *The Life of Emily Dickinson*, London, 1976.
Richard B. Sewall, *Emily Dickinson: A Collection of Critical Essays*, Englewood Cliffs, NJ, 1963.
Denis Donoghue, *Connoisseurs of Chaos*, London, 1965.

5

Mark Twain (1835-1910)

Once I said to myself it would be a thousand times better for Jim to be a slave at home where his family was, as long as he'd *got* to be a slave, and so I'd better write a letter to Tom Sawyer and tell him to tell Miss Watson where he was. But I soon give up that notion, for two things: she'd be mad and disgusted at his rascality and ungratefulness for leaving her, and so she'd sell him straight down the river again; and if she didn't, everybody naturally despises an ungrateful nigger, and they'd make Jim feel it all the time, and so he'd feel ornery and disgraced. And then think of *me*! It would get all around, that Huck Finn helped a nigger to get his freedom; and if I was to ever see anybody from that town again, I'd be ready to get down and lick his boots for shame. That's just the way: a person does a low-down thing, and then he don't want to take no consequences of it. Thinks as long as he can hide it, it ain't no disgrace. That was my fix exactly. The more I studied about this, the more my conscience went to grinding me, and the more wicked and low-down and ornery I got to feeling. And at last, when it hit me all of a sudden that here was the plain hand of Providence slapping me in the face and letting me know my wickedness was being watched all the time from up there in heaven, whilst I was stealing a poor old woman's nigger that hadn't ever done me no harm, and now was showing me there's One that's always on the lookout, and ain't agoing to allow no such miserable doings to go only just so fur and no further, I most dropped in my tracks I was so scared. Well, I tried the best I could to kinder soften it up somehow for myself, by saying I was brung up wicked, and so I warn't so much to blame; but something inside of me kept saying, 'There was the Sunday school, you could a gone to it; and if you'd a done it they'd a learnt you, there, that people that acts as I'd been acting about that nigger goes to everlasting fire.'

It made me shiver. And I about made up my mind to pray; and see if I couldn't try to quit being the kind of a boy I was, and be better. So I kneeled down. But the words wouldn't come. Why wouldn't they? It warn't no use to try and hide it from Him. Nor from *me*, neither. I knowed very well why they wouldn't come. It was because my heart warn't right; it was because I warn't square; it was because I was playing double. I was letting *on* to give up sin, but away inside of me I was holding on to the biggest one of all. I was trying to make my mouth *say* I would do the right thing and the clean thing, and go and write to that nigger's owner and tell where he was; but deep down in me I knowed it was a lie – and He knowed it. You can't pray a lie – I found that out.

So I was full of trouble, full as I could be; and didn't know what to do. At last I had an idea; and I says, I'll go and write the letter – and *then* see if I can pray. Why, it was astonishing, the way I felt as light as a feather, right straight off, and my troubles all gone. So I got a piece of paper and a pencil, all glad and excited, and set down and wrote:

> Miss Watson your runaway nigger Jim is down here two mile below Pikesville and Mr Phelps has got him and he will give him up for the reward if you send.
>
> Huck Finn

I felt good and all washed clean of sin for the first time I had ever felt so in my life, and I knowed I could pray now. But I didn't do it straight off, but laid the paper down and set there thinking – thinking how good it was all this happened so, and how near I come to being lost and going to hell. And went on thinking. And got to thinking over our trip down the river; and I see Jim before me, all the time, in the day, and in the night-time, sometimes moonlight, sometimes storms, and we a floating along, talking, and singing, and laughing. But somehow I couldn't seem to strike no places to harden me against him, but only the other kind. I'd see him standing my watch on top of his'n, stead of calling me, so I could go on sleeping; and see him how glad he was when I come back out of the fog; and when I come to him again in the swamp, up there where the feud was; and such-like times; and would always call me honey, and pet me, and do everything he could think of for me, and how good he always was; and at last I struck the time I saved him by telling the men we had small-pox aboard, and he was so grateful, and said I was the best friend old Jim ever had in the world, and the *only* one he's got now; and then I happened to look around, and see that paper.

It was a close place. I took it up, and held it in my hand. I was a trembling, because I'd got to decide, forever, betwixt two things, and I knowed it. I studied a minute, sort of holding my breath, and then says to myself:

'All right, then, I'll *go* to hell' – and tore it up.

The Adventures of Huckleberry Finn (1885)[1]

* * *

In this passage, Huck Finn arrives at the toughest spot, the closest place, in all his adventures on the Mississippi river, while Mark Twain uses the scene to bring his novel to its moral crisis. Huck has just learned that Jim, the runaway slave who has been his companion on the river, has been betrayed. The 'King' who, with his friend the 'Duke', had earlier taken control of their raft, has sold Jim back into slavery for a mere forty dollars.

The passage reports and recreates the movement of Huck's consciousness as he thinks his way through the consequences of the new situation that the King's characteristic duplicity has produced. Huck's first thought is that, for Jim, capture will mean permanent separation from his family, because he has been wrongly identified as a runaway from a plantation below New Orleans. The boy he has just been talking to has told him there is no question about the identification; he has seen the handbill; 'It tells all about him, to a dot – paints him like a picture' (p. 177). Twain's point, of course, is that to the white Southerners all Negroes, being invisible as individuals, look alike. So Huck worries about Jim being sold down the river, away from his family – it was everywhere believed that the treatment of slaves grew progressively harsher the further south in the Southern states they were located – apparently forgetting that Jim's original reason for running away was that Miss Watson was in fact about to sell him down the river to New Orleans for 800 dollars. The worry is an unrealistic one – as Huck immediately recognizes. There is no chance that Miss Watson will take Jim back. But what is important is that Huck's first thoughts in the new situation have been for Jim and his predicament. And he is still thinking about Jim when he decides that, anyway, it would not be a good thing for Jim to be taken back by Miss Watson; Jim would be identified by everyone as a runaway; he would be looked down on, and so his feelings would be hurt. The hint here that Huck sees Jim as sharing a slave-owning society's evaluation of him is an important indication of how far the boy is from understanding the actual situation of a slave in the South, and of how far he himself shares the attitudes and assumptions of a slave-holding society. Suddenly, however, Huck stops thinking about Jim and his fate, and turns instead to himself. Jim the person is forgotten, lost sight of; in his place emerges the runaway slave, an object; Jim even loses his name – he becomes simply 'a nigger,' 'a poor old woman's nigger', 'that nigger'. Even in the letter that Huck writes, Jim is 'runaway nigger Jim'. Coincident with this characteristic Southern reification of Jim, the individual human being, the previous hint of Huck's sharing in his society's attitude and opinions is made overwhelmingly explicit in the series of self-exhortations he goes on to propound.

What follows has been carefully prepared for by Twain. Huck now puts more forcibly doubts which have already assailed him. At the end of Chapter 15, Huck had played a thoughtless and hurtful trick on Jim. In a thick fog the two had got separated. When they are reunited, Huck exercises all his by no means limited powers of invention and persuasion to convince Jim that he has only dreamed of the separation that has in fact just ended. But the joke goes sour, and Huck's frivolity is made to seem a trivial thing beside the concern and love that Jim shows for him. For once Huck is abashed. 'It was fifteen minutes before I could work myself up to go and humble myself to a nigger – but I done it, and I warn't ever sorry for it afterwards, neither' (pp. 73–4). Huck is still unable to disentangle Jim from the stereotype 'nigger', but this beautifully modulated scene is none the less a crucial one in Huck's gradual recognition, despite what he has been taught all his life, that his slave companion is an ordinary human being just like himself. Immediately following this incident, however, Twain presents a scene which clearly delineates the limits of Huck's understanding. At the beginning of Chapter 16, the two voyagers are nearing Cairo, Illinois, at the junction of the Mississippi and Ohio rivers; to Jim's mind, Cairo spells freedom, entry to a non-Southern, free state. But now that Jim's escape is in sight of success, Huck is suddenly filled with doubt. His conscience rebels, 'scorching' him, reminding him that what he is doing in assisting Jim to freedom, is robbing Miss Watson: 'What did that poor old woman do to you, that you could treat her so mean? Why, she tried to learn you your book, she tried to learn you your manners, she tried to be good to you every way she knowed how. *That's* what she done' (p. 75). Huck feels 'mean' and 'miserable' and almost wishes he was dead. His conscience-struck self-condemnation intensifies when Jim suddenly begins talking about how once he has gained his own freedom, he will rescue his wife and children from slavery, either by buying them or, if necessary, by stealing them with the help of an 'Ab'litionist'. Huck is horrified by such talk. 'Thinks I, this is what comes of my not thinking. Here was this nigger which I had as good as helped to run away, [is that *which* just an example of Huck's bad grammar, or a necessary reversal to the neuter form?] coming right out flat-footed and saying he would steal his children – children that belonged to a man I didn't even know; a man that hadn't ever done me no harm' (p. 75). The tragi-comic ironies here are entirely at the expense of Huck and the society whose teaching he reflects; unlike Twain – and the reader – Huck has no sense whatsoever of the awfulness of what he is saying. He really does believe these things, just as he really does believe in Chapter 22 that the circus ring-master does not know that the drunk who emerges from the crowd, and rides the circus horse, is one of his own performers. But believing, and acting on that belief, are different things. Huck's earlier decision to salve his conscience, in Chapter 16, by betraying Jim, however attractive at the moment he came to it – 'I felt easy, and happy, and light as a feather, right off' (p. 76) – cannot survive a reminder of Jim's gratitude, trust, and love. That, of course, is the incident he recalls towards the end of the extract: 'at last I struck the time I saved him by telling the men we had small-pox aboard, and he was so grateful, and said I was the best friend old Jim ever had in the world, and the *only* one he's got now.' At the time, in Chapter 16, Huck had not been at all sure afterwards that he had done the right thing. He had struggled to utter the words of betrayal that his conscience had told him he ought to utter; but somehow 'the words wouldn't come'. 'I tried, for a second or two, to brace up and out with it, but I warn't man enough – hadn't the spunk of a rabbit' (p. 76). Huck's conscious self, that is, remains convinced that in assisting Jim to freedom, he is doing wrong. Not to betray Jim, is perceived by him as an act of self-betrayal.

What the incident in Chapter 16 reveals is a head-on collision between Huck's instincts, his natural impulses and spontaneous feelings, and what can accurately be called his social self, represented by the attitudes, values, assumptions, he has imbibed from the world in which he has lived. It is a basic error to assume that because Huck is a 'bad boy', a social outcast who prefers the freedom of the river to the civilizing constraints of the shore, he is therefore free from the determining pressures of his social environment. Twain did not write his novels to articulate a particular or consistent view of man's position in the universe; he did not consciously ally himself with those later writers – like

Frank Norris or Stephen Crane or Theodore Dreiser – who saw man as largely the helpless victim of biological and environmental forces outside his control. But he was wholly persuaded of the immense influence of its social environment on the great mass of mankind, and he wrote at least one novel – *Pudd'nhead Wilson* (1889) – to explore, for deeply ironic purposes, the question of the influence of environment and heredity on the individual in the context of Southern racial prejudice. Huck Finn, just as much as the characters in *Pudd'nhead Wilson*, is the product of a particular society at a particular historical moment. His thinking, conscious self is in no way independent of society and history. What happens in the novel is that that conscious self, with its socially acquired attitudes and assumptions, comes increasingly into conflict with a new structure of feeling, that life on the raft, sailing down the Mississippi with Jim, brings vividly and beautifully into being. Twain himself was quite explicit on the point. In 1895, some ten years after the publication of the novel, he described it in a Notebook entry as 'a book of mine where a sound heart and a deformed conscience come into collision and conscience suffers defeat'. Some early readers had been quick to identify the centrality of just this theme. In 1885 Robert Louis Stevenson wrote to J. A. Symonds: 'Have you read *Huckleberry Finn*? It contains many excellent things, above all, the whole story of a healthy boy's dealings with his conscience, incredibly well done.' When Stevenson describes Huck as a 'healthy boy' he is thinking of Twain's 'sound heart': the essential goodness of Huck's natural feelings, constantly manifested throughout the novel, and allowing him in the end even to feel pity for the King and the Duke, treacherous, dishonest, uncaring as they are, when their luck finally runs out and they are brutally tarred and feathered.

It is, then, Huck's soundness of heart which makes the words of betrayal freeze on his lips in Chapter 16. None the less, he remains convinced that he has been cowardly and weak, that he has failed to do the right thing. In the extract, after Huck switches his attention from Jim to his own position, similar feelings seem to be about to overwhelm him. He begins to think about his own role as one who has aided and abetted a runaway slave in his dash for freedom. As we have seen, Jim's reality fades, as Huck's consciousness is flooded with a sense of the heinousness of the crime he has just about committed. To help Jim escape would be a shameful act; but he realizes he has more than social disgrace to fear. His awakened conscience tells him that what he is doing is a sin – a sin for which he will be duly punished. Suddenly he is thinking in terms of the traditional morality and the conventional religious world-view he has been exposed to by such characters as Miss Watson and the Widow Douglas. Twain is at his most brilliant here, indicating the change in perspective by allowing Huck's natural and spontaneous vernacular to be infiltrated by a rhetoric of a quite different register. In fact the sentence beginning, 'And at last . . .' is uncharacteristically long and complex, partly because Huck is struggling to argue out a logical case proving his own wickedness, and partly because it is filled out with the cant phrases of a familiar Puritan-Calvinist sermonizing kind: 'the plain hand of Providence . . . my wickedness was being watched all the time from up there in heaven . . . there's One that's always on the lookout.' In the notion of the plain hand of Providence 'slapping me in the face', just as in such a phrase as 'I most dropped in my tracks I was so scared', the authentic Huck, on the other hand, comically survives. But for the moment Huck thinks he has seen the light – and as a result is scared stiff. He struggles for an excuse, a let out; but his conscience is riding much too high – his destiny is the 'everlasting fire' of the Calvinist tradition. Like some youthful Faust, he seeks relief in prayer; in the revivalist spirit of the frontier camp meeting he will gain salvation by a personal reformation; he will be a 'better' boy. But the magic refuses to work. Just as in Chapter 16, the words freeze on his lips; and just as on that occasion, Huck blames and chastises himself. He knows what the trouble is and condemns himself for it in the short, harsh terms and phrases of the popular religion of the South: 'my heart warn't right,' 'I warn't square,' 'to give up sin,' 'the right thing,' 'the clean thing.' Particularly striking is the use of repetition, and parallel phrasing: 'It was because . . . it was because . . . it was because . . .' and, 'I was . . . I was . . . I was. . . .' It is the technique of the popular preacher, carrying his audience along, as he builds to his climax: 'You can't pray a lie – I found that out.'

Huck's conscience, that objectification of the religious and cultural mores of the world in which he lives, has driven him down into what for him is a dark night of the soul: 'so I was full of trouble, full as I could be.' He is a sinner, unable to escape his sin, unable to repent. But with the thought of actually writing a letter to Miss Watson comes a transformation. Salvation is at hand. The religious vocabulary reaches a climax of its own. Having made his decision, Huck, like any other born-again Christian, feels 'as light as a feather' – the very phrase he had used when deciding to betray Jim in Chapter 16 – his 'troubles all gone'. The burden of sin and guilt that has been weighing him down is taken away. Once the letter has been written, Huck tells us he 'felt good', 'washed clean of sin' for the first time in his life. So purified, he is confident that he will be able to pray. At this stage in the passage, Huck would have been welcomed with open arms by the St Petersburg Sunday School as a shining example of a converted sinner.

Now, however, the passage and its language begin to change direction. Huck's heart – however 'weary' – has not been entirely silenced. Gradually Huck ceases thinking about himself and instead, as in the opening sentences of the extract, begins to think about Jim. Instead of praying, Huck turns to thinking, and remembering. Notions of 'being lost' and 'going to hell' are soon overtaken by images and memories of an altogether more immediate and more compelling kind. The movement of the passage becomes slower, its rhythm more gentle and flowing: 'I see Jim before me [no mention of 'nigger' now] all the time, in the day, and in the night-time, sometimes moonlight, sometimes storms, and we a floating along, talking, and singing, and laughing.' Much earlier, at the beginning of Chapter 19, Twain had explicitly linked the passage of time, for the voyagers, with the flowing movement of the river: 'Two or three days and nights went by; I reckon I might say they swum by; they slid along so quiet and smooth and lovely' (p. 99). And the passage that follows this observation is one of the novel's most vivid and lyrical evocations of the freedom afforded Huck and Jim by life on the river. Huck's recollection now of 'a floating along' with Jim 'talking, and singing, and laughing' begins to evoke a similar quality of feeling. Huck's memory flows like the river itself, and what is created is an extraordinary lyrical intensity of feeling. Formal, rhetorical phrasing, the conventional diction of evangelical religion, even the restrictions of traditional grammar – all have disappeared. The successive memories are linked by the simplest of 'and' constructions. As a result they seem to float into Huck's consciousness with a wholly natural, irresistible spontaneity. The boy's awareness is filled with reminiscences and recollections of an essentially similar kind; several relate to moments of restoration and renewed compansionship after periods of separation, danger, even apparent death; and all suggest Jim's fundamental, caring goodness, his concern, humanity, and love. Last of all, Huck recalls that crucial moment in Chapter 16 when Jim, at the very moment when Huck was teetering on the edge of betrayal, had affirmed his total belief in his companion's friendship and loyalty.

Just before, Huck had remembered how he and Jim had been reunited after being separated by a dense fog that had covered the river. Now, here, in a moment of intense, emotional realization, Huck emerges out of the fog created by the false consciousness of a deformed conscience, and the choice dictated by fire and brimstone, sin and damnation, is rejected in favour of loyalty, love, and Jim's individual existence: 'I studied a minute, sort of holding my breath, and then says to myself: "All right, then, I'll *go* to hell."'

*

Twain's problem is where to go from here. Life with Jim on the raft, floating down the Mississippi, has clearly had a remarkable effect on Huck; at the very least, the experience has been a sentimental education. Despite everything he has been taught, or has assumed, or has taken for granted, about negro slaves, Huck has come to see Jim as an individual human being to whom he owes an immense debt of loyalty and love. But we need to be as careful here as Twain has been. Huck chooses to go to hell. That is, he still believes that what he is doing, in deciding not to write to Miss Watson, is wicked, immoral, sinful. It is simply that not even the threat of the everlasting fire is enough to make him deny his heart's feelings, and betray his friend. In other words, there is no question of Huck's seeing through, and therefore repudiating, what he has been taught. He has in no way whatsoever arrived at a decision that Southern society is wrong about slaves and slavery. He has acted as he has done, not as a result of a process of rational analysis, but simply on the basis of natural impulse. That he has not in fact arrived at any new moral maturity and understanding concerning the position of the Negro in Southern society, is beautifully suggested, only a page or two *after* the episode of the letter, by this exchange about the accident aboard a steamboat that Huck pretends has occurred: 'We blowed out a cylinder-head.' 'Good gracious! Anybody hurt?' 'No'm. Killed a nigger' (p. 185). That he opts to protect Jim, the individual negro slave, while continuing to accept the conventional Southern attitude towards the negro in general, seems mainly to heighten the irony, both comic and frightening, of the situation. Huck chooses the 'wickedness' of loyalty and love, rather than the 'goodness' of an act of betrayal on behalf of the institution of slavery.

In fact Jim is now a captive on the Phelps's farm, awaiting the arrival of his alleged owner from New Orleans, so Huck decides that his next act of wickedness will be to 'steal Jim out of slavery again' (p. 180). The difficulty for Twain, just as much as for Huck, is to find a way of achieving this. Given the realities of the slave society of the ante-bellum South, revealed in all their callousness, violence and brutality in a variety of episodes in previous chapters, how is the youthful Huck to act out the bond of love and caring that links him to Jim? The problem remains even if one agrees that it is wrong to exaggerate the degree of maturity, moral or otherwise, that the river experience has produced in Huck. What Twain does is skilfully to evade the issue by finding a solution which, while sufficiently entertaining and diverting, has struck a great many readers as less than wholly satisfactory. Once before, in the writing of *Huckleberry Finn*, Twain had faced an equally major structural and thematic problem, centrally involving Jim, and on that occasion he finally arrived at a truly brilliant solution.

Twain began writing *Huckleberry Finn* in the summer of 1876. The work went rapidly, and by the end of the summer Twain had reached the point, towards the end of Chapter 16, when Huck and Jim on their raft are run down by the Mississippi steamboat. Here the manuscript came to an abrupt halt. More than two years elapsed before Twain took it up again and added Chapters 17 and 18, the account of Huck's involvement, away from the river, with the Shepherdson-Grangerford feud – this is the feud Huck recalls near the end of the extract. Subsequently, the manuscript was again set aside, and it was not until the summer of 1880 that the writing of the second half of the novel began with the introduction of the two new characters, the King and the Duke.

The causes of these delays are reasonably clear. Up to Chapter 16 the basic structure of the novel had been provided by the journey down the Mississippi undertaken by Huck and Jim; both characters are making the journey because they are in flight, in search of freedom – in Huck's case, from both the 'sivilizing' attentions of Miss Watson and the Widow Douglas, and the brutality and violence of his drunken Pap; in Jim's case, from his bondage as a slave. But in Chapter 16 the two escapees reached the point at which the Mississippi is joined by the Ohio river. Here, as we have already noted, freedom for Jim means leaving the Mississippi, and turning up the Ohio into the free state of Illinois. For Jim, to proceed down the Mississippi would be to proceed 'down the river', deeper and deeper, that is, into slave territory. Yet this was the world, the society, Twain wanted to write about; this was the world he remembered from his childhood, and from his years as a steamboat pilot on the lower Mississippi. Illinois, on the other hand, he did not know. Down the Mississippi was the imaginative journey to which

Twain was committed, but he needed to find a way of making such a journey compatible with his original plot. Clearly the answer for long eluded him. But the invention of the King and the Duke produced a brilliant solution. At the level of plot they simply take over the raft – and its occupants – and the journey south continues because they wish it to. At the level of theme, King and Duke, shameless tricksters and con-men, allow Twain to develop the penetrating, cogent, and often bitter, satirical analysis of ante-bellum Southern society, which occupies much of the second half of the novel. The journey itself is now of little significance: it is a journey going nowhere, and therefore it ceases to provide the novel's basic structure. That role is taken over by the contrast between River and Shore. Despite its natural dangers, the River is more than ever identified with freedom, companionship, integrity, and love; the Shore, on the other hand, is marked by violence, cruelty, cowardice, falsity and corruption in a multitude of forms. In fact the analysis of Shore society that Twain undertakes in the later sections of the novel allows us to recognize how Jim's literal slavery in the ante-bellum South is itself a metaphor for society's denial of freedom to the individual such as Huck. Thus the novel's two structures finally blend marvellously together, supporting and reinforcing each other.

None the less, once the junction with the Ohio has been left behind, the problem of what to do with Jim remains. For a time the King and the Duke take over not only the raft, but the novel – as Twain uses the antics of the two con-men to delineate the corrupt state of Southern society. Huck and Jim remain for a time in the background. But at the end of Chapter 31, with Jim's recapture and Huck's determination to free him, the problem resurfaces, and this time has to be resolved. Twain's solution is the resurrection of Tom Sawyer. Tom had already appeared in the early chapters of the novel, acting very much in the manner of the Tom Sawyer of Twain's earlier novel. Tom is portrayed, comically, as a boy who confuses what he has read in romantic adventure stories with real life. For Tom, reality has to be made to conform to what he has read in books. In the final section of *Huckleberry Finn* what this means is that Tom and Huck have to effect Jim's escape according to the conventions established by popular, romantic fiction. Huck, who, highly significantly in the context of the role he now plays, has been mistaken at the Phelps's farm for Tom Sawyer, takes only a minor part in these antics; but he offers no serious objection to them. And that is the critical problem. Given the decision he makes at the end of the extract, in Chapter 31, and its implications, why does he allow Tom Sawyer to play his elaborate games with the captive Jim?

The problem is a complex one because, at one level, what Twain is doing in this closing section of his novel is developing what has been all along one of its major items: the way in which language, and literary language in particular, can be used to manipulate and distort, deceive and betray. In *Huckleberry Finn* reality is frequently the victim of language. In this context, through the extravagant absurdity of Tom Sawyer's boyish antics over the release of Jim, Twain is simply poking fun at the distortions of reality liable to be produced by an excessive devotion to the world of romance and adventure to be found in certain kinds of fiction. But in *Huckleberry Finn* it is not only Tom Sawyer who is seduced by language. In the extract we have seen how the conventional language of a Puritanical, Calvinist, evangelical revivalism is powerful enough to persuade Huck's conscience that black is white, evil good. The same language can be deployed at will by the King and the Duke to dupe and deceive a Southern audience. (It should be recalled that while old-style Calvinism and Puritanism were losing their hold on nineteenth-century New England, broadly similar forms of popular religious belief were still spreading out into the frontier states of the south and west.) The comic element present in Huck's decision to go to hell does not negate the underlying serious point. And the same is true of the King and the Duke. There is high comedy in the Duke's Shakespearian lesson to the King in Chapter 21:

> To be, or not to be; that is the bare bodkin
> That makes calamity of so long life. . . .

But a calculated manipulation of language – 'flapdoodle' as Huck calls it – is the key to the pair's ability to bamboozle, cheat, and defraud those who listen to them. In the feud between the Grangerford and Shepherdson clans linguistic and cultural debasement is revealed as producing still more frightening consequences. The families shoot and kill each other apparently out of some perverse sense of honour which compels them to maintain a meaningless 'feud' whose origin has been long forgotten.

The society that Twain depicts in *Huckleberry Finn* is thus a society characterized by linguistic corruption. This is why it is so vulnerable to any form of linguistic 'sleight-of-hand'. Distinctions between the true and the false, the sham and the real, have been blurred and lost. Linguistic posturing and attitudinizing successfully pass for genuine feelings.

The language of religion and of feeling has been pre-empted by a conventionalized sham rhetoric and a sham gentility; as a result, a gulled society is ready to act out the falsities of the shabby rhetoric it is taken in by. In such a context as this, Tom Sawyer's play-acting over the escape of Jim should come as no great surprise.

Complex as the situation may be, the problem of Huck and Jim and the novel's ending remains. *Huckleberry Finn* offers a positive alternative to the linguistic corruption of the society which it portrays. The vernacular language in which Huck narrates the novel, and which Twain sustains so beautifully throughout, challenges the distortions of thought and feeling produced by society's more genteel linguistic modes. The realism of Huck's speech, that is, acquires a powerful moral authority; the naturalness of the vernacular is the only remaining source of honesty, integrity, truth. William Dean Howells, who was friendly with Twain just as he was with almost every other contemporary American writer, championed the cause of realism in American letters in part for moral reasons; he believed that the idealizing strain in much popular, sentimental fiction offered readers false models of human conduct. Realism was the answer. But Howells did not read the linguistic situation of his society as profoundly as Twain did, which is why Twain's legacy of the vernacular to later American writers has proved a more enduring one even than Howellsian realism. However, the closing section of *Huckleberry Finn* at Phelps's farm represents a retreat from Twain's profounder realism: honesty, integrity, and truth are largely sacrificed to comic effect. Tom Sawyer rules, and Huck (and Twain) are leagued with him. The situation is not improved when we learn that Jim has been free all along anyway, because of a fortuitous and sentimental death-bed decision by the Widow Douglas.

Honesty, integrity, and truth have been sacrificed – for nothing. But perhaps we should not be surprised. All that has happened is that Huck has reverted to his normal pattern of Shore behaviour. Throughout all his adventures, Huck has constantly engaged in lying, fabrication, shamming, inventing; his true self, even his identity, has to be constantly disguised and concealed. For Huck this is the only way; survival is impossible on any other terms. In the violent social world in which he exists, honesty, integrity, truth, and vernacular realism are of little avail. The pessimistic implications of such a view are confirmed by the comic ending Twain has devised for his novel. Twain cannot see any way in which the humanly desirable values, achieved in the pastoral world of the River, can be made to work within actual, human society.

This is the explanation of Huck's final decision to 'light out for the Territory'. Where James sought for ways of preserving the values of freedom, spontaneity, and integrity, within society, Twain came to see society as inevitably destructive of such values. What this means is that if Huck had tried to sustain, on the shore, the relationship with Jim that had developed by the end of their Mississippi journey, the ending of the novel would have had to be quite different. Given the realities of Southern society, which the novel has already charted, such a relationship could only have ended tragically. Twain's sense of his audience, or perhaps his own temperament, made him shy away from any such tragedy. Hence the comic, clever, but flawed ending he wrote.

*

The Adventures of Huckleberry Finn is a great comic novel. But its comedy exists within a fictional world which constantly emerges as cruel and unfeeling. The picture of Southern society that Twain draws in the novel is one that allows the South its traditional hospitality, generosity and communal concern, but insists much more strongly on its violence, brutality and corruption. Such paradoxes and contradictions are characteristic of Twain himself and his work in general. Of all the writers discussed in this volume, Twain best epitomizes the contradictions of the period. He is the age's representative man. He possesses all its energy, its drive, its inventiveness, its self-confidence – but equally its self-doubt, its sense that somehow everything has gone wrong, that progress is an illusion. Twain rather enjoyed his role as the brash American, the Westerner, totally dismissive of Europe and the past and all its traditions and outworn conventions. Yet a novel like *A Connecticut Yankee at the Court of King Arthur* (1889), which starts out by mocking, belittling and satirizing the medieval past, ends by raising serious questions about the superiority of the modern, industrial present. Through the Connecticut Yankee, Hank Morgan, Twain satirizes medieval ignorance, superstition, inhumanity, tyranny, cruelty and snobbery, as well as medieval styles of thinking, writing and speaking. But in the end Hank himself emerges as no more than a naive, complacent, intolerant, unsympathetic, culturally-deprived, nineteenth-century American; he has no sense of values other than business, commercial, practical ones; he is morally prudish, ignorant of art and linguistically corrupt. His knowledge of technology alone gives him any superiority over the medieval world, and in the end even that technology is used only for purposes of mass destruction. The problem of the book is the problem of Twain's own position; as so often in his work, rather than confront the issues being raised, Twain tends to retreat into an evasive flippancy of tone, or cynicism, which undermines the potential significance of what he has written.

Despite having written, early in his career, *The Gilded Age* (1873, in collaboration with Charles Dudley Warner) and given post-bellum America a defining label that it has never lost, Twain was not prepared to speak out openly against the *status quo* in America's social and economic life. After all, for much of his career he was complicit with it, riding high, earning a fortune, socially mobile – even if most of his money was lost in what proved to be a bad gamble on future printing technology. However, towards the end of his career, at the time when so many others were coming to feel that, unless there were radical changes in its social and economic structure America was about to explode into violence and anarchy, Twain's vision of man and society grew progressively darker. The American realist writers were frequently accused by contemporary critics of presenting a view of human life altogether too dark and pessimistic; but they produced little to match the despairing bleakness of vision present in Twain's *The Man Who Corrupted Hadleyburg* (1900) or *The Mysterious Stranger* (1916). At the end of his life Twain was convinced that the average man was worth no more than Colonel Sherburn suggests he is when he cows the lynch mob in Chapter 22 of *Huckleberry Finn*. We have every reason to be grateful that the creation of Huck Finn allowed Twain, on one occasion at least, to sustain a superb equilibrium between the comic and tragic realities of human life.

Note

1 The text of the extract from Chapter 31 of *The Adventures of Huckleberry Finn* is taken from the Riverside edition, ed. Henry Nash Smith, Boston, 1958. The novel was published in England in 1884, but the first American edition was in 1885.

Further reading

Justin Kaplan, *M. Clemens and Mark Twain*, New York, 1967.
Walter Blair, *Mark Twain and Huck Finn*, Berkeley, 1960.

6

William Dean Howells (1837–1920)

Miss Kingsbury leaned forward and asked Charles Bellingham if he had read 'Tears, Idle Tears,' the novel that was making such a sensation; and when he said no, she said she wondered at him. 'It's perfectly heart-breaking, as you'll imagine from the name; but there's such a dear old-fashioned hero and heroine in it, who keep dying for each other all the way through and making the most wildly satisfactory and unnecessary sacrifices for each other. You feel as if you'd done them yourself.'

'Ah, that's the secret of its success,' said Bromfield Corey. 'It flatters the reader by painting the characters colossal, but with his limp and stoop, so that he feels himself of their supernatural proportions. You've read it, Nanny?'

'Yes,' said his daughter. 'It ought to have been called "Slop, Silly Slop."'

'Oh, not quite *slop*, Nanny,' pleaded Miss Kingsbury.

'It's astonishing,' said Charles Bellingham, 'how we do like the books that go for our heart-strings. And I really suppose that you can't put a more popular thing than self-sacrifice into a novel. We do like to see people suffering sublimely.'

'There was talk some years ago,' said James Bellingham, 'about novels going out.'

'They're just coming in!' cried Miss Kingsbury.

'Yes,' said Mr Sewell, the minister. 'And I don't think there ever was a time when they formed the whole intellectual experience of more people. They do greater mischief than ever.'

'Don't be envious, parson,' said the host.

'No,' answered Sewell. 'I should be glad of their help. But those novels with old-fashioned heroes and heroines in them – excuse me, Miss Kingsbury – are ruinous!'

'Don't you feel like a moral wreck, Miss Kingsbury?' asked the host.

But Sewell went on: 'The novelists might be the greatest possible help to us if they painted life as it is, and human feelings in their true proportion and relation, but for the most part they have been and are altogether noxious.'

This seemed sense to Lapham; but Bromfield Corey asked: 'But what if life as it is isn't amusing? Aren't we to be amused?'

'Not to our hurt,' sturdily answered the minister. 'And the self-sacrifice painted in most novels like this –'

'Slop, Silly Slop?' suggested the proud father of the inventor of the phrase.

'Yes – is nothing but psychical suicide, and is as wholly immoral as the spectacle of a man falling upon his sword.'

'Well, I don't know but you're right, parson,' said the host; and the minister, who had apparently got upon a battle-horse of his, careered onward in spite of some tacit attempts of his wife to seize the bridle.

'Right? To be sure I am right. The whole business of love, and love-making and marrying, is painted by the novelists in a monstrous disproportion to the other relations of life. Love is very sweet, very pretty –'

'Oh, *thank* you, Mr Sewell,' said Nanny Corey in a way that set them all laughing.

'But it's the affair, commonly, of very young people, who have not yet character and experience enough to make them interesting. In novels it's treated, not only as if it were the chief interest of life, but the sole interest of the lives of two ridiculous young persons; and it is taught that love is perpetual, that the glow of a true passion lasts forever; and that it is sacrilege to think or act otherwise.'

'Well, but isn't that true, Mr Sewell?' pleaded Miss Kingsbury.

'I have known some most estimable people who had married a second time,' said the minister, and then he had the applause with him. Lapham wanted to make some open recognition of his good sense, but could not.

The Rise of Silas Lapham (1885)[1]

* * *

What Howells is doing in this dinner-party exchange is reflecting more or less directly upon his own convictions about fiction and its status. So doing he is writing what amounts to a somewhat apologetic manifesto on behalf of the kind of fiction he wants, and which, in *The Rise of Silas Lapham*, he is attempting to write. More than this, the damaging effects of the kind of fiction that comes under attack here are about to be demonstrated within the pattern of social relationships in Howells's own novel. The passage, then, has a self-reflexive quality, exceedingly familiar within the context of more recent fiction, less so in the nineteenth-century novel. *The Rise of Silas Lapham* is not a novel about the writing of novels; none the less, one of its significant themes is the relationship between art and life, and in particular the way in which expectations of life can be conditioned by art. In Howells's view, just such a conditioning was evident in the America in which he was writing – with unfortunate results. We have already seen how Twain implies, in *Huckleberry Finn*, that one of the sources of the corruption of the society of the Old South was the distortion of language and feeling produced by a sentimental and degenerate romanticism; the Civil War itself, Twain argued in *Life on the Mississippi* (1883), was caused by the South's acquiring a bogus sense of aristocracy, medieval notions of chivalry and nobility, and a romantic nationalism, from the pages of the romances of Walter Scott. In *The Rise of Silas Lapham*, Howells sees what is essentially the same sentimental, romantic, tradition as responsible for an equally specific moral corruption of post-bellum American society. To recognize this is to recognize an important moral dimension to Howells's championing of the cause of realism in American fiction. The new mode of realism deserves support because, rejecting romantic falsifications and distortions of human experience, it allows American fiction a new moral authority.

'Tears, Idle Tears' is deployed as an example of the kind of fiction which the school of realism saw itself as above all challenging. Miss Kingsbury's description of the impact of the novel is marked by a superficial, self-protective irony; she has enjoyed the novel, but simultaneously wishes to suggest that she sees through its manifest absurdities: its 'perfect' heart-break is produced by 'such a dear old-fashioned hero and heroine' whose sacrifices for each other are 'the most wildly satisfactory and unnecessary'. The cosy humour of such phrases is clearly meant to demonstrate to Miss Kingsbury's audience the superiority of her own aesthetic and critical sense. At the same time, the emphasis on *self-sacrifice* is one that will recur in the subsequent discussion, and it will also prove a major issue in Howells's own novel. The discussion moves to an explanation of the success of novels of the type Miss Kingsbury has described – Howells of course is right in insisting that, in the post-bellum period, sentimental, romantic fictions were of immense, popular appeal. Lew Wallace's *Ben Hur* (1880), for example, a romantically exciting account of the rise of Christianity in the late Roman Empire, sold some 2 million copies. Success of this kind, it is argued, depends upon the readers' ability to identify with the idealized, superhuman characters portrayed, and to respond to the simplest kind of sentimental appeal: such as that afforded by unnecessary acts of self-sacrifice. These again are characteristics that the realistic novel, at whatever price in terms of popular appeal, will firmly reject.

James Bellingham's reference to the idea, 'some years ago', that novels were going out, is problematical. What Howells has in mind is perhaps the continuing strain in much orthodox moral and religious philosophy in the nineteenth century which saw novel-reading as a morally dangerous activity serving no useful or instructive purpose. Certainly the reaction of orthodox, traditional believers to the exciting, visionary aspect of Emersonian transcendentalism involved a renewed resistance to works of the imagination of every kind. Whether such views could possibly have reduced the size of the novel-reading public seems highly dubious; and, in any event, the idea gets no support from Mr Sewell, the clergyman present at the dinner-table. Howells's own view, no doubt based on his experience as editor of the Boston magazine *Atlantic Monthly* from 1871 to 1881, is clearly that novel-reading is on the increase. In the post-bellum period, a growing population and increasing literacy were certainly producing a new and expanding reading-public; one perhaps less well-educated than that which had existed in an older America, and one which could be a source of huge profits for editors and publishers willing to furnish it with whatever seemed to be to its taste. There is in fact some evidence to suggest that the general level of America's literary taste did decline in the later decades of the nineteenth century.[2]

Mr Sewell, the clergyman who here, as elsewhere in the novel, seems to voice Howells's own point of view, agrees that there is now a whole class of people for whom novels provide the sole source of intellectual sustenance; hence the importance of the quality of that sustenance. For Sewell, novels could be sources of benefit, of moral illumination. The problem is that popular fiction is the reverse. These novels, with their 'old-fashioned heroes and heroines' are no less than 'ruinous'. This is precisely Howells's own point of view, and the underlying premise of his complete rejection of all romantic, sentimental fiction. In July 1887, in *Harper's Magazine*, Howells wrote at length of how romantic novels provide their readers with no more than an escape from the realities of existence. Such novels 'make one forget life and all its cares and duties;

they are not in the least like the novels which make you think of these, and shame you into at least wishing to be a helpfuler and wholesomer creature than you are.' Such novels substitute for reality a world of dream and make-believe:

> No sordid details of verity here, if you please; no wretched being humbly and weakly struggling to do right and to be true, suffering for his follies and for his sins, tasting joy only through the mortification of self, and in the help of others; nothing of all this, but instead a great, whirling splendor of peril and achievement, a wild scene of heroic adventure . . . with a stage 'picture' at the fall of the curtain, and all the good characters in a row, their left hands pressed upon their hearts, and kissing their right hands to the audience in the good old way that has always charmed and always will, Heaven bless it!

Howells's attack is directed here at the forms and conventions of a particular writing mode; it is these forms and conventions which are the source of the dangers which the prevalence of this kind of writing – in the theatre, as Howells's closing metaphor suggests, as well as in fiction – represents. The Rev. Mr Sewell makes the same point: the failure of most fiction to be morally educative springs from the limitations inherent in its mode of writing. Above all its failure is a failure of realism: 'The novelists might be the greatest possible help to us if they painted life as it is, and human feelings in their true proportion and relation, but for the most part they have been and are altogether noxious.' Novelists, that is, are guilty of distorting the realities of life, and of human feeling in particular.

To the novel's protagonist, Silas Lapham, an uncultured hard-headed New England businessman, Mr Sewell's arguments seem convincing: that the novelist should describe life as it is, is no more than common sense. But at this point Howells uses Bromfield Corey, a member of the traditional upper-class élite of Boston, himself a cultural dilettante and erstwhile amateur painter, to raise some obvious objections to the clergyman's ideology of realism. Sewell's assumption is that literature should maintain a didactic relationship with life. But what the novelist should do is entertain us – and to describe life as it is may not be entertaining. Contemporary critics repeatedly levelled just this charge against Howells and his followers: their work did not entertain; it was merely gloomy and depressing. As one contemporary put it – he had probably read Howells's onslaught on romantic fiction in the July 1887 *Harper's*: 'people who marry and live happily ever after are the very salt of the earth, and it is good to know them; it is good to find them at the close of a fiction. They are real people.' Howells's answer to the charge that the novelist has an obligation to delight us – however much teaching he may wish to do – is that the delighting and amusing should not be of such a nature as to do us harm; and, in the view of Howells-Sewell, immensely harmful is precisely what the vision of life and experience offered by popular, romantic fiction, is. In the remainder of the passage, Howells allows Mr Sewell to develop this point of view, while justifying the overt didacticism of his comments by alluding to the clergyman's wife's attempts to cut her husband short. Love and passion in particular, in Sewell's view, are distorted, and their importance inflated, by the way they are treated in romantic fiction. Silas Lapham, once again, is represented as being impressed by the plain good sense of the clergyman's views.

In the exchanges, what Howells does not seem to refute is the view, very frequently put by upholders of the tradition of novel-writing under attack here, that the behaviour of 'old-fashioned heroes and heroines', even if untrue to the realities of ordinary everyday experience, none the less provides the reader with a model of lofty, high-principled, moral idealism, towards which he or she may at least aspire. And what we have to keep reminding ourselves of is the fact that, in the 1880s, critics, commentators and editors who shared such a view were very much in the majority. In fact, ironically, and wholly mistakenly, it was the fate of *The Rise of Silas Lapham* to be attacked by contemporary reviews for its lack of high-principled, moral idealism. Most reviewers agreed that the story lacked any 'spiritual' quality, and that Howells's interest in the 'passionless everyday' ensured that his novel was unable to 'inspire' the reader. As one reviewer put it, Howells 'always pleases, often charms us, but he never inspires'.[3] Underlying these criticisms is the view that Silas Lapham cannot be seen as a romantic hero providing the reader with an ideal of high-minded, moral behaviour.

The irony is, as I have implied, that whatever contemporary reviewers may have thought, *Silas Lapham* does indeed present the reader with a model of moral and ethical idealism. Furthermore, a page or two later, Howells specifically rejects the sentimental novel's presentation of heroic self-sacrifice as something wholly exceptional, the prerogative of such superhuman characters as appear in dramatic fiction. James and Charles Bellingham, as well as Silas Lapham himself, had fought in the Civil War. Over their coffee and cigars the men discuss their experiences, and agree that then acts of heroic self-sacrifice had been commonplace, almost a shared experience. All that is needed is an appropriate occasion; ordinary men are quite capable of heroism. Peace-time of course provides fewer such occasions, but Mr Sewell is prepared to redefine heroism in the context of everyday life: 'I dare say we shall have the heroism again if we have the occasion. Till it comes, we must content ourselves with the every-day generosities and sacrifices. They make up in quantity what they lack in quality, perhaps' (pp. 201–2). Bromfield Corey wonders, however, whether art is capable of expressing such generosities and sacrifices: 'They're not so picturesque. . . . You can paint a man dying for his country, but you can't express on canvas a man fulfilling the duties of a good citizen' (p. 202). In Howells's opinion, of course, this is precisely what the aim of the American novelist should be. He uses Charles Bellingham to articulate his point of view. The ordinary, the every-day, the commonplace – these are exactly what, until now, novelists have entirely failed to register: 'The commonplace is just that light, impalpable, aërial essence which they've never got into their confounded books yet. The novelist who could interpret the common feelings of commonplace people would have the answer to "the riddle of the painful earth" on his tongue' (p. 202). For Mr Sewell and those who think like him, to render imaginatively the ordinary and commonplace, and to interpret 'the common feelings of commonplace people', are exactly what the aims of the novelist should be – of the novelist committed to observing the precepts of Howellsian realism in particular.

*

Such a discussion of the art of fiction as Chapter 14 of *The Rise of Silas Lapham* contains may strike the reader as too obvious and heavy-handed, too great an intrusion of the author's own concerns into the fictional world he is trying to create. In fact, as part of a dinner-table conversation in a cultured Bostonian home, the exchanges in the extract do not seem to be seriously lacking in verisimilitude. In addition, the consideration that Silas Lapham himself listens in a state of increasingly befuddled incomprehension helps the reader to accept their naturalness. These exchanges, however, point not only outward to Howells's determined championship of the cause of realism in the novel, but inward to the plot and theme of the novel he himself is writing. The dinner-party itself is occasioned by the fact that Bromfield Corey's son, in the brave new democratic world of post-bellum America, is working for Silas Lapham in his paint business. He also happens to be falling in love with one of Silas's daughters. Circumstances thus bring together two traditionally alien worlds – the old world of cultured, upper-class Boston, and the new world of booming, energetic American business. Howells succeeds admirably in evoking the ambience of both these worlds, and also maintains a delicate balance in suggesting the value of each. The drive, energy and directness of the Lapham world are missing in the somewhat effete way of life enjoyed by the Coreys; but the Coreys possess a fund of taste, knowledge and understanding remote from the Laphams. (Silas, we learn, likes a play as long as it makes him laugh. He has no time for tragedy: 'I think there's enough of that in real life without putting it on the stage' (p. 88).) Clearly Howells expects us to approve of a future in which Tom Corey (who is determined to earn his own living) is united with Penelope Lapham (who is anxious to read *Middlemarch*).

Before such a happy consummation can be arrived at, a major hurdle has to be surmounted. It is here that Howells works into his novel the theme which he sees popular romantic fiction as so frequently and dangerously distorting. For most of the novel, the Lapham family assume that Tom Corey's attentions are directed, not towards Penelope, but towards Irene, her beautiful sister. Irene herself shares this view. When the truth comes out, all is confusion, and there is much talk and protestation about the desirability of that kind of high-minded self-sacrifice which 'Tears, Idle Tears', and works of that ilk, so admiringly portrays. Penelope cannot think of marrying Tom (although she loves him) because of the hurt it will cause her sister, etc., etc. It is, inevitably, Mr Sewell who makes the family see the simple truth that there is no sense in making three suffer instead of one: 'that's sense, and that's justice. It's the economy of pain which naturally suggests itself, and which would insist upon itself, if we were not all perverted by traditions which are the figment of the shallowest sentimentality.' Mr Sewell, and thus Howells, uses this opportunity to reiterate his view that it is a corrupt literary mode that is responsible for the Laphams' moral confusion. 'We are all blinded, we are all weakened,' says the minister, 'by a false ideal of self-sacrifice.' The notion of self-sacrifice in such a situation runs wholly counter to common sense: 'But in such a case we somehow think it must be wrong to use our common sense. I don't know where this false ideal comes from, unless it comes from the novels that befool and debauch almost every intelligence in some degree.' 'Your daughter believes,' the clergyman continues, 'in spite of her common sense, that she ought to make herself and the man who loves her unhappy, in order to assure the lifelong wretchedness of her sister, whom he doesn't love, simply because her sister saw him and fancied him first! And I'm sorry to say that ninety-nine young people out of a hundred – oh, nine hundred and ninety-nine out of a thousand! – would consider that noble and beautiful and heroic; whereas you know at the bottom of your hearts that it would be foolish and cruel and revolting' (pp. 241–2). Here, with an appealing and impressive niceness and precision, Howells's commitment to realism in literature is afforded all the authority of a moral crusade. Morality and aesthetics – both demand, above all, realism.

*

The problems associated with moral idealism, and self-sacrifice, become crucial not only in the lives of Lapham's daughters, but in the rise and fall (and rise again?) of Lapham himself. By the 1880s, few Americans were unaware that business and businessmen had come to dominate American life. But American writers had been exceedingly slow to depict the world of business in their work. For writers within the genteel tradition in particular – Bromfield Corey, with his carefully cultured aestheticism, is a not unfavourable picture of a representative of genteel, New England culture – business and businessmen were not acceptable as proper subjects of serious literary concern. For writers of the school of realism, the reverse was true. Committed to depicting the every-day attitudes of American life, Howells and his followers were inevitably drawn to portray business life. Even Bromfield Corey is compelled to admit that money and big business have become the distinguishing features of American life, that indeed money is now at the heart of the American romance: 'there's no doubt but money is to the fore now. It is the romance, the poetry of our age. It's the thing that chiefly strikes the imagination' (p. 64). By 1900, in fact, some sixty novels had been published on the business theme, and in the great majority of these, the businessman was portrayed in a critical or hostile manner. *The Rise of Silas Lapham* is an exception to this general rule. What is in question is a limit to Howells's realism at least in the sense that Silas Lapham hardly emerges as a typical businessman of the new, booming, post-bellum world. Lapham does not belong to the world of the Rockefellers, the Vanderbilts, or the Andrew Carnegies. That is, he has little or nothing in common with Dreiser's Frank Algernon Cowperwood, portrayed in *The Financier* (1912) and *The Titan* (1914) as the archetypal robber-baron figure, powerful, ruthless, totally unscrupulous. Despite the contrast that Howells's novel provides between the old, genteel world of upper-class Boston, and the new, thrusting world of business enterprise, Silas Lapham himself belongs to an older, traditional America. He is a product of rural New England, and retains most of the character traits of his origins. He is shrewd, hard-headed, independent, self-confident; he has made his fortune, not by ruthless exploitation and corruption, but through his own business acumen and hard work. Nevertheless, not even Silas's moral probity is absolute. Early in his career he had had a business partner whose capital he had needed to develop the paint business. Subsequently, Silas squeezed him out. When a crisis comes in Silas's business life this man, Rogers, plays a crucial part. For most of the novel Silas's business fortune seems secure; and he begins to build a grand new mansion-house for his family in the fashionable Beacon Street area of Boston. However, his fortunes suddenly change. There is an economic recession; paint sales fall; Silas is tempted into unwise speculations; the new house burns down; worst of all, a new paint has appeared on the market, equal to Silas's in quality, and cheaper to produce. In this crisis Rogers reappears with a tempting solution: an opportunity for a piece of typical business sharp practice, which would save Silas without in any way infringing the law. The situation is handled extremely well by Howells. In the end we learn that while Silas, Rogers and his shady associates would benefit from the deal, no one would suffer except a large group of investors in England. Silas is tempted, but does not fall. Rather than take advantage of this opportunity – and indeed of a later one, involving a new, wealthy partner – he chooses bankruptcy. Even with his back to the wall, Silas cannot persuade himself that there can be any distinction between unethical behaviour in his business and his private life; to both spheres, the same rules of right and wrong apply.

Some critics have tried to argue that Howells has contradicted himself in the business and romance plots of his novel. In the plot involving the entanglements in the relationships between Tom Corey and Silas's daughters, he has fiercely attacked the notion of unrealistic self-sacrifice; but in the business plot he invites us to approve of Silas's act of principled self-sacrifice at the expense of his family and his own fortune. But in fact there is no contradiction. Silas's is no romantic gesture; it is not modelled on the conventions of a decadent culture; rather it is the real thing – an act of commonplace heroism, one of those 'everyday generosities or sacrifices' that Mr Sewell had previously asked for. Further,

Silas has learned the lesson of the economy of pain preached by the clergyman. The common good takes precedence over individual need. Just as it is better, more realistic, that Irene alone should suffer, rather than that Irene, Penelope and Tom should all suffer, so it is better that Silas and his family should suffer loss, rather than all those whose investments would have been ruined had Silas agreed to Rogers's proposition. It is an utilitarian ethic, infused with moral idealism and a hint of a Tolstoyan sense of the brotherhood of man. As Howells in the 1880s became increasingly uneasy over what the economic and political power structures of America were doing to ordinary American society, these were the directions in which his convictions were moving.

*

It was in 1886, just after the publication of *The Rise of Silas Lapham*, that Howells made what proved to be his most famous pronouncement on the new mode of realism in American fiction: 'Our novelists . . . concern themselves with the more smiling aspects of life, which are the more American. It is worth while, even at the risk of being called commonplace, to be true to our well-to-do actualities.'[4] Native writers, Howells insisted, who wished to depict normal, rather than abnormal, American life, were bound to emphasize the happier characteristics of their world. In fact, Howells was always anxious that the pursuit of realism should not become a cloak under which a novelist could exploit and appeal to the baser human instincts: realism should involve 'no unnatural straining after the intenser and coarser emotions of blood and fire, no intentional effort to drag in murder, crime, or fierce interludes of passion without adequate reason'. What Howellsian realism meant then, was the rendering of no more than the everyday surfaces of life, of what Howells referred to, in *The Rise of Silas Lapham*, as the commonplace. Such a definition of realism is clearly somewhat limiting and one is compelled to admit that the level of realism actually achieved in *Silas Lapham* is also limited. The surfaces of different levels of Boston life are certainly meticulously rendered and effectively presented; but the levels themselves do not range very widely. As late as 1885, Howells is still able to believe that the social and political consequences of the economic developments in American life, which *The Rise of Silas Lapham* does to a degree acknowledge, are not such as to disturb the even surface of American life. The American norm, he implies, is still a well-to-do one; it is still the 'smiling aspects of life' that are characteristically American.

A minor aspect of the plot of *Silas Lapham* concerns the Millom family. Jim Millom had been a soldier in Silas's Civil War regiment, and had been killed by a bullet which Silas believed had been aimed at him. Characteristically Silas accepts full responsibility for the dead soldier's family, even though the widow is a worthless harridan who has married her daughter to a drunken sailor. The reader is expected to applaud Silas's charitable good-heartedness in this business, but he is kept at a very genteel distance from the presumably harsh realities of the Milloms' actual life. More seriously, there is a sense in which the entire Lapham–Corey romance side of *The Rise of Silas Lapham* appeals to the very sentimental taste in popular fiction which Howells's realism was intended to replace. Howells may have felt that the cause of realism was sufficiently advanced by the way in which in his novel common sense prevails over sentimentalized notions of romantic self-sacrifice. Nevertheless, the impression remains that the work is to a degree trapped by the very tradition it seeks to deny. For example, in the major section of the novel during which Penelope Lapham is not portrayed as the object of Tom Corey's love, she is shown to possess considerable independence of mind – she even rejects the notion of *fictional* self-sacrifice – and a capacity for sardonic humour. Such characteristics and attitudes hardly prepare us for the romantic excesses of which she is guilty when she discovers that she, rather than her sister, is the object of Tom's attentions.

Such limitations in *The Rise of Silas Lapham* explain why later exponents of realism in American fiction became dissatisfied with the Howellsian model. Yet Howells does occupy a position of vital importance in the history of American culture. As editor and critic, as well as novelist, he came to be a major influence on the world of American letters; he used that influence consistently to promote the cause of realism. Particularly during the five years between 1886–91, when he wrote a regular 'Editor's Study' section in *Harper's Monthly*, he worked tirelessly to make a recalcitrant American cultural establishment accept the fact that realism was the way ahead for American writing. Immensely to his credit is the manner in which he helped and defended those younger writers – Garland, Crane, Norris, Harold Frederic – who carried their realism a great deal further than he was prepared to do, trespassing against the rules of that genteel New England culture which he himself was never entirely able to escape, and which his somewhat pallid language and style frequently suggests. Yet, in his own generation, Howells was nothing less than a revolutionary writer. The effort we have to make is to recognize the strength and scale of the opposition to his views. The genteel tradition, with its commitment to a romantic, idealizing view of literature, did not yield easily. Literature ought indeed to be elevating and inspiring, full of 'noble instances of human self-sacrifice, of lofty aspiration and of soul-stirring passion'. Howells's interest in the ordinary and every-day is frequently seen as an interest in 'the vulgar, the commonplace and the insignificant' which is itself 'the last stage of vulgarity, hopelessness, and decadence'. When Boswell tried to defend Henry Fielding to Dr Johnson by suggesting that at least he wrote of real life, he was told that it was of 'low life' that Fielding wrote. Howells's fate was not very different. If realism did in the end come to dominate American fiction in the later nineteenth and early twentieth centuries, it was not without a prolonged and hard-fought struggle.

Howells triumphed in the end by using the intellectual weapons with which the contemporary world provided him. Paradoxically, he defended realism by drawing on the identical ideologies which were being used to buttress those aspects of America's economic and social life which, as the 1880s passed, were troubling him more and more deeply. Realism, Howells showed, was the modern way, a modern instance. Literature, he argued, following the French critic Hippolyte Taine, was not created in splendid isolation; it emerged out of a particular background at a particular time; the artist was conditioned by the society and age and nationality to which he belonged. Further, evolutionary science had proved that reality could not be regarded as fixed or static; flux and change were the nature of things. Finally, from Herbert Spencer and John Fiske, Howells learned that the principles of Darwinist evolutionary change could and should be applied to all aspects of experience – not only to human society, but to the moral and intellectual life of that society. The conclusion was obvious. All those who argued that literature should continue in the good old-fashioned way, that it should not be encouraged to develop and move in new directions, and that it should stick to traditional modes and themes, were simply refusing to face the scientifically verifiable facts. Change was of the nature of things; literature, and literary criticism, were part of the inevitable process of evolutionary development. Realism in America should be seen as the inevitable next stage in the development of American literature.

Realism, in Howells's view, was not only inevitable; it was also in tune with the spirit of modern America. It was scientific in its concern for the detailed, documentation of every aspect of American life; it was democratic in its commitment to the depiction of the ordinary, commonplace, every-day face of American society. Determined to do justice to the actualities of America, it was bound to take notice of the distinctive, democratic features of the nation's society, which were themselves part of America's social and political evolution. Once again, in every aspect of the defence of realism, it is the evolutionary metaphor that provides the crucial, intellectual concept: literary evolution has produced realism, and realism embodies the contemporary ideals of both science and democracy. These were the principles upon which Howells and his supporters – Hamlin Garland, Thomas Sergeant Perry and George Pellew, for example – conducted the campaign on behalf of realism in the later 1880s and early 1890s. The limitations so clearly present in Howells's practice of realism in his novels, should not prevent us from recognizing the major part he played in changing the direction of America's literary culture.

In fact, after the publication of *The Rise of Silas Lapham*, Howells's own attitudes continued to evolve. On 4 May 1886, a bomb was thrown in Chicago's Haymarket Square, killing a policeman. In the violence that followed several more policemen, and an unknown number of citizens, were killed. Eight anarchists were charged with the bomb-throwing, and in the summer of 1886 Howells followed their trial with increasing perturbation. The trial was conducted in a context of mounting public hysteria, and Howells was convinced that the radicals, innocent in his view, would be victims of the public mood. When the anarchists were in fact condemned, Howells was among those who appealed publicly for clemency, and when four were hanged on 11 November, he described the act as civic murder. The existing social and political power structure had perpetrated an irreparable injustice. Just as the trial and execution of Sacco and Vanzetti in the 1920s would clarify contemporary social and political issues for a great many American artists and intellectuals, so the Haymarket affair compelled Howells to re-think his fundamental attitudes. As a result, his thinking veered sharply towards a form of radical, Tolstoyan, Christian socialism. In his later fiction the consequence is a considerably sharper and deeper analysis of the ills of American society in an age of *laissez-faire* capitalism: 'the smiling aspects of life' cease to be the typically American ones.

A Hazard of New Fortunes (1890) is the best product of the new, more radical, Howells. This novel's analysis of American society, with its massive economic injustices, and ruthless unconcern for the individual, is both penetrating and comprehensive. Set in New York, but with characters representing all the important sections of the United States, the novel successfully explores a whole range of social options from capitalism to revolutionary socialism. Through his use of Basil March, the artist-observer figure in the novel who doubles for the author himself, Howells is able to explore not only the complexities of the social issues confronting America, but also the ambivalences and uncertainties in his own feelings about these issues. March is half-in, half-out, of the world he observes. His fringe role almost certainly reflects Howells's doubts about the position of art and culture in an American society whose harsh economic realities he now perceives quite clearly. Where Henry James, a friend and correspondent, was convinced that detachment was part of the price the artist willingly paid to preserve the pearl of his art, Howells seems to have remained much less sure about the appropriate stance of the artist confronting social injustice on a grand scale. Like Tennyson's persona in 'The Palace of Art', a poem that increasingly obsessed him, he wrestled with the problem of whether 'the riddle of the painful earth' could only be solved by abandoning the palace of art in favour of 'a cottage in the vale'.

A Hazard of New Fortunes is an excellent, important, and under-rated novel. Nevertheless, the radicalism of its ideas and analysis is once again partially muted by somewhat genteel elements of plot and style. Where Twain contrived an American vernacular language with which to subvert established society and its values, Howells never managed to win entirely free from the language of the culture and society whose attitudes and values he wished desperately to move in new directions.

Notes

1 The text of this extract from Chapter 14 of *The Rise of Silas Lapham* is taken from Walter J. Meserve and David J. Nordloh (eds.), *A Selected Edition of W. D. Howells*, Volume 12, Bloomington and London, 1971.
2 See 'Introduction', p. viii.
3 Meserve and Nordloh, op. cit., p. xxvi.
4 The comment was originally made in the 'Editor's Study' section of *Harper's Monthly* in 1886. Howells subsequently published most of the material from *Harper's* in *Criticism and Fiction* (1891).

Further reading

Donald Pizer, *Realism and Naturalism in American Literature*, Carbondale, Ill., 1966.

Edwin H. Cady, *The Road to Realism: The Early Years, 1837–1885, of William Dean Howells* 1956.

——, *The Reader at War: The Mature Years, 1885–1920, of William Dean Howells* 1958.

7

Edward Bellamy (1850–98)

I sat in silence until Edith began to rally me upon my sombre looks. What ailed me? The others presently joined in the playful assault, and I became a target for quips and jests. Where had I been, and what had I seen to make such a dull fellow of me?

'I have been in Golgotha,' at last I answered. 'I have seen Humanity hanging on a cross! Do none of you know what sights the sun and stars look down on in this city, that you can think and talk of anything else? Do you not know that close to your doors a great multitude of men and women, flesh of your flesh, live lives that are one agony from birth to death? Listen! their dwellings are so near that if you hush your laughter you will hear their grievous voices, the piteous crying of the little ones that suckle poverty, the hoarse curses of men sodden in misery, turned half-way back to brutes, the chaffering of an army of women selling themselves for bread. With what have you stopped your ears that you do not hear these doleful sounds? For me, I can hear nothing else.'

Silence followed my words. A passion of pity had shaken me as I spoke, but when I looked around upon the company, I saw that, far from being stirred as I was, their faces expressed a cold and hard astonishment, mingled in Edith's with extreme mortification, in her father's with anger. The ladies were exchanging scandalized looks, while one of the gentlemen had put up his eyeglass and was studying me with an air of scientific curiosity. When I saw that things which were to me so intolerable moved them not at all, that words that melted my heart to speak had only offended them with the speaker, I was at first stunned and then overcome with a desperate sickness and faintness at the heart. What hope was there for the wretched, for the world, if thoughtful men and tender women were not moved by things like these! Then I bethought myself that it must be because I had not spoken aright. No doubt I had put the case badly. They were angry because they thought I was berating them, when God knew I was merely thinking of the horror of the fact without any attempt to assign the responsibility for it.

I restrained my passion, and tried to speak calmly and logically that I might correct this impression. I told them that I had not meant to accuse them, as if they, or the rich in general, were responsible for the misery of the world. True indeed it was, that the superfluity which they wasted would, otherwise bestowed, relieve much bitter suffering. These costly viands, these rich wines, these gorgeous fabrics and glistening jewels represented the ransom of many lives. They were verily not without the guiltiness of those who waste in a land stricken with famine. Nevertheless, all the waste of all the rich, were it saved, would go but a little way to cure the poverty of the world. There was so little to divide that even if the rich went share and share with the poor, there would be but a common fare of crusts, albeit made very sweet then by brotherly love.

The folly of men, not their hard-heartedness, was the great cause of the world's poverty. It was not the crime of man, nor of any class of men, that made the race so miserable, but a hideous, ghastly mistake, a colossal world-darkening blunder. And then I showed them how four fifths of the labor of men was utterly wasted by the mutual warfare, the lack of organization and concert among the workers. Seeking to make the matter very plain, I instanced the case of arid lands where the soil yielded the means of life only by careful use of the watercourses for irrigation. I showed how in such countries it was counted the most important function of the government to see that the water was not wasted by the selfishness or ignorance of individuals, since otherwise there would be famine. To this end its use was strictly regulated and systematized, and individuals of their mere caprice were not permitted to dam it or divert it, or in any way to tamper with it.

The labor of men, I explained, was the fertilizing stream which alone rendered earth habitable. It was but a scanty stream at best, and its use required to be regulated by a system which expended every drop to the best advantage, if the world were to be supported in abundance. But how far from any system was the actual practice! Every man wasted the precious fluid as he wished, animated only by the equal motives of saving his own crop and spoiling his neighbor's, that his might sell the better. What with greed and what with spite some fields were flooded while others were parched, and half the water ran wholly to waste. In such a land, though a few by strength or cunning might win the means of luxury, the lot of the great mass must be poverty, and of the weak and ignorant bitter want and perennial famine.

Let but the famine-stricken nation assume the function it had neglected, and regulate for the common good the course of the life-giving stream, and the earth would bloom like one garden, and none of its children lack any good thing. I described the physical felicity, mental enlightenment, and moral elevation which would then attend the lives of all men. With fervency I spoke of that new world, blessed with plenty, purified by justice and sweetened by brotherly kindness, the world of which I had indeed but dreamed, but which might so easily be made real. But when I had expected now surely the faces around me to light up with emotions akin to mine, they grew ever more dark, angry, and scornful. Instead of enthusiasm, the ladies showed only aversion and dread, while the men interrupted me with shouts of reprobation and contempt. 'Madman!' 'Pestilent fellow!' 'Fanatic!' 'Enemy of society!' were some of their cries, and the one who had before taken his eyeglass to me exclaimed, 'He says we are to have no more poor. Ha! ha!'

'Put the fellow out!' exclaimed the father of my betrothed, and at the signal the men sprang from their chairs and advanced upon me.

Looking Backward 2000–1887 (1888)[1]

* * *

Looking Backward is not a novel likely to appear in courses devoted to the art of fiction. Edward Bellamy was a man with a message, and he wrote with no other aim than to drive it home. But art and didacticism are not always at odds with each other, and here, in a sequence near the end of his book, Bellamy shows how fictional and imaginative skills can be used to give additional weight and power to what a deeply committed writer wishes to say.

Julian West, the reader is led to believe, has returned from his dream of the year 2000 to the reality of 1887. But he returns possessed of the enlightenment of the future, determined to illumine the real world from the perspective of the ideal one. Like an early version of Kurt Vonnegut's Billy Pilgrim, he feels compelled to pass on to the present the message his vision of the future has vouchsafed him. Julian had fallen asleep in the year 1887 and awakened in the year 2000. All that has gone before in *Looking Backward* has been taken up with Julian's learning of the transformation of every aspect of society that has occurred between the two dates. By 2000 a utopian ordering of society has been achieved and Julian, in the chapters of *Looking Backward*, listens, like the reader, to a detailed exposition of the new world and all its social, political and economic arrangements. Bellamy, of course, makes some effort to fictionalize and dramatize the situation. Some attention is paid to the psychological effects resulting from an individual's going to sleep in one world and waking up in a very different one – but not very much; there is a mild romantic interest that overleaps the chasm of time – but it is wholly conventional. Bellamy's heart is clearly not in such matters. What he requires is simply a framework within which to portray, in considerable detail, the lineaments of the new world, the new society, which he believes the America of the 1880s could, in time, produce. The great bulk of his novel, occupying the space created by the framework, is concerned with the delineation and definition of the utopian future.

Now, however, almost at the end, the dream is over. Julian has returned to the Boston of 1887, which he sees, a new man, with the eyes of the year 2000. One of Bellamy's more effective devices is to make Julian West himself something of a Boston Brahmin, the kind of man who would have been perfectly at home at Bromfield Corey's dinner-table in *The Rise of Silas Lapham*. Julian has been a wholly conventional member of the Boston élite, part of that upper-class American society whose social and cultural power remained absolute. That it is a man from such a background who is persuaded by his experiences of the total desirability of a broadly socialist future makes the point all the more telling. The reformed conservative is a more challenging figure than the long-term radical. What is crucial, though, is that the reformed, radicalized conservative has returned to the nineteenth century. What the book is doing *in toto* is now enacted within its own structure. Bellamy aimed *Looking Backward* at his contemporaries; his concern was with the *now*, not with the future, near or distant. In its closing pages, Bellamy's confrontation with his contemporaries is acted out for us; Julian West confronts his former friends as Bellamy confronts, with his novel, contemporary society. The result is a noticeable change in imaginative and fictional intensity. The long and sometimes tedious chapters of exposition and explanation are over. The pace quickens. There is a new element of drama. In the year 2000 Julian has spent his time asking questions, listening to lengthy answers, raising mild objections, and being gently put right. The temperature of the book much of the time remains surprisingly low. Not so here. Because he is, as it were, talking straight; because he has devised a situation in which Julian can speak directly to his own kind; because he is at last making a direct comparison between things as they are and as he believes they could and should be, Bellamy writes with a passion and intensity of feeling all the more striking because of their apparent absence from so much of what has gone before. A *saeva indignatio* suddenly replaces the expository tone of the academic lecturer. Furthermore, since Julian is trying to explain what he feels about the present to an audience who know nothing of his experience of the future, what he offers is inevitably a kind of distillation of all that he has learned. For a moment or two Bellamy, that is, stops pretending he is looking backward, and looks forward instead. The result is a dramatic summary of the entire novel bounced off a section of the existing power structure of American society in 1887. The fact that in the novel's closing paragraphs Bellamy lets Julian off the hook by telling us that 'his return to the nineteenth century had been the dream', his 'presence in the twentieth . . . the reality', in no way destroys the impact and power of the section from which the extract comes. Julian himself, despite initially feeling like a convict who has made good his escape, experiences a deep sense of guilt and remorse at such a fortuitously happy ending: 'There suddenly pierced me like a knife a pang of shame, remorse, and wondering self-reproach.' He feels guilt over the kind of person he had been in 1887; he had failed 'to help forward the enfranchisement of the race which was even then preparing'; he had failed even to plead for a 'crucified humanity'. What right had he 'to hail a salvation' which reproached him, at whose dawning he had mocked (p. 310)? To the society of the year 2000 Julian's contribution is to become – what else? – a lecturer in history; to the society of 1887, Bellamy's is the writing of *Looking Backward*.

*

'Ailed', 'quips and jests', 'dull fellow' – such words and phrases belong to the genteel world of Bostonian culture. Here they are perfectly appropriate in so far as Julian has joined his fiancée at dinner with her family and friends. But in fact there is little in the writing of *Looking Backward* to offend the social and cultural world in which Julian originates. Bellamy's prose is for the most part correct and inoffensive; Dr Leete, the principal spokesman of the Utopia of the future, would have been completely at home, in manner and style at least, in the upper-class Boston of 1887. In Julian's answer to the question about his whereabouts, however, the prose moves into a different register. Coolness and rationality are replaced by a rather shrill, emotional intensity; the language is overwrought, scarcely under control. Given Julian's exceptional state of mind and feeling, his rhetoric is perhaps understandable; but one suspects that Bellamy does not have at his command a language of feeling more effective and less clichéd than this. Hence the resort to the 'grievous voices', 'the piteous crying of the little ones', 'the hoarse curses of men', 'these doleful sounds'. None the less, the paragraph is not devoid of power. The opening allusion to the Crucifixion, particularly in the context of the conventionally-minded audience Bellamy has in mind, is dramatic and arresting. Soon the notion of a crucified American humanity will become a reformer's commonplace, and countless thousands of Americans will listen to the Populist and Democratic presidential candidate, William Jennings Bryan, telling them that, through the gold standard policy of the government, they are being crucified upon a cross of gold. The rhetorical questions, and in particular the notion that the suffering and misery and poverty of the masses are all sounds – 'voices', 'crying', 'curses', 'chaffering', 'sounds' – to be listened and attended to, are also sufficiently effective.

In the paragraph that follows, Bellamy anticipates the coming reaction to Julian West's enlightened views and, by implication, the reaction of established society to his book. Such passion as has appeared in Julian's words offends against good manners. The company is not so much shocked by what he has said as scandalized by the indecorousness of speaking in such a manner. Julian recognizes the error he has made, and reverts from passionate outcry to reason and logic. Bellamy, however, before turning to a kind of résumé of his main theme, cannot resist a lengthy aside on the folly of the rich in nineteenth-century American society. They may not be wholly responsible for the entire state of society, but their mode of life does nothing to alleviate it. The point is driven home in a series of sentences, biblical in their diction, which, in their tone and movement, are very much in the mode of the popular sermon. But it has to be recognized that *Looking Backward* is in no major sense designed either to expose the cruelties and injustices of post-bellum, capitalist American society, or to denounce the wealthy class it has produced. In this sense, as has already been suggested, Julian's passionate outburst concerning the dreadful existence of the Boston poor is an exceptional passage. At the beginning of the novel, Bellamy is content to define the contemporary situation. Society is likened to a coach, containing a privileged minority, which is pulled along by the great mass of humanity straining at its harness of ropes. Later, in a more striking image, the contemporary social order is compared to the Black Hole of Calcutta which, 'with its press of maddened men tearing and trampling one another in the struggle to win a place at the breathing holes' is 'a striking type of the society' of late nineteenth-century America. But Bellamy does not choose to elaborate such images. What he is interested in is an alternative vision. What he offers in *Looking Backward* is an account, not of the old, but of a new America, which has evolved from it. It is this utopian vision of the new America that Julian West now offers, in summary form, to his audience of wealthy Bostonians.

The main emphasis falls on the one overriding source of all the flaws in the contemporary social mechanism. This is the 'hideous, ghastly mistake', the 'colossal world-darkening blunder' of which West speaks. What it is, is competition. It is competition, and the competitive instinct it creates, which, in Bellamy's view just as in Henry George's, is the crucial flaw in the capitalist system. What competition creates is 'mutual warfare'; it sets workers against workers in such a way that all their efforts are wasted. This was another idea that was picked up and widely repeated. A spokesman for the Farmers' Alliance in 1891, for example, announced that 'competition is only another word for war'. In Bellamy's view, only by rejecting competition and working co-operatively can labour produce the wealth and abundance needed to support all of society. Labour is the water that fertilizes the earth, but under the present social organization, the water is largely wasted through the greed or spite or cunning or strength of those who compete against each other. Bellamy was convinced of the overwhelming influence of environment on human behaviour; men are 'good' or 'evil', not because of any fixed, natural disposition, but because of the circumstances in which they find themselves. An economic system based on a spirit of competition – 'on the pseudo self-interest of selfishness' – encourages the development of the anti-social and brutal side of human nature. A changed environment, with institutions 'based on the true self-interest of a national unselfishness', has the reverse effect and encourages 'the social and generous instincts of men' (p. 275). Bellamy, that is, typifies the optimistic side of the coin of environmental determinism. If, as the literature of realism and naturalism often suggests, man is not master of his destiny, but rather the victim of external circumstances, then there can be rational hope for the future. In the fictional worlds created by the realists and, particularly, the naturalists, man is frequently brutalized or destroyed by his environment; but the implication of hope survives, human nature is not irredeemably fallen; innate depravity does not exist. Take away the ugliness and oppression and violence of the present, and man can be transformed. Bellamy shows us a world in the year 2000 that validates the environmental determinist's dream.

What is needed is no more than a re-marshalling of existing forces. *Looking Backward* is a product of its times – and this also helps to explain its enormous success – fundamentally because it advocates evolution, not revolution. Bellamy anticipates no need for the violent overthrow of the existing capitalist system. He sees a broadly socialist society as evolving naturally from the existing one; it is simply the logical culmination of a process that is already in evidence. An ultimate state monopoly is the logical outcome of the movement towards monopoly capitalism already under way. In historical terms Bellamy was right; capitalism was moving in the direction he described. 'Competition', in the classical economic sense, was ceasing to exist. Through price agreements, voluntary associations, combinations of independent companies, and mergers, market forces could be controlled in the interest of the capitalist class. The creation of larger and larger companies and corporations intensified the movement towards monopoly situations. By the end of the 1880s, public utilities and the railways were already, in many areas, local monopolies. And, by 1890, the production of a substantial range of industrial products had become monopolies: refined petroleum, refined sugar, cotton and linseed oil, matches, tobacco, whisky, cordage, and lead production, were each largely controlled by a single firm.[2] The movement of capitalism was, then, in the direction of monopoly; Bellamy's point was that the natural outcome of such a movement was one in which the state became 'the one great business corporation in which all other corporations were absorbed' (p. 127). The doctrine of evolutionary progress is thus enlisted by Bellamy on the side of radical economic and social reform.

Bellamy's central image for the new harmony of effort which will emerge when the old, destructive need for competition has been swept away, is a surprising one. It is that of an army. The entire work-force of the nation will be organized as an 'industrial army'. Bellamy – perhaps on the basis of his view of the Union forces in the Civil War – regards an army as an aggregate of individuals all united under a common purpose, and willing to perform acts of heroic self-sacrifice to achieve its ends. So, in the utopian future, the workers will be united. The result will be the ideal world, a vision of which Julian West offers his Bostonian audience. Now back in the real world, as he believes, he recognizes it as no more than that, a vision or a dream, but one which, he insists, 'might so easily be made real'. A world of plenty, and of justice and brotherly love, is readily attainable, and in *Looking Backward* Bellamy has shown his readers how. The key concept is brotherly love, the power that unites all men and women – Bellamy provides for a great advance in the rights and freedom of women in the year 2000 – and produces social harmony. This is the power that requires the competitive spirit, which sets man against man, to be cast aside. As Dr Leete has told Julian: 'If I were to give you, in one sentence, a key to what may seem the mysteries of our civilization as compared with that of your age, I should say that it is the fact that the solidarity of the race and the brotherhood of man, which to you were but fine phrases, are, to our thinking and feeling, ties as real and as vital as physical fraternity' (p. 179). Like Howells's radicalism, Bellamy's socialism has a strongly Christian and Tolstoyan flavour. (There is even a possible Christian dimension to the romance structure of *Looking Backward*: Julian West 'dies' in 1887 to be 'born again' in the year 2000.)

In any event, as the ending of the extract demonstrates, the notion of the universal brotherhood of man has yet to make its appearance in the Boston of 1887. After the vision of 'physical felicity, mental enlightenment, and moral elevation' comes the reality of 'Madman', 'Pestilent fellow', 'Fanatic', and 'Enemy of society'. The effect is dramatic, but the contrast upon which it is based is a device that writers of the year 2000 will no longer be able to exploit. *Looking Backward* makes it clear that Bellamy shared Howells's view on the harmful nature of the great mass of contemporary popular romantic fiction, with its emphasis upon the incitement of 'morbid sympathy' for the 'sentimental selfishness of lovers' (p. 271). The novelists of the future will provide a healthier stimulus, abandoning these decadent sentiments, as well as many other effects dear to the hearts of the popular writers of 1887. Bellamy insists that the new social structures, and the new social realities, will produce a new fiction. Excluded from this novel of the future will be 'all effects drawn from the contrasts of wealth and poverty, education and ignorance, coarseness and refinement, high and low, all motives drawn from social pride and ambition, the desire of being richer or the fear of being poorer, together with sordid anxieties of any sort for one's self or others' (pp. 204–5). The obvious difficulty is how such a fiction, from which so much is excluded, could avoid being anything other than upliftingly boring. Bellamy concedes that the serious literature of his own day was a literature of protest and compassion; the novelist of the future seems dangerously close to having nothing to write about. *Looking Backward* itself, with its emphasis on exposition and explanation, and its failure to dramatize or vivify the future, often seems all too like the anti-novel that is to come.

Julian West's address to his fellow Bostonians, however, possesses something of the drama missing from most of the book. And in the vision of the male guests advancing menacingly upon the hapless Julian, Bellamy hints at the reality of the stores of violence latent in American society in the 1880s. That there is a crisis in the America of the 1880s, *Looking Backward* underlines. Twice Bellamy uses Carlyle's famous phrase 'the signs of the times' to indicate his awareness that America is undergoing a crisis in the 1880s just as serious as that experienced by Great Britain in the 1840s. But his evolutionary and religious optimism sees the crisis as leading not to violence, anarchy, or revolution, but to the peaceful Utopia *Looking Backward* describes. Threatened by the violence of his fellow-guests, Julian wakes up to find himself back in the Boston of the year 2000. Just this, the novel suggests, can be the glorious fate of the threatened America of the 1880s.

*

Looking Backward was a sensational success. Of books published in America in the second half of the nineteenth century it was outsold only by *Uncle Tom's Cabin* and *Ben Hur*. In the first year of publication 60,000 copies were sold, 400,000 in the United States alone by 1897. Translations quickly appeared in German, French, Italian and Norwegian, and a variety of American reform movements, social and political, took up, distributed, and sold cheap editions of the book. Magazines like the respectable *Ladies' Home Journal* and the *People's Health Journal* offered it free to new subscribers. *Looking Backward* also set a new fashion for utopian fiction. By 1900 some forty other utopian novels had appeared, the great majority, significantly, like *Looking Backward*, repudiating notions of an inevitable class conflict in American society, maintaining instead that some form of collectivist state could be achieved through education or political and religious appeals. None of these later novels, however, achieved anything remotely comparable to the impact of *Looking Backward*.

Bellamy's book became one of that select band that can be said to have changed men's lives. Writers and thinkers and politicians like William Dean Howells – whose early enthusiastic review in *Harper's Monthly* was immensely important in launching the novel – Upton Sinclair, John Dewey, Thorstein Veblen, Eugene Debs and Norman Thomas, were all deeply influenced by it. Thomas, indeed, who was to run for the presidency of the United States as a socialist on numerous occasions, regarded *Looking Backward* as his introduction to socialism. But the book's appeal was in no sense limited to coteries of intellectuals. Most extraordinarily of all, *Looking Backward* created a mass political movement which came close to capturing the presidency of the United States. Within three years of its publication, 162 Nationalist Clubs – 'nationalist' because they were dedicated to the nationalization of all the means of production – were operating in twenty-seven states with the purpose of spreading Bellamy's message. The Nationalist movement, supported by the *New Nation*, a weekly paper edited by Bellamy, flourished for several years, but was in the end taken over by the Populist party, itself a coalition of farm and labour reform groups all determined to destroy the existing capitalist system, and all broadly sympathetic to Bellamy's ideals. In 1896 the Populists' moment of destiny seemed to have come when they successfully won control of the Democratic party; however their candidate for the presidency, William Jennings Bryan, was narrowly defeated by the Republican McKinley.

What the phenomenal, spiralling impact of *Looking Backward* shows is that by 1888, the feeling that something was fundamentally amiss with the structure of American society was shared by an ever-increasing number of Americans. Much had happened between 1879 and 1888 to confirm the fears that Henry George had expressed in *Progress and Poverty*. As we have seen, George's conviction that, if nothing were done, American society was heading for destruction, was firmly based on the scale of industrial unrest, strikes and violence evident in so many areas of America in the late 1870s. After 1879 had come an economic upturn, and a corresponding temporary decrease in social tensions. But in the 1880s bad times returned for enormous sections of the American population. For farmers and industrial workers, for Southerners, for Negroes and immigrants, the story was the same; their economic position, never particularly strong, seemed to be growing progressively worse. Farmers in the west and south saw the prices they received for the crops they grew falling steadily, while their debts in capital and interest to eastern banks and loan companies mounted. The Grange movement, the Farmers' Alliance, and the Populist party all represent attempts by farmers to fight back. Industrial workers in the east, miners and railwaymen, all faced wage-cuts and an apparently declining standard of living. In such a climate, new immigrants, and other minority groups, inevitably suffered; the land of opportunity must have often seemed like a broken promise. That the distressed and discontented masses should have tried to resist is hardly surprising. In 1883 the telegraph operators came out on strike; in 1885 it was the turn of the steel-workers in Pittsburgh and Cleveland. But it was in the following year that American society once again reached a point where a total collapse into violence and anarchy seemed a distinct possibility. A union-sponsored campaign for an eight-hour day had been launched in 1884. Initially it gained little support, but in 1885 and 1886 the situation changed. Strikes multiplied: coke workers in Pennsylvania; coal miners in Pennsylvania, Maryland, West Virginia, and Ohio; textile and boot and shoe workers in New England; even nail-makers went on strike. A new spirit of militancy among the railway unions achieved some improvements in the conditions of their members. But the great railroad strikes in the spring of 1886, involving derailments, sabotage, and violent confrontations between union men and non-union strike-breakers, inevitably led to widespread violence and rioting which, in several states, required the calling out of militia to put down. Nowhere was the campaign for the eight-hour day pursued more aggressively than in Chicago, a centre both of the railroads and heavy industry. Serious trouble had threatened since February 1886, when the McCormick mechanical reaper company, one of the largest employers in the city, had locked out its workers in an attempt to break the union. It had subsequently reopened with non-union labour, but the union men maintained an active picket around the plant. On 3 May, during a speech by a prominent anarchist, violence erupted between union and non-union workers; the police were called, and in the resulting confrontation two union men were shot dead, and several wounded. This was the prologue to the Haymarket tragedy of the following day when, after the explosion of an anarchist bomb had killed one policeman, the police fired into the crowd and in the fighting that followed six more policemen and an unknown number of demonstrators were killed. This, and the summary trials and executions that followed, were the events that, as we have said, radicalized William Dean Howells. In a wider context, they were the events that convinced Bellamy, and the increasing number of Americans who felt like him, that the divisions in American society were growing so wide and bitter that, if nothing were done, further and greater violence was inevitable.

Against such a background, the astonishing enthusiasm with which so many readers greeted *Looking Backward* becomes more explicable. Bellamy's book represented a head-on attack on the competitive spirit of capitalism – an attack he carried on in *Equality* the sequel to *Looking Backward* he published in 1897 – and his endorsement of collectivism as the way of the future involved a direct challenge to the old American traditions of self-reliance, and the individual's right to carve out his own future, come what may. But by 1888 substantial numbers of Americans were convinced that the problems of their society were so vast and urgent that new ideas, new solutions, however 'un-American' they might appear, were desperately needed. Every day in their newspapers they read of strikes, lock-outs, industrial unrest and conflict of an increasingly widespread and violent nature. They could see all around them how small businesses were being squeezed out by the great corporations and monopolies. They could hear the increasingly vociferous views of the labour unions, the farmers' groups, and other committed reformers, all attacking the existing system. Many wondered whether that system was indeed collapsing, and even whether democracy itself was breaking down. For all such Americans, *Looking Backward*, with its recognition that in 1887 America was facing 'an impending social cataclysm' (p. 101), both reflected a current crisis and suggested an acceptable solution. The book was a challenging tract for the times, addressing the central issues of America's social and economic life, and pointing a way forward. Hence its amazing success.

Needless to say, the chorus of approval was not universal. Defenders of the *status quo* were prepared to fight back. Their leading spokesman was Francis A. Walker, the period's best-known academic economist, and President of Massachusetts Institute of Technology. Walker's bitter attack on Bellamy was published in *Atlantic Monthly*. He rejected utterly Bellamy's criticisms of the current state of society, 'that state of society in which all of us live, and which most of us cordially support'. He described Bellamy's views on the equal distribution of wealth as involving 'the grossest violation to common honesty, as every plain man understands it'. The unequal distribution of wealth, he argued, was essential as a spur to individual achievement. And he reiterated, in the baldest of terms, the orthodox, Social Darwinist view, that the competitive struggle was the key to human social development. Walker considered a man 'very shallow in his observation of the facts of life, and utterly lacking in the biological sense, who fails to discern in competition the force to which it is mainly due that mankind have risen from stage to stage, in intellectual, moral, and physical power'. Finally, he suggested that if there was anything amiss with the current state of things, the blame lay with nature or human wilfulness, in no way with the capitalist economy or the behaviour of the business interest.[3] Whether such views, expressed in such terms, could have had any influence on anyone prepared to go as far as reading *Looking Backward* (or *Progress and Poverty* which Walker also assailed) is a very open question.

In England, *Looking Backward* proved to be not to the taste of a distinguished fellow reformer and radical. William Morris disliked Bellamy's vision of a wholly industrialized future, and argued, correctly enough, that Bellamy's utopia involved a large measure of undemocratic, bureaucratic and managerial control over the life of the individual. Morris's *News from Nowhere* was written in part at least as a rejoinder to *Looking Backward*. But despite these and other arguments about the defects in Bellamy's vision of the future, *Looking Backward* like, say, Emerson's early essays, was an inspiration to the young and radical. It represented another major leap forward in the task, begun by *Progress and Poverty*, of making radical criticism of the *status quo* in America's social and economic arrangements both possible and popular.

The depth of William Dean Howells's own perplexities over the American scene must be reflected in the obsessional way he kept returning to and quoting Tennyson's line from 'The Palace of Art' about 'the riddle of the painful earth'. Hence perhaps the appropriateness of quoting the tribute he paid to both Bellamy and George in the new Preface to *A Hazard of New Fortunes* he wrote in 1911. Thinking of the late 1880s, when he was at work on the novel, he said: 'In those days, the solution of the riddle of the painful earth through the dreams of Henry George, through the dreams of Edward Bellamy, through the dreams of all the generous visionaries of the past, seemed not impossibly far off.'

Notes

1 The text of this extract from Chapter 28 of *Looking Backward 2000–1887* is taken from the Belknap Press edition, ed. John L. Thomas, Cambridge, Mass., 1967.

2 See Thomas C. Cochran, 'Business in Veblen's America', in Carlton L. Qualey (ed.), *Thorstein Veblen*, New York and London, 1968, pp. 47–71.

3 See Joseph Dorfman, *Thorstein Veblen and his America*, London, 1935, p. 71.

Further reading

Sylvia E. Bowman, *The Year 2000, A Critical Biography of Edward Bellamy*, New York, 1958.

8

Hamlin Garland (1860-1940)

Howard, being the lion of the evening, tried his best to be agreeable. He kept near his mother, because it afforded her so much pride and satisfaction, and because he was obliged to keep away from Grant, who had begun to talk to the men. Howard talked mainly about their affairs, but still was forced more and more into talking of life in the city. As he told of the theatre and the concerts, a sudden change fell upon them; they grew sober, and he felt deep down in the hearts of these people a melancholy which was expressed only elusively with little tones or sighs. Their gayety was fitful.

They were hungry for the world, for life – these young people. Discontented and yet hardly daring to acknowledge it; indeed, few of them could have made definite statement of their dissatisfaction. The older people felt it less. They practically said, with a sigh of pathetic resignation:

'Well, I don't expect ever to see these things *now*.'

A casual observer would have said, 'What a pleasant bucolic – this little surprise-party of welcome!' But Howard, with his native ear and eye, had no such pleasing illusion. He knew too well these suggestions of despair and bitterness. He knew that, like the smile of the slave, this cheerfulness was self-defence; deep down was another self.

Seeing Grant talking with a group of men over by the kitchen door, he crossed over slowly and stood listening. Wesley Cosgrove – a tall, raw-boned young fellow with a grave, almost tragic face – was saying:

'Of course I ain't. Who is? A man that's satisfied to live as we do is a fool.'

'The worst of it is,' said Grant, without seeing Howard, 'a man can't get out of it during his lifetime, and *I* don't know that he'll have any chance in the next – the speculator'll be there ahead of us.'

The rest laughed, but Grant went on grimly:

'Ten years ago Wess, here, could have got land in Dakota pretty easy, but now it's about all a feller's life's worth to try it. I tell you things seem shuttin' down on us fellers.'

'Plenty o' land to rent,' suggested some one.

'Yes, in terms that skin a man alive. More than that, farmin' ain't so free a life as it used to be. This cattle-raisin' and butter-makin' makes a nigger of a man. Binds him right down to the grindstone and he gets nothin' out of it – that's what rubs it in. He simply wallers around in the manure for somebody else. I'd like to know what a man's life is worth who lives as we do? How much higher is it than the lives the niggers used to live?'

These brutally bald words made Howard thrill with emotion like some great tragic poem. A silence fell on the group.

'That's the God's truth, Grant,' said young Cosgrove, after a pause.

'A man like me is helpless,' Grant was saying. 'Just like a fly in a pan of molasses. There ain't any escape for him. The more he tears around the more liable he is to rip his legs off.'

'What can he do?'

'Nothin'.'

The men listened in silence.

'Up the Coulé' in *Main-Travelled Roads* (1891)[1]

* * *

Main-Travelled Roads holds an honourable position in one of the few, genuinely distinctive, formal traditions in American literature: the collection of short stories which has a degree of unity far beyond what the term 'collection' suggests. From the nineteenth century on, the short story seems always to have had a special attraction for American readers and writers, and perhaps it was this guarantee of popularity that led, in turn, to the development of the genre of the group of stories, discrete in terms of action and plot, but unified in terms of over-all design. What that design is, and how it is achieved, will of course vary from book to book, but in the hands of such modern masters as Hemingway and Faulkner the genre itself has proved aesthetically rich and satisfying. A common location, consistent atmosphere, recurring characters, linked or contrasting themes, a single narrator, all of these, separately or in combination, have been used to produce a unity and coherence that transcends the diversity of the individual narratives. As a result this genre can be seen as embodying at least one of the American challenges to received notions about the necessary form of the novel.

Main-Travelled Roads itself could hardly be regarded as a novel. But the book, particularly in its original 1891 edition when it was composed of six stories, does have a remarkable unity of effect. That unity is produced by a consistency of theme, linked to a consistency of place and atmosphere. The stories in *Main-Travelled Roads* are all concerned with the life of the American farmer in Wisconsin and Iowa – what Garland called the Middle Border. All are equally concerned to demonstrate that the life of the farmer – and his wife – is one of unremitting harshness, hardness, and a back-breaking struggle for economic survival. And all insist on the bleakness, dreariness and narrow provinciality of the lives of those condemned to farm the American West. The extract chosen from 'Up the Coulé' precisely defines Garland's central, unifying theme: the definition of the life of the farmer offered here by Grant McLane is one which all the stories in *Main-Travelled Roads* unite in authenticating. This is the truth which Garland – a trifle uneasily present in the figure of Howard in the extract – was determined to communicate.

Such a determination makes Garland's literary allegiance abundantly clear. From the outset of his literary career in the 1880s, Garland was a single-minded adherent of the school of realism in American fiction of which Howells was the pioneer. His contribution to that school, however, was original and distinctive. What he did was to radicalize the post-bellum, so-called 'local color' movement in American writing. Just as Maria Edgeworth and Walter Scott had once conceived of their novels as spreading greater understanding of the Irish and Scots among English readers, so in the aftermath of the Civil War, American local colour writers tried to explore and explain the characteristics of the different sections of America for the benefit of the population as a whole. Thus writers like Bret Harte and, to a degree, Mark Twain, in the West, George Washington Cable and Joel Chandler Harris in the South, Sarah Orne Jewett and Harriet Beecher Stowe in New England, all produced work centrally concerned to delineate the distinctive character and manners of their varied regions of the United States. A kind of nascent realism is often present in such writing, particularly in its use of traditional types of humorous story-telling, folklore material, and the registering of local vernaculars and dialect. None the less, realism was not on the whole characteristic of a local colour movement frequently inclined to dwell on the past, in a mood of nostalgic reminiscence, and readier to emphasize the genial, the humorous and the sentimental, rather than the harsh or sordid or tragic.

Whatever its limitations in terms of realism, the local colour movement was, in Garland's view, the best hope for the future of American literature. Like so many of his contemporaries, Garland was a convinced evolutionist. He had read Herbert Spencer's *Synthetic Philosophy* in Iowa in 1884, and once he had arrived in Boston in 1885 to embark on a literary career, all his reading and thinking about literature was influenced by the Spencerian model. Thus, like Howells and his supporters, he rejected any notion of literary modes or values being fixed or static: literature and literary criticism should be seen as evolving, like all other phenomena. Like Taine, he saw literature as largely determined by the social conditions under which it was produced. Thus American literature should reject traditional models and evolve towards increasingly native or local forms. It should embody and portray the everyday life of ordinary Americans, as Howells had argued: inevitably, therefore, it should reflect the progressive and democratic ideals of America itself. In Garland's view, Whitman was the truly representative American writer, but as far as the novel was concerned, it was the local colour writers, with their concern for the particularities of individual areas, who promised to be most in key with the evolutionary development of a national American literature. Herbert Spencer had propounded the theory of an evolutionary progression from incoherent homogeneity to coherent heterogeneity; Garland believed that it was the local colour movement that best reflected the application of this 'law of development' to American writing.

Garland developed these views in the essays and reviews he wrote in the 1880s. In 1887 he finally met Howells in Boston, and the two men became friends for life. It is the date, however, that is significant. The Howells whom Garland met was the newly radicalized Howells; the Howells who saw in the public reaction to the anarchist bomb in Haymarket Square, Chicago, in May 1886, an abandonment of American ideals of justice and the rights of the individual. This was the Howells who has ceased to believe that the 'smiling aspects of life are the most American' and whose own fiction was changing accordingly. In 1888 Garland wrote a review of *Annie Kilburn*, a novel by Howells which reflected the new kind of social awareness he had arrived at. Garland praised it precisely for its social concern: 'social regeneration is a living issue – it is in the air and as a living present problem, is the properest of all subjects for the pen of our greatest novelist.'[2] Such praise indicates very clearly the kind of emphasis that would appear in the stories Garland was at work on in the period 1888–90, and which would be published as *Main-Travelled Roads*.

In *Main-Travelled Roads* Garland takes over the local colour movement, retaining its outward forms, as it were – the preoccupation with a particular section of America and its typical inhabitants – but he will portray the farming communities of the Middle Border, not in a mood of gentle nostalgia and reminiscence, but with the harshness of a new and powerful realism. In these stories of the Middle Border, realism conquers new territory. There had been little in earlier American writing to suggest that the lot of the farmer was anything other than an enviable one. Indeed in the conventional mythology of America, the farmer, from the earliest days of the republic, had been a quasi-legendary figure, the sturdy, independent yeoman, the authentic inhabitant of the golden West, the garden of America. Garland's farmers are certainly men of unyielding strength, of rock-like endurance and heroic toil, but they know nothing of Eden, nor even any longer of a Jeffersonian vision of sturdy independence and self-reliance. Long expelled from Eden, they struggle for survival by the sweat of their brow. It is the truth of this struggle that it is Garland's aim to communicate.

As a realistic portrayal of middle-western country and small town life, *Main-Travelled Roads* has only one possible antecedent: Edgar Watson Howe's strange novel, *The Story of a Country Town* (1883). Having been turned down by various publishers, the novel was finally published by its author, who was the editor and owner of a Kansas newspaper. It immediately became something of a sensation, and was reprinted in the next year or two some twenty-five times. The power of the novel lies in its suggestion of how the lives of its characters are largely determined by the narrow, restricting circumstances in which they find themselves. The story becomes increasingly one of failure, non-communication, sadness and sorrow, for which no one is really to blame: the characters seem driven to act as they do, however self-destructively. Garland found much to admire in Howe's work, but, reasonably enough, he was less impressed by Howe's somewhat melodramatic action and plot, and his resort, on occasion, to stereotyped characters. In its powerful anti-pastoral strain, *The Story of a Country Town* does anticipate Garland's own work, but he could see that in other areas the realism of the novel was badly flawed.

Howe's failure is ultimately a failure of artistic control. He cannot find a narrative form and structure that is appropriate to what is new and radical in his imaginative insight into American rural experience. When Garland came to write his own anti-pastoral, he was to encounter the same difficulty. He had spent his early life in the farming communities of Iowa and South Dakota. In 1885, he had come east to Boston and begun to prepare himself for a literary career; in 1887 and 1888, however, he made trips back to the west, with every intention of using the experiences and observations occasioned by these return visits as material for his writing. Once he had obtained the material, the problem remained of how best to use it. How was he to tell the truth about the life of the western farmer and his wife in a realistic, but imaginatively satisfying form? The conventional novel he distrusted. Like Howells, he saw its forms and structures as determined by the demands of a harmful, sentimental, romanticism. 'The time will yet come,' he wrote, 'if it has not already, when the public will recognize Mr Howells as a public benefactor for replacing morbid, unnatural and hysterical fiction with pure, wholesome and natural studies of real life.'[3] What Garland regarded as 'natural studies of real life' were just not compatible with the elaborate plots and narrative complications readers expected to find in a novel. Hence the preference he developed for the sketch or short story, centred on a single character or group of characters, and simply set down. In 1892, after the appearance of *Main-Travelled Roads*, he was still prepared to insist that the short story or 'novelette' was 'the most perfect form of writing'.[4]

No more than Howe, though, was Garland finally able to resolve the problem of finding a wholly satisfactory form through which to say what he was determined should be said. What the example of Garland reveals, with particular clarity, is the dilemma facing the writer who espouses a literary mode that seems to suggest that art falsifies or distorts reality. Garland did not believe that life needed to be 'worked up' into art. But the truth about life he wished to communicate had none the less to be articulated with imaginative power and effectiveness. For Garland, as for other followers of Howells, realism's relationship to life was far less problematical than realism's relationship to Art. The particular nature of Garland's aesthetic problem is neatly suggested by a passage from a different story in *Main-Travelled Roads*. In 'Among the Corn Rows', a young Norwegian girl is guiding a corn-plough while her young brother rides the horse. Garland's description emphasizes the terrible, relentless, heat of the sun, and the overwhelming, exhausting, physical demand the ploughing makes. The girl's heart, we are told, 'was full of bitterness, her face flushed with heat, and her muscles aching with fatigue' (p. 122). Garland is determined to draw an ironic contrast between this picture of human weariness and exhaustion, and the beauty of the natural world within which such inhuman demands upon the girl's strength are being made. So he ends the descriptive paragaph thus: 'What matter to her that the king-bird pitched jovially from the maples to catch a wandering blue-bottle fly, that the robin was feeding its young, that the bobolink was singing? All these things, if she saw them, only threw her bondage to labor into greater relief' (p. 122). The problem here is clearly an unresolved one of point of view; the gap between the author's perception and the character's is so wide – as Garland's commitment to realism requires it to be – that there is no way in which the ironic point can be made except by the crude authorial intervention to which he resorts. The result is aesthetically and imaginatively unsatisfying. The text even questions its own validity ('if she saw them') and the anger and bitterness that the author so clearly feels have not been integrated into the created scene.

The one device that Garland discovered to give his material an independent life, and some measure of dramatic impact, amounted to no more than allowing his own point of view, his own experience, to exist within the fictional world he was creating. The best stories in *Main-Travelled Roads* involve the return to the Middle Border of a character who, having been brought up in the region, has been away for a number of years. The character is then a kind of inside outsider. He looks at his native region with a sympathetic familiarity, but from a perspective created by his experience of a wider world. Also, because he has escaped from the limiting circumstance of farming life, he can be appropriately presented as better educated, more intelligent, more perceptive. Garland, in other words, had come to realize that one of the limitations of Howellsian realism was the role it allowed the author. The art that was concerned above all to render the commonplace, the everyday, the ordinary actualities of American life, was a highly impersonal art. How were the author's own attitudes and feelings to be communicated? The passage from 'Among the Corn Rows' shows Garland precisely failing to resolve this problem. But he did see that there was a problem, and in his best stories coped with it more successfully. His theoretical answer was to modify realism, with its commitment to the neutral rendering of the observable realities, by shifting it towards what he called 'veritism', a mode of writing which he conceived of as combining accuracy and truth in the portrayal of the facts of experience with a form of impressionism in the way in which the perception of such facts was mediated through the personality of the artist. In *Crumbling Idols* (1894), in which he set out his literary theories and beliefs, Garland wrote, '. . . in carrying on the fight for truth in American fiction, I had adopted Veritism as the word which best described my theory, a word which I gained from reading Eugene Veron's "Esthetics".'[5] Veritism accommodated fact and impression, objectivity and subjectivity; ultimately it could do equal justice to life and art. In practice, in the context of the structure of his stories, what this means is that the character, for example, who is returning home – a double of the author – serves both as realist and impressionist. Howard McLane, in 'Up the Coulé', is just such a character.

*

Howard is a successful actor and playwright who is returning home to visit his mother and brother after a ten-year absence. His impressions of the familiar landscape of western Wisconsin is rendered in a 'veritist' mode: because he is returning home, the scene has a special, personal vividness for him. Garland writes: 'It had a certain mysterious glamor to him; the lakes were cooler and brighter to his eye, the greens fresher, and the grain more golden than to any one else, for he was coming back to it all after an absence of ten years' (p. 59). Howard retains this alert responsiveness to the natural beauties of the La Crosse valley, but as the story develops the natural landscape is increasingly set in ironic contrast to Howard's awareness of the harsh severity and sordidness of those who toil for a living amid these magnificent surroundings. The first hint of the contrast comes with the little town where Howard leaves the train. The hills, richly wooded, surrounding the town, are as beautiful and majestic as he remembered them: 'gracious, lofty in their greeting, immortal in their vivid and delicate beauty.' But the town, squalid and sleepy, with its 'unpaved street, drab-colored, miserable, rotting wooden buildings' (p. 60) was changed, if at all, for the worse. The same point is made when Howard reaches his brother's farm. As he had approached it, the 'dazzling sunlight', 'the green and purpled slopes', 'the luscious velvety grass', and 'the rounded, distant, purple peaks' had made his heart swell 'with pleasure almost like pain' (p. 64). But the stark reality of the farm drives all sense of pleasure out of his consciousness; its drab dreariness overwhelms him. 'Instantly,' writes Garland, 'the beautiful, peaceful valley was forgotten.' In its place, 'a sickening chill struck into Howard's soul as he looked at it all.' 'The longer he stood,' we read, 'absorbing this farm-scene, with all its sordidness, dullness, triviality, and its endless drudgeries, the lower his heart sank' (pp. 66–7).

The rhythm established here of hopes and expectations raised and then destroyed by two contrasting kinds of reality is sustained throughout 'Up the Coulé'. Howard experiences a constant pattern of wishes and anticipations being thwarted and frustrated by bitter and destructive realities. He is burdened by the guilt of his past neglect, but he believes all the same that his return can be a joyful one. When he understands what has gone wrong, why his family had to leave the farm that had been his boyhood home, he longs to help, to make up for the past. As circumstances change, he allows his hopes to rise, renews his efforts; but in vain. It is too late for anything to be done. This pattern of conflicting hopes and frustrations within Howard is paralleled by a wider pattern of inevitable and unchangeable contrasts. Howard is successful, famous, well-off. He is accustomed to a life of comfort and ease, foreign travel, a share in the warmth and luxury of civilized, cultured life. His farming family belong to a different world. Trapped by economic circumstances over which they have no control, theirs is a life of ceaseless toil for little or no return: Grant McLane, unable to meet the mortgage payments, has been forced to leave the old family farm. The letter of appeal for help to Howard had never reached him – he had been travelling abroad. As a result, Grant regards his brother's return with bitterness and anger. In one scene of angry confrontation Grant takes exception to his brother's spoiling his fine clothes by trying to help in the fields. Howard retaliates by listing the exact price of everything he is wearing: shirt – six dollars; pants – fifteen dollars; shoes – six-fifty; the ring on his cravat – sixty dollars. Grant retorts with his own list: pants, eighty-five cents; hat, twenty cents; shoes, a dollar fifty; 'stockin's I don't bother about' (pp. 78–9). The two worlds of progress and poverty in American society in the 1880s meet here in classic confrontation. And Garland succeeds superbly in rendering Howard's anger and frustration at being forced to acknowledge the truth of the fundamental and devastating injustice that lies at the heart of Grant's resentment.

The occasion of the extract, however, reveals a more smiling aspect of Middle Border life, its traditional hospitality and popular culture. The neighbours have gathered at the McLane's farm for an impromptu welcome home party for Howard. In the opening paragraph Howard remains beside his mother, talking to the women. His mother, of course, takes a natural pride in his achievements, even though she knows that relations between her elder and younger son remain strained. But there is a greater significance in Howard's position; rejected by Grant, he is denied admission to the serious business of the men's world. He may be able to entertain the women and girls, but, in Grant's view, he has nothing important to say. Even in the second half of the extract he is allowed only to overhear, not to participate. Howard, like Garland, has become an uneasy observer of Middle Border life, in it but no longer of it. Nevertheless, what he does have to say has its own appeal. He is able to bring a report from that larger world that the farming people know exists, but of which they have no experience. Howard has done what the young among them may still dream of doing: escape. The sadness Howard senses in them is the sadness of lost opportunities, the identical sadness that, a generation later, Sherwood Anderson will register in his account of Middle-Western life, *Winesburg, Ohio*, another story collection. For Garland, however, it is not enough to communicate Howard's sense of the inarticulate yearnings of the young people which make them listen with such fascination to his talk of the city, of theatres and concerts. Garland has to intervene directly himself, to define the young people as hungry for life, discontented, dissatisfied. He has to spell things out. In fact Howard's 'native ear and eye' is an altogether more reliable guide; we can accept his understanding of the current of melancholy and despair, underneath the superficial gaiety of the occasion, because once he had shared the life of his auditors.

At this point in the extract, Howard leaves the young people and crosses the room to listen to the men. He has observed that the outward gaiety of the first group is self-defensive, 'like the smile of the slave'. This image of the slave proves to be the link between the two sections of the passage. It is Grant McLane now who does the talking; Howard, standing on the edge of the group of men, is allowed only to overhear. Grant talks not of the excitements of city life, with its theatres and concerts, but of the life of the farmer. Thus what follows is a powerful statement of Garland's anti-pastoral theme. With bitter energy, Grant defines the circumstances that have reduced the life of the farmer to a form of slavery. The discontent of the young people has been expressed in terms of their longing for that wider world of which the city is a potent image; Grant's discontent is with the realities of the farming life itself: its harsh injustices above all. For Grant farming has become a trap, a prison: 'a man can't get out of it during his life-time.' (That he *has* got out explains Howard's deep-seated sense of guilt.) And in

Grant's sardonic joke about the next life there is an indication that he blames the entrapment that he feels on the financial exploitation of which he is the victim. The position of the farmer has deteriorated. The era of free land is over; rents are rising: 'I tell you things seem shuttin' down on us fellers.'

Historically speaking, Grant McLane was undoubtedly right. In the late 1880s, when Garland was writing, the position of the western and southern farmer was worse than it had been at any time since the Civil War. At the close of the war, farming had boomed. The Homestead Act of 1862 had granted 160 acres of public land free to anyone who asked for it; further Acts in the 1870s offered the same or a larger amount of land free on certain conditions. But these Acts had not in fact worked out as their proponents had hoped. Huge areas of public land, often of superior quality, had fallen into the hands of speculators and monopolists. Farmers and settlers often found it better and more advantageous to buy land – because it was near a railway, for example – than to accept the free land. None the less, the land hunger of so many Americans meant that the total area of land being farmed doubled between 1860–1900. The increase in output that this expansion produced was a major factor in the plummeting farm prices that were the primary cause of the problems facing all the farmers represented by Grant McLane. In 1866, wheat was worth $2.06 a bushel; in 1894 the corresponding figure was 48.9 cents. In 1866 corn was worth 65.7 cents a bushel; in 1896, the figure was 21.4 cents. These statistics tell the same story in economic terms that Garland tells in human ones. By the end of the 1880s, the plight of the western farmer was often desperate. The return he got on the crops he produced was constantly declining; but the fixed cash interest he had to pay on the money he had borrowed to buy land or materials or equipment remained the same. Therefore he had to work harder, grow and sell more, simply to meet his debts. It is hardly surprising that the struggle often proved an impossible one; mortgage payments could not be met, and the farmer's land was lost. In 1886 and 1887, in a section of Kansas, more than half the outstanding mortgages were foreclosed; in one area the figure rose as high as nine out of ten. All too often the farmer was being skinned alive.

Such an economic squeeze had obviously meant a decline in the average farmer's quality of life. As Grant McLane puts it, 'farmin' ain't so free a life as it used to be.' At this point Garland allows the image of entrapment and loss of freedom to culminate in a parallel between the position of the farmer and that of the slave: 'This cattle-raisin' and butter-makin' makes a nigger of a man. Binds him right down to the grindstone. . . .' Ironically Grant is conceding the South's old argument that there was little to choose between chattel slavery in the South and wage or economic slavery in the North. And the irony of Grant's insisting that the farmer's life is worth no more than that of the Negro slave is all the more bitter when one recalls that these are the very men, as the story 'The Return of a Private' in *Main-Travelled Roads* shows, who fought and died in the Union armies to free the Negro. What above all else powers Grant's sense of anger and frustration is his awareness that the relentless toil demanded of him is to no avail. Like the Negro slave, he is working for someone else: he 'wallers around in the manure for somebody else'. Who that is is the land speculator or mortgage holder: the man who buys up farms, rents them out, waits for the farmer to improve the land by his own heroic efforts, then promptly doubles the rent or offers to sell the land to the man who has improved it at two or three times the price he originally paid for it. This is the theme of the most famous story in *Main-Travelled Roads*: 'Under the Lion's Paw', which Garland used to read to audiences in Boston with the actor James A. Herne. To the question of how much higher is the life of the farmer than that of the Negro slave there is no answer. For Grant and his audience the freedom promised by America's democratic system has ceased to exist. They are all enslaved, all victims of economic circumstances over which they have no control. Like the fly in the pan of molasses, they are helpless. There is no escape. And the grammatical ambiguity over the antecedent of 'him' – whether it is 'a man like me' or 'a fly in a pan' – serves only to drive home the brutal effectiveness of the image; man and fly are equally trapped. To the question, 'What can he do?' the answer is 'Nothin'', and the acquiescent silence of the listening group of men is more eloquent than anything they might have said.

It is Howard McLane's fate in the story to discover that there is nothing that can be done. In the struggle for survival he has happened to succeed, while his brother has failed. In Garland's view, questions of merit or ability do not arise. The success of one brother is no more praiseworthy than the failure of the other is culpable. It is circumstance alone, as Howard says, that has made one and destroyed the other; Howard feels he is no different, no better, than the boys and girls he used to know who have stayed at home on the farms. He is ready even to consider the possibility that to succeed in the fiercely competitive world of American society is in fact morally culpable. What is the price of success? 'Struggle, strife, trampling on some one else. His play crowding out some other poor fellow's hope. . . . So, in the world of business, the life of one man seemed to him to be drawn from the life of another man, each success to spring from other failures' (p. 83). The indictment spreads out from the particular situation of the McLane brothers, beyond the circumstance of the farming communities, to the entire capitalist system of American society.

Howard goes on hoping that something can be done to save his brother. He plans to raise the money to buy back the old family farm. When he puts his plan to Grant in the final scene of the story, however, it collapses just like all his earlier hopes. 'Money can't give me a chance now,' says Grant. 'What do you mean?' 'I mean life ain't worth very much to me. I'm too old to take a new start. I'm a dead failure. I've come to the conclusion that life's a failure for ninety-nine per cent of us. You can't help me now. It's too late!' (p. 109). What Garland registers with considerable power in *Main-Travelled Roads* is the failure, near the end of the nineteenth century, of yet another aspect of the American Dream.

*

Yet Garland was not satisfied simply to register failure. He is the Howard of the scene, not the Grant. Nor was he content to listen in silence. Both in his life and his art he struggled to preserve the progressive, democratic, American ideal, to find reasons for believing that American society need not go on rewarding the few at the expense of the many. The protagonists of his stories are all heroic figures: heroic in their powers of endurance, their determination and strength of will. Grant McLane is heroic in his acceptance of failure, others are heroic in their resistance to it. What they fight against is not necessity, something inherent in the nature of things. In Garland's view, what is grinding them down is the massive injustice of an economic system which is interfering with the natural law of evolution. As we have seen, Garland was an early convert to Herbert Spencer's progressive evolutionism. In 1884, however, he read George's *Progress and Poverty* and responded enthusiastically, believing that he could now see how to apply Spencer's theory to the American economic system. As he wrote subsequently of George's book: 'I read it all and some of it I read many times. It fitted in with my sense of justice, with my enthusiastic belief in the doctrine of Evolution as set forth by Herbert Spencer.'[5] From the mid-1880s,

Garland became a dedicated campaigner for Henry George's 'single tax' policy. The single tax would sweep away the injustices and inequalities of the landlord system and thus allow the natural law of evolution to proceed unchecked. For Garland, this was the answer to the problems of the farmers of the Middle Border: once the problem of land ownership had been solved, then the American farmer would regain his individual freedom and be carried forward by the evolutionary process.

What Garland proposed was an 1880s (evolutionary) solution to a major 1880s problem. The weakness of his subsequent writing stems from the fact that he was unable to see that the circumstances which had produced the difficulties of the 1880s were themselves subject to change. For a few years in the early 1890s, Garland remained the leading exponent of American literary realism. But there his progress stopped. His later autobiographical writing is of interest, *A Son of the Middle Border* (1917) in particular. But it is on his early stories, and especially those in *Main-Travelled Roads*, that his literary significance rests.

Notes

1 The text of the extract from 'Up the Coulé' is taken from Hamlin Garland, *Main-Travelled Roads*, New York, 1961.
2 See Donald Pizer, *Hamlin Garland's Early Work and Career*, Berkeley and Los Angeles, 1960, p. 63.
3 ibid., p. 28.
4 ibid., p. 103.
5 ibid., p. 39.

Further reading

Donald Pizer, *Hamlin Garland's Early Work and Career*, Berkeley and Los Angeles, 1960.

9

Stephen Crane (1871–1900)

The column that had butted stoutly at the obstacles in the roadway was barely out of the youth's sight before he saw dark waves of men come sweeping out of the woods and down through the fields. He knew at once that the steel fibers had been washed from their hearts. They were bursting from their coats and their equipments as from entanglements. They charged down upon him like terrified buffaloes.

Behind them blue smoke curled and clouded above the tree-tops, and through the thickets he could sometimes see a distant pink glare. The voices of the cannon were clamoring in interminable chorus.

The youth was horrorstricken. He stared in agony and amazement. He forgot that he was engaged in combating the universe. He threw aside his mental pamphlets on the philosophy of the retreated and rules for the guidance of the damned.

The fight was lost. The dragons were coming with invincible strides. The army, helpless in the matted thickets and blinded by the overhanging night, was going to be swallowed. War, the red animal, war, the blood-swollen god, would have bloated fill.

Within him something bade to cry out. He had the impulse to make a rallying speech, to sing a battle hymn, but he could only get his tongue to call into the air: 'Why – why – what – what's th' matter?'

Soon he was in the midst of them. They were leaping and scampering all about him. Their blanched faces shone in the dusk. They seemed, for the most part, to be very burly men. The youth turned from one to another of them as they galloped along. His incoherent questions were lost. They were heedless of his appeals. They did not seem to see him.

They sometimes gabbled insanely. One huge man was asking of the sky: 'Say, where de plank road? Where de plank road!' It was as if he had lost a child. He wept in his pain and dismay.

Presently, men were running hither and thither in all ways. The artillery booming, forward, rearward, and on the flanks made jumble of ideas of direction. Landmarks had vanished into the gathered gloom. The youth began to imagine that he had got into the center of the tremendous quarrel, and he could perceive no way out of it. From the mouths of the fleeing men came a thousand wild questions, but no one made answers.

The youth, after rushing about and throwing interrogations at the heedless bands of retreating infantry, finally clutched a man by the arm. They swung around face to face.

'Why – why –' stammered the youth struggling with his balking tongue.

The man screamed: 'Let go me! Let go me!' His face was livid and his eyes were rolling uncontrolled. He was heaving and panting. He still grasped his rifle, perhaps having forgotten to release his hold upon it. He tugged frantically, and the youth being compelled to lean forward was dragged several paces.

'Let go me! Let go me!'

'Why – why –' stuttered the youth.

'Well, then!' bawled the man in a lurid rage. He adroitly and fiercely swung his rifle. It crushed upon the youth's head. The man ran on.

The youth's fingers had turned to paste upon the other's arm. The energy was smitten from his muscles. He saw the flaming wings of lightning flash before his vision. There was a deafening rumble of thunder within his head.

Suddenly his legs seemed to die. He sank writhing to the ground. He tried to arise. In his efforts against the numbing pain he was like a man wrestling with a creature of the air.

There was a sinister struggle.

Sometimes he would achieve a position half erect, battle with the air for a moment, and then fall again, grabbing at the grass. His face was of a clammy pallor. Deep groans were wrenched from him.

At last, with a twisting movement, he got upon his hands and knees, and from thence, like a babe trying to walk, to his feet. Pressing his hands to his temples he went lurching over the grass.

The Red Badge of Courage (1895)[1]

* * *

The first sentence of this passage, which opens Chapter 12 of the novel, carries us immediately into a young soldier's awareness of the confused and changing reality of a battle-field. In the previous chapter, the youth, Henry Fleming, had seen a new column of infantry advancing purposefully towards the front-line, from which he himself had recently fled, forcing its way through a vast mass of retreating Union forces – wagons, horses, men. The youth had been immensely impressed by the resolution and unswerving determination of the forward-moving column of men. These characteristics are repeated in the extract's opening phase: the column 'had butted stoutly at the obstacles in the roadway' and the description suggests the slow but regular, purposeful, forward movement. Now, however, that vision of controlled purpose is blotted out by a wholly contrary one; into the youth's sight come 'dark waves of men' 'sweeping out of the woods'. The fixed, firm, purposeful intent contained in words like 'butted', 'stoutly' and 'obstacles' is replaced by the sense of blind, fast, uncontrolled movement of 'waves', 'sweeping out' and 'down'. It is just this sensation of uncontrolled and uncontrollable movement that a large part of the passage will, above all, convey. This first sentence is uncharacteristically long because it looks back to the previous vision, while also beginning to create the new. The typically short sentences that follow enlarge the impression of an irresistible, oncoming movement by developing the metaphors latent in the first sentence. The 'steel fibers' in their hearts look back to the hard, fixed, almost static quality of their purposeful, forward march; 'steel fibers', that is, like 'butted stoutly' and 'obstacles' belongs to the earlier vision – the vision that is 'washed away' as the fleeing men are imaged as a great wave of overwhelming water. The marvellously vivid 'bursting from their coats and their equipment as from entanglements' contains in 'bursting' a hint of the water image, while 'bursting' and 'entanglements' also suggest images of the warfare they are fleeing: the bursting of shells and the difficult terrain of woods and thickets over which the battle is being fought. What the soldiers seek is unimpeded movement – like that possessed by the charging buffaloes of the final sentence in the paragraph. In that final sentence, Crane deploys one of his favourite images of war: war converts man into an animal fighting for its survival. The image is traditional enough, but Crane's use of it in *The Red Badge of Courage* is so frequent and insistent that it acquires a new significance. It grows out of Crane's determinedly naturalistic vision: man's place in the universe is no different from that of the rest of the animal world, and man too is engaged in a brutal Darwinian struggle for survival.

Momentarily the young soldier's consciousness becomes aware of the setting out of which the stampeding soldiers are emerging: the tree-tops and thickets, the blue smoke and pink flashes of the cannon. But it is the unbelievable significance of what is happening that rivets and horrifies Henry Fleming. His 'agony' and 'amazement' are a consequence of the overwhelming and terrifying contrast between what he is seeing now and how these same men had impressed him when they had been pressing forward to the front in the previous chapter. It is the feelings and train of thoughts sparked off by that sight – it has occurred just seconds before – that Crane mocks in what now seems to be a somewhat heavy-handed intervention by the omniscient narrator. But the use of the stiffly formal phraseology – 'combating the universe' and especially 'mental pamphlets on the philosophy of the retreated' and 'rules for the guidance of the damned' – is intentional and deliberately ironic.

Fleming's first reaction to his sight of the fresh column of infantry, so proud and resolute in its forward march, had been one of shame and envy. He longs to be one of them, and blames, not himself, but 'the indefinite cause', 'it', 'whatever it was' (p. 67) for his own failure and desertion. For a moment he manages to forget himself and what he has done (turning tail and fleeing in blind panic) and instead imagines himself in a series of grandly heroic postures. Such sweet imaginings seem to have a transforming power: 'He felt the quiver of war desire. In his ears, he heard the ring of victory. He knew the frenzy of a rapid successful charge. The music of the trampling feet, the sharp voices, the clanking arms of the column near him made him soar on the red wings of war. For a few moments he was sublime' (p. 68). On the brink of a decision to rush back to the front, doubts return to assail him: he has no rifle; he will not be able to find his regiment; he will be asked to explain his absence. His new-found courage drains away. He is tired, hungry, footsore. He is not like those others; he is not a hero. His rationalizations carry him in new directions: if the army is defeated the confusion will be such that his individual failure will not be noticed; defeat will be a vindication of his decision to run. But what if there is a victory? He wishes he were dead; in a victory all the dead will be seen as glorious; and victory for the determined men in Union blue is inevitable. These are the kinds of thought processes, racing through Fleming's mind, that Crane now mocks and derides; and the stilted, formal, academic language of that mockery and derision reflects the fact that what Henry Fleming had been engaged in was an attempt to come up with neatly rational justifications, or logical excuses, for his own craven behaviour.

Throughout *The Red Badge of Courage* there is a wide gap between the author and his main character; Crane rarely shares Fleming's attitude towards himself, or anything else. That potentially ironic gap is being exploited here.

What is being thrust upon Henry Fleming is a recognition that he has been wrong. Wrong about these men; and therefore wrong in all the conclusions he had drawn. The battle is lost. War is the only victor. The 'dragons' are not the onrushing soldiers, nor their victorious opponents, hot in pursuit; the dragons are the dragons of war itself: war is the enemy, the blind, chaotic, destructive enemy; the army, paradoxically, its victim. Two of Crane's favourite images are deployed here: war as an all-powerful all-devouring, irresistible animal, and war as a fierce, primitive, pagan god demanding constant, bloody sacrifice. Such deliberately atavistic images have two effects; they challenge modern man's assumption of his own advancing civilization, and they deny the exceptionality of war – war, however primitive, becomes a general principle, a principle of destructive power inherent in the nature of things. Crane's use of this kind of universalizing imagery in *The Red Badge of Courage* has led some critics to argue that the precise setting of the novel in the American Civil War is of little significance: this could be any war at any time. A generalizing impulse is certainly present in the novel; another of its manifestations is Crane's preference for semi-allegorical names for most of the characters: 'the tall soldier', 'the tattered soldier', 'the loud soldier', even 'the youth'. And Crane's focus is certainly on the nature, experience, and significance of war in a general sense. Nevertheless, *The Red Badge of Courage* does not dissolve into pure allegory; it is full of minute particulars of the utmost vividness and clarity. Much of this detail anchors the novel firmly in the historical reality of the Civil War. On occasion it may do even more: the reference here to a 'plank road' (paragraph seven of the extract) is one of various details which have encouraged some scholars to identify the occasion of the novel as the Battle of Chancellorsville, fought in northern Virginia in 1863.[2] The major point is that, like much great literature, *The Red Badge of Courage* successfully combines the immediate and particular with a constant suggestion of the permanent and universal.

Henry Fleming's momentary impulse to protest, to halt and rally the unbelievable rout of the blue-clad men, is useless. There is no way in which the rational world he had imagined can be put back together again. All he can articulate is his horrified amazement at what has occurred. For him, there has to be a reason. 'Why – why – what – what's th' matter?' But in the confused and rapid movement that now envelops him (suggested above all by the past participles of verbs of motion: 'leaping', 'scampering', 'running', 'fleeing', 'rushing') logical communication is the first casualty. His 'incoherent questions' were lost; the galloping soldiers 'gabbled insanely', and 'from the mouths of the fleeing men came a thousand wild questions' – but no answers. The blind panic that grips these men has swept away all notions of logic or reason; the structures of meaning that Henry Fleming is seeking for have ceased to exist. Incoherence, the failure of communication – 'Say, where de plank road? Where de plank road!' – have become the norm. Simultaneously with this breakdown of reason and logic, the passage insists on the youth's increasing sense of physical disorientation: the men were running 'hither and thither in all ways'; the artillery booming 'forward, rearward, and on the flanks'; landmarks 'had vanished into the gathered gloom'; all sense of direction is 'made jumble'. Mentally and physically Henry Fleming is trapped in a world from which all sense of order and meaning has disappeared.

What the first half of the extract communicates through its extraordinarily vivid flashes of action and movement, is no more than an intensification of Fleming's experience of war throughout *The Red Badge of Courage*. The reality of battle is invariably meaningless confusion; a savage and brutal anarchy acquires a momentum of its own. The mechanism of war catches up the individual and processes him like so much raw material. He is marched up and down, forwards and backwards; he advances or retreats (and thus wins or loses, is hero or coward) according to no comprehensible plan or pattern. In this situation of incoherence, confusion and violence, the individual soldier is invariably the random and helpless victim. As Crane builds up such an impression of the world at war in which Henry Fleming finds himself, it is inevitable that it should begin to close in upon the reader as an impression of the nature of reality itself. For Crane, as for so many twentieth-century writers, war is a revelation of ultimate truth: in its fearful incoherence, its confusion and violence, and ever-present threat of death, war is a uniquely powerful image of life. Man struggles for survival in a universe as brutal, primitive, hostile and uncaring as that which Henry Fleming encounters in his experience of the American Civil War. Such is the bleakly naturalistic vision that Crane communicates in *The Red Badge of Courage*.

It is not a vision, however, that Henry Fleming, whatever his experiences, is capable of understanding or accepting. So here, in the second half of the extract, he attempts once more to rationalize the chaos around him. Dramatically, he attempts to interrupt, impede, the on-rushing sense of movement that until now has dominated the scene. This sudden intervention is both a physical and a metaphysical challenge. The demand for order, for understanding, confronts and conflicts with a heedless, chaotic reality. Fleming's amazed bewilderment is communicated by the 'stammered' and 'stuttered' series of 'whys' that he utters: he is still seeking desperately for a reason, an explanation for the wholly irrational and inexplicable. Simultaneously, the conflict between the contrary impulses towards movement and arrest is defined by a series of verbs suggesting struggle and resistance: 'clutched', 'grasped', 'tugged', 'compelled', 'dragged'. Thus the struggle between Henry Fleming and the anonymous soldier is extraordinarily vivid and immediate, enacted both in its language and the visual scene that language creates. But the collision between a moving force and a static opposition can end only in one way: the violence of the blow that 'crushed upon' the young soldier's head. ('Crushed', uniting as it does notions both of crashing and crushing, typifies Crane's capacity to write with the compressed economy of style characteristic of his poetry.)

In the third and final section of the passage, Crane evokes with vivid and meticulous detail Fleming's reaction to the stunning blow he has received. The flashing, roaring, cannonades of battle that have surrounded him are suddenly located inside his head. After the speed of the opening, and the tug-of-war of the middle section, the pace of the passage dramatically changes. It is as though a fast-moving film is suddenly slowed down almost into a series of stills, as Henry's fall and attempts to rise are rendered in a kind of visual slow motion. He 'sank writhing'; he 'tried to arise', he was 'like a man wrestling'; as before the sentences are short, but each one now suggests a separate effort spaced out in time. In fact the movement seems to be spiralling downwards towards a final stasis. 'There was a sinister struggle' stands as a single sentence paragraph, and slows the movement of the passage still further. The struggle is 'sinister' because it is one from which Henry may not recover. His 'clammy pallor', 'deep groans' and repeated falls all suggest the onset of death. But, in the closing sentence, the young soldier comes back from the dead. He rises, born again, and lurches off, 'like a babe trying to walk', pressing his temples, no doubt to lessen the numbing pain, but also perhaps to hold fast to the reality of the red badge of courage he has finally acquired.

*

The last section of the extract is a mirror-image in miniature of the movement of the entire novel. Just as here Henry Fleming sinks beneath the blow but contrives to rise again, so the novel as a whole charts the decline and fall of its protagonist followed by his apparent redemption and restoration. The opening of the novel records how Fleming joined the Union army in a spirit of romantic exultation. He had always thrilled to the idea of war, but had come to believe that martial glory was a thing of the past. 'Secular and religious education', he decided, 'had effaced the throat-grappling instinct, or else firm finance held in check the passions' (p. 4). Such simple-minded notions of the social controls imposed by moral evolution and economic self-interest, Crane's novel will effectively subvert. Now, in any event, with the coming of the Civil War, there is after all to be an opportunity for glory and 'breathless deeds' (p. 4). Life in the Union army, however, quickly shatters such romantic illusions. At first all is humdrum monotony; then, when conflict seems near, there is only rumour and counter-rumour, doubt and uncertainty. In this situation, Henry's dreams of heroic deeds quickly fade, replaced by despondency and self-doubt. But the baptism of fire, when at last it comes, is successfully survived, and Henry experiences an 'ecstasy of self-satisfaction' (p. 41). But such exultation is misplaced and short-lived; at the next encounter, Henry turns and runs. In the following sequences – some of the finest in the novel – Henry agonizes through a dark night of the soul in which self-reproaches, self-justifications, a damning sense of guilt, and determined rationalizations mingle confusedly.

Immediately following the desertion, Crane devises a brilliant scene which undermines the romantic and rational illusions which Fleming clings on to in an attempt to justify his actions. At the same time, the scene defines Crane's vision of the true nature of the reality that surrounds the young soldier. In the heart of a wood into which he has fled, Fleming believes he has finally escaped the horror and violence of war. Here, in calm tranquillity, nature rules, serene and beneficent. He throws a pine cone at a squirrel who runs away; a sign from nature, he believes, telling him he has done the natural thing in fleeing from the battle. Nature's lesson that he does not take is provided by an animal he observes pouncing into a pool of water, and emerging with a gleaming fish. He comes upon a chapel-like shelter of over-arching branches of boughs, invested with 'a religious half-light' (p. 50). But the seductive atmosphere of religious serenity and stillness is shattered by the reality the leafy chapel contains: the mouldering remains of a soldier, still with the stillness of a frightening death. Neither in religion nor in nature is there the comfort and consolation that Henry Fleming seeks.

For a time the youth finds a refuge among the walking wounded. But guilty fear over his lack of a wound drives him to a second, more heinous act of desertion and betrayal. Frightened of his questions, he chooses to abandon the sorely-wounded, delirious 'tattered soldier' who has befriended and trusted him. Thus, at the time of the extract, Fleming has reached a spiritual and moral nadir. The blow from the rifle, however, changes everything. Now he can rejoin his regiment, and be accepted back without question. In fact, from this point on, his career as a soldier goes from strength to strength. Under attack, he stands his ground. When his regiment advances, he is in the forefront. Indeed, in the final episode of the battle in which his regiment participates, he takes the lead in a desperate charge, and captures the enemy's battle colours. So in the end Henry Fleming is a hero. He puts the memory of his flight from the battle-field firmly behind him, and even the sin of his abject desertion of the 'tattered soldier' is finally put 'at a distance' (p. 139). He has come to terms with himself and with reality.

Such an account of Fleming's progress through *The Red Badge of Courage* suggests a highly positive reading of the novel: a young man finds his youthful illusions shattered by contact with the harshness of reality; almost destroyed, he survives to acquire a new maturity of understanding and acceptance. *The Red Badge* thus takes its place as a version of the archetypal story of the young man growing up into a full awareness of the nature of life and experience. In the closing paragraphs of the novel there is further textual support for such a reading. Henry Fleming, we are told, feels he has left his old, false self behind: 'With this conviction came a store of assurance. He felt a quiet manhood, non-assertive but of sturdy and strong blood. He knew that he would no more quail before his guides wherever they should point. He had been to touch the great death, and found that, after all, it was but the great death. He was a man.' As a man he understands that 'the red sickness of battle', the 'sultry nightmare' of 'the heat and pain of war' are but a passing phase of reality: 'He turned now with a lover's thirst to images of tranquil skies, fresh meadows, cool brooks – an existence of soft and eternal peace' (p. 140).

The evidence for the 'youth into manhood' theme is clear enough. But is it wholly convincing? The probability of 'an existence of soft and eternal peace' is hardly suggested by the total experience that is *The Red Badge of Courage*. The proffered images of peace are themselves tired clichés, not at all like Crane's own sharply realized images. Finally there is the central fact that redemption for Henry Fleming is wholly dependent on his wound, his red badge of courage. Without that wound, he would have been branded a cowardly deserter. But the reader has seen how the youth receives his hurt: not in circumstances of courage, heroism, and heroic purpose, but in a moment of confusion, panic, and headlong flight. He may find it easy to forget the irony of the manner in which he gained his red badge of 'courage', but Crane does not necessarily expect the reader to be equally forgetful. The possibility remains, therefore, that the attitudes articulated at the end of the novel are those of Crane's protagonist, not Crane's own. For Henry Fleming, 'scars faded as flowers' (p. 139). The question is whether they do so for Stephen Crane or for us?

Henry Fleming has unquestionably 'come through' in some sense. He has successfully reintegrated himself into the society of his regiment and army. He has learned to adjust to the reality that surrounds him. But what is the nature of that reality? It is a reality of conflict; of contradictory and irresistible forces, within and without the individual, in terms of which he is a helpless victim, borne this way and that. The blind, passionate rage that makes Henry lead the successful charge, that makes him a hero, is no more nor less a purely animal impulse than the panic and fear that had earlier driven him to ignominious flight. Accepting his new-found status, forgetting his past, the youth is deceiving himself; he has learned nothing from his experience, unless it is collaboration with the destructive element within reality. Crane might well treat such a version of maturity with a certain irony.

After the publication of his earlier short novel, *Maggie, A Girl of the Streets* (1893), Crane said that his aim had been to show 'that environment is a tremendous thing in the world and frequently shapes lives regardless'.[3] In this aim he succeeds: Maggie, a young and innocent girl, is shown to be the helpless victim of the physical degradation of the Bowery slum in which she lives, and of the destructive, inflexible rules of a conventional morality shared by rich and poor alike. But even in *Maggie*, Crane insists that the characters are complicit in their own destruction. Unable to face the harshness of reality, they cling on to illusions, and act out self-indulgent romantic and moral roles which ensure their defeat. Maggie's life ends in pathetic suicide. Henry Fleming survives. But it is less than certain that Fleming is free of illusions, or that Crane shares his reassuring confidence about himself and the universe in which he exists.

*

Stephen Crane's writing career was short, and very little of what he wrote equalled the power and artistry of *The Red Badge of Courage*. His problems as a writer seem to have centred on the question of the relationship between art and life, between imaginative experience and actuality. When he wrote *The Red Badge of Courage* he had had absolutely no experience of the realities of war; later in the 1890s, however, as a newspaper war correspondent in Cuba and Greece, he seems to have sought out violence and danger. Similarly, when he began the writing of *Maggie*, he had had no first-hand experience or knowledge of New York's Bowery slums; later, when he was writing a short story called 'An Experiment in Misery', also set in the Bowery, he insisted on spending a night in a Bowery flop-house.

Despite the success of *The Red Badge of Courage* (it was everywhere assumed that the author was a veteran of the Civil War) Crane seems to have come to believe that the sincerity and truth he sought as an artist could only be achieved by basing his work on actual, personal experience. That sincerity and truth were his main concerns emerges from the relatively few remarks that he was ever prepared to make on his aims and interests as a writer. In a letter of 1896 he wrote: 'a man is born into the world with his own pair of eyes, and he is not at all responsible for his vision – he is merely responsible for his quality of personal honesty.'[4] Again, not long after the appearance of *The Red Badge of Courage*, he wrote that the one thing in his literary life which had given him pleasure was the fact that 'men of sense [he had in mind William Dean Howells and Hamlin Garland in particular] believe me to be sincere'.[5] Crane's difficulty was that, despite the wholly convincing and authentic imaginative sincerity he achieved in *Maggie*, and especially *The Red Badge of Courage*, he seems to have come to believe, perhaps as a result of his work as a newspaper-man, that sincerity for the artist meant writing about what he himself had seen or done. On occasion, Crane was ready to believe that it was enough – enough for sincerity and truth to be achieved – if the artist was genuinely committed to what he was saying, and if what he was writing meant something important to him. As he commented once to a friend: 'You've got to feel the things you write if you want to make an impact on the world.'[6] But the pattern of his hectic life in America, Mexico, Greece, Cuba, Puerto Rico and England – where he was known to Conrad, Henry James, and H. G. Wells – suggests that this aesthetic position was increasingly set aside in favour of the view that the artist needed to pursue life itself. Ironically, Crane's own pursuit brought him little artistic success. Only on one occasion did a real-life experience – shipwreck off the coast of Florida – give him material to produce a work equal in power and artistry to his earlier achievements: 'The Open Boat' (1897) is the finest of all his short stories. Crane did write a handful of other successful stories, but the great bulk of his later writing is of disappointing quality. Outside *The Red Badge of Courage*, and the few successful stories, his best work is contained in his two, strangely modernist, volumes of poetry: *The Black Riders* (1895) and *War is Kind* (1899).

Crane's poems – short, intense, lyrical and possibly influenced by Emily Dickinson – are strongly imagist and symbolist in their method and form. At its best, his vivid, impressionistic prose in *The Red Badge of Courage* is similar. As has been hinted, Crane wrote according to no carefully formulated plan or programme. He liked to suggest that his writing was natural and spontaneous. But the 1896 letter, quoted above, linking 'eyes', 'vision' and 'honesty', goes a long way towards explaining his writing mode. Crane's aim is to convey to the reader what the eye sees, with absolute fidelity. Conrad's summary of his aims as a writer, in the Preface to *The Nigger of the Narcissus*, could well have been Crane's: 'My task . . . is, by the power of the written word to make you hear, to make you feel – it is, before all, to make you *see*.' *The Red Badge of Courage* is at its greatest when, focusing on Henry Fleming's consciousness, and articulating his impressions in a richly imagistic style, it does precisely this.

Crane's art may well have been more spontaneous than learned, but it would be quite misleading to deduce from this that he was a writer in isolation, wholly detached from, and uninfluenced by, his contemporaries. He was familiar with Hamlin Garland's theory of veritism,[7] and was deeply sympathetic towards it. Garland's notion of a writing mode combining the artist's own individual impression with an accurate rendering of observable reality, was obviously closely related to Crane's own practice. Perhaps this explains Crane's subsequent readiness to identify himself wholly with the realist movement in American fiction. In an 1894 letter, surveying his literary development, he says that in 1892 he had decided to renounce 'the clever school in literature', by which he probably meant the kind of writing that was no more than a game, with no urgent meaning for the author. Instead, 'I developed all alone a little creed of art which I thought was a good one.' Crane's 'little creed' clearly involved his notions of truth and sincerity, and in his letter Crane goes on to link this creed with the realism of Howells and Garland: 'Later I discovered that my creed was identical with the one of Howells and Garland and in this way I became involved in the beautiful war between those who say that art is man's substitute for nature and we are the most successful in art when we approach the nearest to nature and truth, and those who say – Well, I don't know what they say . . . they fight villainously and keep Garland and I out of the big magazines.'[8] In the struggle for realism in American fiction in the 1890s, Crane at least had no doubt which side he was on! His own success did in fact owe a great deal to the support and encouragement he received from Garland and Howells. Garland wrote a favourable review of *Maggie* in 1893, and was largely responsible for persuading Howells, by then becoming established as America's most important man of letters, to do the same a year later. Crane subsequently acknowledged his debt to Howells in a revealing inscription he included in a copy of *Maggie* presented to the older writer: 'as a token of the veneration and gratitude of Stephen Crane for many things he has learned of the common man and, above all, for a certain re-adjustment of his point of view victoriously concluded some time in 1892.' Just as in the 1894 letter, quoted above, Crane insists on linking the development of his own art with the example of Howellsian realism.

Of course one has to allow for a certain element of over-statement here. Crane needed the support of men like Garland and Howells. And it is perfectly obvious that in *Maggie, A Girl of the Streets*, and *The Red Badge of Courage*, Crane carried realism in directions wholly unknown to Howells. Howells's review described *Maggie* as 'a remarkable book'. But its realism was such, he thought, as to unfit it for general reading, even though 'once in a while it will do to tell the truth as completely as *Maggie* does'.[9] Crane's fiction communicates a vision that is darker and bleaker than anything in the fiction of the earlier realists. In 'The Open Boat' (1897), Crane wrote: 'When it occurs to a man that nature does not regard him as important, and that she feels she would not maim the universe by disposing of him, he at first wishes to throw bricks at the temple, and he hates deeply the fact that there are no bricks and no temples.' Such a vision annihilates the significance of man, of individual human existence, and even of significance itself. It is a vision of the universe as a meaningless void in which man's survival or non-survival is a purely random matter. Whatever Henry Fleming may believe, it is just this kind of truth that *The Red Badge of Courage* also conveys. How far such a vision is reinforced by Crane's sense of the fate of the individual in American society in the 1890s is perhaps problematical. But the image of the machine – vast, all-powerful, destructive, inhuman – is sufficiently dominant in *The Red Badge of Courage* to lead one to believe that Crane sees the truth to be discovered in the battle-fields of the Civil War as equally evident in the social and economic strife characteristic of the violent, divided and machine-dominated America in which he lived.

Notes

1 The text of this extract from Chapter 12 of *The Red Badge of Courage, An Episode of the American Civil War* is taken from the Library of Literature edition, ed. Frederick C. Crews, 1964. *The Red Badge of Courage* appeared in a shortened, serialized form in various newspapers in December 1894. In book form it was first published in 1895.
2 See Crews's Introduction in the above edition.
3 R. W. Stallman and L. Gilkes (eds), *Stephen Crane: Letters*, New York, 1960, p. 14.
4 ibid., p. 110.
5 Quoted by R. W. Stallman (ed.), *Stephen Crane: Stories and Tales*, New York, 1955, p. xxiii.
6 ibid., p. xxi.
7 See p. 121–2 of this volume.
8 *Letters*, p. 31.
9 Quoted by Stallman, op. cit., p. xxv.

Further reading

R. W. Stallman, *Stephen Crane: A Biography*, New York, 1968.
Edwin H. Cady, *Stephen Crane*, New York, 1962.

10

Harold Frederic (1856–98)

The three visitors had completed their survey of the room now; and Loren Pierce emitted a dry, harsh little cough, as a signal that business was about to begin. At this sound, Winch drew up his feet, and Gorringe untied a parcel of account-books and papers that he held on his knee. Theron felt that his countenance must be exhibiting to the assembled brethren an unfortunate sense of helplessness in their hands. He tried to look more resolute, and forced his lips into a smile.

'Brother Gorringe allus acts as Seckertary,' said Erastus Winch, beaming broadly upon the minister, as if the mere mention of the fact promoted jollity. 'That's it, Brother Gorringe, – take your seat at Brother Ware's desk. Mind the Dominie's pen don't play tricks on you, an' start off writin' out sermons instid of figgers.' The humorist turned to Theron as the lawyer walked over to the desk at the window. 'I allus have to caution him about that,' he remarked with great joviality. 'An' do *you* look out afterwards, Brother Ware, or else you'll catch that pen o' yours scribblin' lawyer's lingo in place o' the Word.'

Theron felt bound to exhibit a grin in acknowledgement of this pleasantry. The lawyer's change of position had involved some shifting of the others' chairs, and the young minister found himself directly confronted by Brother Pierce's hard and colorless old visage. Its little eyes were watching him, as through a mask, and under their influence the smile of politeness fled from his lips. The lawyer on his right, the cheese-buyer to the left, seemed to recede into distance as he for the moment returned the gaze of the quarryman. He waited now for him to speak, as if the others were of no importance.

'We are a plain sort o' folks up in these parts,' said Brother Pierce, after a slight further pause. His voice was as dry and rasping as his cough, and its intonations were those of authority. 'We walk here,' he went on, eying the minister with a sour regard, 'in a meek an' humble spirit, in the straight an' narrow way which leadeth unto life. We ain't gone traipsin' after strange gods, like some people that call themselves Methodists in other places. We stick by the Discipline an' the ways of our fathers in Israel. No new-fangled notions can go down here. Your wife'd better take them flowers out of her bunnit afore next Sunday.'

Silence possessed the room for a few moments, the while Theron, pale-faced and with brows knit, studied the pattern of the ingrain carpet. Then he lifted his head, and nodded it in assent. 'Yes,' he said; 'we will do nothing by which our "brother stumbleth, or is offended, or is made weak."'

Brother Pierce's parchment face showed no sign of surprise or pleasure at this easy submission. 'Another thing: We don't want no book-learnin' or dictionary words in our pulpit,' he went on coldly. 'Some folks may stomach 'em; we won't. Them two sermons o' yours, p'r'aps they'd do down in some city place; but they're like your wife's bunnit here, they're too flowery to suit us. What we want to hear is the plain, old-fashioned Word of God, without any palaver or "hems and ha's." They tell me there's some parts where hell's treated as played-out, – where our ministers don't like to talk much about it because people don't want to hear about it. Such preachers ought to be put out. They ain't Methodists at all. What we want here, sir, is straight-out, flat-footed hell, – the burnin' lake o' fire an' brimstone. Pour it into 'em, hot an' strong. We can't have too much of it. Work in them awful deathbeds of Voltaire an' Tom Paine, with the Devil right there in the room, reachin' for 'em, an' they yellin' for fright; that's what fills the anxious seat an' brings in souls hand over fist.'

Theron's tongue dallied for an instant with the temptation to comment upon these old-wife fables, which were so dear to the rural religious heart when he and I were boys. But it seemed wiser to only nod again, and let his mentor go on.

'We ain't had no trouble with the Free Methodists here,' continued Brother Pierce, 'jest because we kept to the old paths, an' seek for salvation in the good old way. Everybody can shout "Amen!" as loud and as long as the Spirit moves him, with us. Some one was sayin' you thought we ought to have a choir and an organ. No, sirree! No such tom-foolery for us! You'll only stir up feelin' agin yourself by hintin' at such things. And then, too, our folks don't take no stock in all that pack o' nonsense about science, such as tellin' the age of the earth by crackin' up stones. I've b'en in the quarry line all my life, an' *I* know it's all humbug! Why, they say some folks are goin' round now preachin' that our grandfathers were all monkeys. That comes from departin' from the ways of our forefathers, an' puttin' in organs an' choirs, an' deckin' our women-folks out with gewgaws, an' apin' the fashions of the worldly. I shouldn't wonder if them kind did have some monkey blood in 'em. You'll find we're a different sort here.'

The Damnation of Theron Ware (1896)[1]

* * *

The Damnation of Theron Ware was written while Harold Frederic was London correspondent of the *New York Times*. Published in England under the title *Illumination*, the novel was an immediate success on both sides of the Atlantic. Frederic had at last achieved his ambition of establishing himself as a literary man: leading figures in the English literary world like George Bernard Shaw, George Gissing, H. G. Wells, Joseph Conrad, and Henry James, made his acquaintance, while Stephen Crane, when he was passing through London in 1897, made a point of seeking Frederic out. The two American writers, with many shared interests, remained close friends for the remainder of their short lives. Like Crane's, Frederic's literary allegiance was to the world of Howellsian realism, and it was the realist dimension of *The Damnation of Theron Ware* that gained it its success; no doubt Crane was among those who responded with enthusiasm to Frederic's firmly realistic treatment of one of the remaining taboo subjects in American culture: contemporary religion.

In more general terms, Frederic's novel, like Edgar Watson Howe's *The Story of a County Town* (1883), gained a conventional reputation as essentially a pioneering work in its revelation of the truth about American rural and small town life. In these novels by Howe and Frederic, the general pattern of American provincial life delineated by such twentieth-century works as Sherwood Anderson's *Winesburg, Ohio* (1919), and Sinclair Lewis's *Main Street* (1920) – its bigotry and narrow-mindedness, its cultural barrenness and hostility to the new or unfamiliar – is already set out.

The general characteristics of Frederic's realism are clearly evidenced by the extract from *The Damnation of Theron Ware*. Theron Ware has just arrived as the newly-appointed Methodist minister for Octavius, a small upstate New York town, clearly modelled on the Utica, New York, in which Frederic grew up. Ware and his wife had been ambitious of an appointment to a larger and more important church in a larger and more important town, but it is to the backwoods Octavius they are sent. None the less, Theron awaits his first encounter with the three trustees of his new church in no spirit of regret or despondency. His career, short as it is, has already known success and failure. His first charge had been in a dairy-farming area which he now looks back upon as a kind of pastoral paradise. After his marriage, he had moved to Tyre where his life at first had been equally ideal. Previously prized – and the reader needs to keep these qualities very much in mind – for 'his innocent candor and guileless mind, for his good heart, his pious zeal, his modesty about gifts notably above the average' (p. 29), marriage had released in him an unsuspected vein of joyful humour. For a year the young couple had been an immense success in Tyre. At the end of that year they find they are eight hundred dollars in debt, and life is no longer funny. Lucky to escape from this financial hole, they come to the Methodist Conference where Theron preaches the sermon of his life and believes he has earned a glittering prize in the form of a prestigious appointment. But it is to Octavius he is consigned. None the less, the Conference has left him with a renewed sense of spiritual zeal: 'the ministry to souls diseased beckoned him with a new and urgent significance' (p. 36). Hence he now faces his trustees in a mood of self-confidence.

Frederic opens Chapter 3, from which the extract is taken, with a sketch of the three trustees. All three religious office-holders are presented with considerable irony; Pierce, the rich quarryman, and Winch, the farm utensils salesman and cheese-buyer, are devotees of the religion of cash, while Gorringe, the lawyer, is an eccentric figure whose tastes are 'startlingly at variance with the standards of Dearborn County Methodism'. Having estimated the value of the furnishings of the room they are in, the three are now ready to get down to business. Their appearance alone is enough to undermine Theron Ware's confidence, while Pierce's 'dry, harsh little cough' is an excellent pointer to the tone of what is to follow. The jocular usurpation of Theron's desk, involving as it does a demotion of the minister, further weakens his position. The jokes over, Theron finds himself confronting Pierce who is made to appear just about as human as the stones he quarries to make his money. In what follows Frederic, with considerable relish and skill, dramatically and devastatingly reveals the Methodism of Octavius as an absurd travesty of Christian values and beliefs. Just in the manner of the persona of Burns's 'Holy Willie's Prayer', which is a brilliant, satirical exposure of Presbyterian Calvinism, every word that Brother Pierce utters condemns him. When he refers to his fellow church members as 'a plain sort o' folks' he means that they, like him, are hide-bound, bigoted and anti-intellectual. The 'meek an' humble spirit' of which he prates, is, given his delight in authoritarian bullying, a quality which he conspicuously lacks. His hatred of 'new-fangled notions' means that the minister's wife is forbidden to wear roses in her hat, and a similar petty-minded, anti-intellectual intolerance is reflected in his objections to 'book-learnin'' and 'dictionary words'. In every case, however, Brother Pierce's vocabulary and turn of phrase, his use of biblical language, his accent and pronunciation, strike the reader as wholly accurate and convincing. Frederic persuades us of the reality of the voice we are hearing. Pierce's demand for fire and brimstone preaching is the logical follow-up to the views he has expressed. Not, of course, that Pierce himself needs to be terrified into repentance. His own salvation is already assured. 'Pour it into 'em', he says, 'hot an' strong.' 'They' are the target, not 'us'.

At this point Frederic himself, or at least an authorial 'I' figure, makes an uncharacteristic intervention in the story. These 'old-wife fables' about death and damnation, we are told, 'so dear to the rural religious heart when he and I were boys', almost tempt a comment from Theron. The effect of the intervention is of course powerfully to align the author with Theron: author and character stand together against Pierce's absurdities. The major critical issue in *The Damnation of Theron Ware* is how far this alignment remains present as the story develops.

The Free Methodists, to whom Brother Pierce refers, were a splinter group who had seceded from the main body of American Methodism because they believed that the church's traditional attitudes and values were being undermined by a new spirit of liberalism. In Octavius, as this extract makes clear, there is no need for a breakaway movement, because the Free Methodist mentality remains in full control of the local church. Such notions as a choir and an organ are dismissed contemptuously as 'tom-foolery.' The final section of the passage, with its derogatory references to nineteenth-century geology and Darwin's theory of evolution, comes in reasonably well, given the fact of Pierce's activities as a quarryman. But the satirical point lies in the logical absurdities contained in an attack on what are no more than populist travesties of serious scientific theories. The rest of the chapter is taken up by a lengthy harangue by Pierce on the evils of the Irish and Roman Catholicism, and the revelation, clear even to Theron Ware, that two at least of the trustees – Pierce and Winch – have manipulated his church's finances to their own advantage. At the end of the meeting, a weary Ware feels like learning a different trade.

*

The nature of Frederic's contribution to the school of American realism is thus reasonably clear. He subjects the face of at least one form of popular American religion to careful scrutiny. The result is a devastating critique. There is much in the rest of the novel to confirm the impression created by this early passage. Whatever its pretensions to godliness, Methodism emerges as hypocritical, uncharitable and corrupt. A major aspect of the plot concerns the activities of the Soulsbys who are professional fund-raisers for the church. They are portrayed, not wholly unsympathetically, as money-raising artists, who succeed through their skill in manipulation, exploitation, and all the other theatrical tricks of their trade. Questions of religious faith or conviction are wholly irrelevant to their performance, which none the less triumphantly extracts blood from the stones of Octavius. One can well understand why this whole dimension of Frederic's novel must have struck readers in the 1890s as challengingly realistic and hard-hitting.

Yet it is scarcely adequate to read *The Damnation of Theron Ware* as no more than a scathing, satirical attack on the excesses of popular American Methodism. Theron Ware's 'damnation', it is true, may be regarded in a wholly ironical light. At the end of the novel he is leaving Octavius and setting out for Seattle, Washington, in the West, having abandoned his Methodist ministry. From the point of view of Brother Pierce this is no doubt ample proof of damnation. However, Brother Pierce and his allies are not the cause of Theron Ware's abandonment of his religious career. Theron does not, that is, give up his ministry because his more liberal Christian feelings and views come into inevitable conflict with the flinty fundamentalism of the quarrymaster and his fellow-believers. The case is more complex than this, and one may in the end even question whether the damnation of the novel's title is to be taken as wholly ironical after all.

At the conclusion of the novel, Theron Ware abandons the Methodist Church because he is made into a new man by the influences brought to bear upon him in Octavius. These influences are represented by three characters, whose presentation seems to have little or nothing to do with the mode of realism, Howellsian or any other kind, but who have a clear symbolical, or even allegorical, significance. First there is Celia Madden, daughter of the richest man in town, organist and pianist, formally a Roman Catholic but in fact an Epicurean, in love with the beautiful paganism of Ancient Greece: she manifestly represents the world of Art and Beauty, particularly in its sensual dimension. Second is Dr Ledsmar, trained as a doctor, but now engaged in scientific experiment and research along Darwinian lines: he represents the world of Science and Learning. And third is Father Forbes, the Roman Catholic priest of Octavius, an unbelievably urbane and cultured figure: he represents Religion in its truly modern, philosophical and sceptical guise. Art, Science, and Religion of a rarefied and refined kind; these are the forces that flood over and transform Theron's life and character. His involvement with these characters gives him an opportunity to enter into the Higher Culture of which his primitive Methodism had allowed him not a glimpse. He is carried away by what he believes to be a richly sophisticated mode of living of whose existence he had scarcely even dreamed. The exquisite delights of the senses – whether in the form of Celia's personal beauty, or the romantic passion and extravagance of the music she plays, or sophisticated food and drink – the expansive world of scholarship and learning so effortlessly displayed by Dr Ledsmar and Father Forbes, the cultured manners of Father Forbes, and even the beauties of Roman Catholicism itself; all of these overwhelm, bewilder and inspire the young and innocent Methodist. The result is a series of sudden changes in his attitudes and values. At first no more is involved than a challenge to some of his most traditional and deeply-rooted prejudices: he quickly learns that the Roman Catholic Church is not the evil he had believed it to be, that the Irish are not the race of drunken criminals and corrupt politicians he had assumed, and that a Democrat is not of necessity inferior to a Republican.

Soon, however, a great deal more is involved. Theron comes increasingly to believe that in justice he too should belong to the world of the Higher Culture which he is now occasionally allowed to observe. What this means is that he becomes increasingly critical of himself, his mode of life, his house and surroundings, and, most serious of all, of Alice, his wife. It might just be possible for a reader to believe that we are at this stage invited to remain sympathetic towards Theron: that we are meant to see him as the talented provincial, desperate to escape to a wider world. But in fact it is soon evident that this is not so. The truth is that the higher Theron believes he is rising, the lower in fact he is falling. While Theron is growing increasingly infatuated with the improbable

Celia, Alice has also gained an admirer: Levi Gorringe, the lawyer trustee. But there is no similarity in the two relationships. On their arrival at the new parsonage in Octavius, Alice had been appalled by the rubbish and litter that had been allowed to take over the parsonage garden; she had determined to set to work and restore it. (Characteristically Theron had been able to avert his eyes from the mess in front and admire the trees behind and the sky above.) The initial description of the garden is firmly realistic: it 'had not been spaded up, but lay, a useless stretch of muddy earth, broken only by last year's cabbage-stumps and the general litter of dead roots and vegetation' (p. 22). But Frederic quite subtly allows the garden, and Alice's commitment to it, to acquire a symbolic meaning almost as Nathaniel Hawthorne might have done. Lawyer Gorringe expresses his admiration and love for Alice by arranging a series of gifts of expensive plants for the new garden; and in due course the rubbish-strewn waste land is transformed into a mass of blooms. The naturalness of this image of the garden and its beauty contrasts sharply with the hothouse artificiality of Theron's romantic passion for Celia, which is even more absurd than Frederic probably realizes. When Theron finally confronts first Gorringe, then Alice, he comes off much the worse on each occasion; the reader recognizes that the shabbiness of feeling is all on his side, however far he may delude himself otherwise.

By the end of the novel, Theron Ware has got pretty well everything wrong. Celia, Dr Ledsmar and Father Forbes, whom he had believed to belong to a world so much superior to his own, have emerged as coldly cruel human beings. The doors they had amused themselves by opening to the naive Theron Ware, they are just as ready to close. But the damage has been done. The Theron Ware who had been prized and admired for his innocence, his good heart, his zeal and his modesty, has been transformed by contact with them into a vain, egotistical and corruptly self-deluded figure. Near the end of the novel, Michael Madden, Celia's dying brother, takes it upon himself to tell Theron precisely how his Octavius experience has corrupted him: 'You are much changed, Mr. Ware, since you came to Octavius, and it is not a change for the good' (p. 437). By this stage, however, Theron is unable to accept criticism of any kind. He insists dogmatically that any change which has occurred has been entirely beneficial: 'I feel myself an infinitely better and broader and stronger man than I was when I came here' (p. 442). Such vanity and misplaced self-confidence are entirely typical of the new, 'improved' Theron Ware. That his final dismissal by

Celia, and a drunken spree from which he is rescued by the ambiguously-presented Soulsbys, brings him partly to his senses, hardly alters the basic fact. What the novel has charted is, after all, precisely the damnation of Theron Ware.

*

The Damnation of Theron Ware is perhaps not a truly great novel. Its form and style suffer from some of Theron's own characteristics: a sense of a rather stiff awkwardness, and too great a contrivance of effect. Then the high culture of the world of Celia, Father Forbes, and Dr Ledsmar exists rather uneasily, and unrealistically, within the context of small-town Methodism, while an element of ambiguity in the author's treatment of his central character worries at least some readers. Frederic's earlier novels, such as *Seth's Brother's Wife* (1887), a broadly Howellsian novel of society and politics in upstate New York, and *In the Valley* (1890), an historical romance set in the period of the American Revolution, reveal similar formal and thematic inadequacies and uncertainties. His last novel, however, *The Market-Place* (1899), published posthumously, is a vigorous analysis of the corruption of English society at the end of the nineteenth century.

Nevertheless, *The Damnation of Theron Ware* is easily Harold Frederic's most fascinating and meaningful novel. Particularly in the context of the 1890s, it is indeed an 'Illumination'. Precisely what it illuminates is bound up with the mode of realism upon which its conception and mode of writing are based. As we have seen, realism is the new literary mode of the new America; it is scientific, progressive, democratic, evolutionary. Realism is closely associated with the forces that are transforming America and American society; it belongs to the world of the new. Frederic seems to have assented to this view. Yet the novel he has written, apparently employing the new realistic mode, is an assault upon the tradition of the new. Theron Ware is a product of rural, agrarian America; his given values and attitudes reflect his background in that older, traditional America. He is a version of Whitman's democratic man, or even of that innocent Adamic figure who has been seen so frequently in American writing as focusing the meaning of America. Certainly the novel's attack on popular Methodism makes it clear that there is much that is wrong with traditional conservative America; its moral uprightness, its honesty and simplicity, have hardened into intolerance and bigotry, and a gross materialism has supplanted true spirituality. But there can be no question that the sources of Theron Ware's corruption are located not in the old world but in the new. It is the world of progressive Science, learning, and Art that undermines and destroys Theron. In other words, it is the modern world, the very world that provides the mode of realism with its intellectual and cultural sanction, that proves to be the cause of Theron's downfall.

What this means is that Harold Frederic has written a book which, as it were, doubles back on itself, and begins to undermine its own foundations. Frederic no doubt did set out to write a novel – and this indeed is how many readers at the time responded to it – which would reveal the narrow-minded bigotry, the anti-intellectualism, and the cultural sterility of rural and provincial American Protestantism. And his book does indeed do this. But the alternative world, with which it presents us, however free of the prejudices and limitations of provincial America, and however advanced, progressive and liberal, is itself, in human terms, corrupt and corrupting. The new Theron Ware of the end of the novel; the man who, having failed as a clergyman, looks forward to a brilliant future in the West as a golden-voiced politician, is an infinitely less attractive figure than the Theron Ware of the novel's opening. His 'innocent candor and guileless mind', his 'good heart', his 'pious zeal' and 'modesty', have gone for ever. Rather than any new maturity of insight and moral understanding, however, his fall from innocence has produced no more than a determination to join in with the ideologies of cynical self-interest and corruption that have destroyed him. Theron Ware has turned his back on his own, and America's past. But the future that beckons to him, and to America, is, Frederic implies, dangerously flawed.

What *The Damnation of Theron Ware* thus reflects, consciously or unconsciously, is less the inevitable onward march of American realism, than the intensifying doubts and uncertainties of the 1890s about the direction in which American society seems to be moving. The deep structures of the novel, both in its plot and its characterization, suggest a radical scepticism about the new world of post-bellum America. Frederic is clearly aware of the powerful, progressive forces that are inevitably transforming America and its culture, and in his literary allegiances at least, he himself is very much part of that process of cultural change. When the forces of change strike at traditional value systems, however, his attitude becomes much more ambivalent. The price to be paid for the emergence of the new, modern America is clearly the collapse of the values of the old; but in its exploitative manipulation, its selfishness, its coldness and inhumanity, and its moral decay, the new world is no improvement on the old. Frederic's pessimistic vision is in the end not far removed from that of Crane or Norris or Dreiser. In Frederic's work, too, the 'smiling aspects' of American life seem to have disappeared for ever, borne back, like Gatsby's dream at the end of Fitzgerald's novel, 'into the past'.

Note

1 The text of this extract from Chapter 3 of *The Damnation of Theron Ware* is taken from the original 1896 edition published by Stone and Kimball in New York.

Further reading

Thomas F. O'Donnell and Hoyt C. Franchere, *Harold Frederic*, New York, 1961.

11

Frank Norris (1870–1902)

The day was very hot, and the silence of high noon lay close and thick between the steep slopes of the cañons like an invisible, muffling fluid. At intervals the drone of an insect bored the air and trailed slowly to silence again. Everywhere were pungent, aromatic smells. The vast, moveless heat seemed to distil countless odors from the brush – odors of warm sap, of pine needles, and of tar-weed, and above all the medicinal odor of witch hazel. As far as one could look, uncounted multitudes of trees and manzanita bushes were quietly and motionlessly growing, growing, growing. A tremendous, immeasurable Life pushed steadily heavenward without a sound, without a motion. At turns of the road, on the higher points, cañons disclosed themselves far away, gigantic grooves in the landscape, deep blue in the distance, opening one into another, ocean-deep, silent, huge, and suggestive of colossal primeval forces held in reserve. At their bottoms they were solid, massive; on their crests they broke delicately into fine serrated edges where the pines and redwoods outlined their million of tops against the high white horizon. Here and there the mountains lifted themselves out of the narrow riverbeds in groups like giant lions rearing their heads after drinking. The entire region was untamed. In some places east of the Mississippi nature is cosey, intimate, small, and homelike, like a good-natured housewife. In Placer County, California, she is a vast, unconquered brute of the Pliocene epoch, savage, sullen, and magnificently indifferent to man.

But there were men in these mountains, like lice on mammoths' hides, fighting them stubbornly, now with hydraulic 'monitors', now with drill and dynamite, boring into the vitals of them, or tearing away great yellow gravelly scars in the flanks of them, sucking their blood, extracting gold.

Here and there at long distances upon the cañon sides rose the headgear of a mine, surrounded with its few unpainted houses and topped by its never-failing feather of black smoke. On near approach one heard the prolonged thunder of the stamp-mill, the crusher, the insatiable monster, gnashing the rocks to powder with its long iron teeth, vomiting them out again in a thin stream of wet gray mud. Its enormous maw, fed night and day with the car boys' loads, gorged itself with gravel, and spat out the gold, grinding the rocks between its jaws, glutted, as it were, with the very entrails of the earth, and growling over its endless meal, like some savage animal, some legendary dragon, some fabulous beast, symbol of inordinate and monstrous gluttony.

McTeague (1899)[1]

* * *

What this passage images and articulates is a sense of immense power, of irresistible force, and inevitable conflict. It begins by powerfully evoking a particular Californian landscape of canyons and mountains, of brush, bushes and trees, a landscape in which, in the first paragraph at least, nature rules supreme. But the description is everywhere pointed and angled to one specific end: an emphatic recognition of the force and power latent in the topography itself. The opening sentences are vividly sensuous; each of our senses is appealed to – sight, smell, hearing, even touch – the day is 'very hot', the silence is 'close and thick' and lies 'like an invisible, muffling fluid', the drone of an insect 'bored the air' (just as later the miners are described as 'boring into the vitals' of the mountains). But the initial emphasis on the still, static, motionless quality of the landscape, the sense of a world weighed down, drowning in heat and silence, proves to be misleading. It is the sense of smell – the odours of sap, of pine needles, tar-weed and witch hazel, rising up from the heat-soaked bushes and trees – which leads us to a recognition of the infinitely potent life force at work within the scene. Trees and bushes are everywhere 'quietly and motionlessly growing, growing, growing', their silent, upward thrust enacted in the incremental repetition of the sentence itself. But this vegetable life is itself only part of a larger, topographical life. Canyons and mountains stretching away into the blue distance distill an atmosphere of tremendous, latent power; the scale of things is immense: the canyons are 'gigantic', 'ocean-deep', 'massive', the forces are 'colossal', 'primeval'. From the depths of the canyons to the mountain peaks 'like giant lions rearing their heads after drinking' (having supped their fill on their latest kill?) there grows an overwhelming sense of the illimitable, living force lying within the natural world. Here in Placer County, California, nature is power, a raw, crude power, unsubdued, untamed, undisguised; she is some huge prehistoric beast, rather than the 'good-natured housewife' she becomes in the civilized world east of the Mississippi. Most significant of all, primitive, primeval, prehistoric nature here makes no acknowledgement even of the existence of man.

At this point Norris's focus switches from nature to man, but the striking fact is the total absence of any significant tonal change when the transition is made. Man is engaged in violent conflict with this landscape, conflict like that between primitive man and some prehistoric beast. 'Like lice on mammoths' hides' (the mammoth flourished in the Pleistocene age, which overlapped with the Pliocene), men bore into the sides of the mountains. But what the description insists on is the violence shared by the opposing powers. Mammoth and man match power with power, force with force. Mammoth and mountain both are assailed in their 'hides', 'vitals', 'flanks', 'blood'. As the lice suck blood from the mammoth's hide, so the men suck gold from the mountain.

The mine, with its 'never failing feather of black smoke', is the weapon with which man ceaselessly opposes and overcomes the resistance of the earth. Like the 'never-failing' smoke is the permanent 'prolonged thunder' of the stamp mill, its thunder echoed in the crush*er*, monst*er*, and powd*er* of the rest of the sentence. Like the natural landscape, the mine with its machinery is a living thing, a monstrous animal with maw, jaws and teeth, and an insatiable hunger which it feeds with 'the very entrails of the earth'. Nature and man's machine are pitted against each other, like two enormous prehistoric monsters, in a living, gigantic, superhuman, struggle. There are no discriminations to be made. One blind force is joined in battle with another. The driving, pulsing life in the essence of things is matched by the monstrous, living machine of man's creation. Nature and human nature both are caught up by a reality that defines itself in terms of power, struggle, strife, and unremitting violence. In the final sentence Norris insists on the symbolic value of his description: the machinery of the mine is a 'legendary dragon' or a 'fabulous beast'. But in fact the entire passage is symbolic, offering a vision of a reality composed of brute forces locked in inevitable, destructive, conflict.

*

McTeague, eponymous protagonist of the novel, has returned to the mining country of Placer County obeying his own natural instincts. He is a murderer in flight from his pursuers, seeking refuge in his natural habitat. In his youth he had been a car boy, working in the Big Dipper mine with his father who, Norris tells us in the opening pages of the novel, for thirteen days of every fortnight was a steady, reliable, shift boss, but who every other Sunday 'became an irresponsible animal, a beast, a brute, crazy with alcohol' (p. 2). McTeague's mother, however, had had ambitions for her son, and he had been sent off with a travelling dentist to learn his trade. For a time McTeague, a shambling giant of a man, strong enough to extract a refractory tooth with thumb and forefinger, enjoys a calm and somnolent life as a dentist in San Francisco. But eventually all goes wrong; the young girl he marries turns into a pathological miser; he is not allowed to continue practising as a dentist because of his lack of paper qualifications; and the violence and brutality deep in his nature erupt in the murder of his wife and the theft of the fortune – won in a lottery – she has so carefully hoarded. In the final scenes of the novel, McTeague, sensing animal-like that his pursuers are closing in on him at the Big Dipper mine, tries unsuccessfully to make his escape by crossing Death Valley.

The characteristics of the landscape of Placer County, California, are thus broadly repeated within the wider context of *McTeague*. The same, naturalistic emphasis on conflict and violence is everywhere apparent; action and plot, and even characterization, play their part in the creation of a grimly naturalistic world dominated by blind and irresistible forces over which man has no control. It is this emphasis on man's impotence and insignificance in a world of violence and conflicting forces that allies Norris to Stephen Crane. The ultimate meaning that Norris discovers in Placer County, California, has much in common with that with which Crane confronts Henry Fleming in the battle-fields of the American Civil War in *The Red Badge of Courage*. For both writers man is engaged in a deadly struggle for survival in a bleakly Darwinian biological universe. Crane, as we have seen, saw himself as belonging to the school of realism in American writing which William Dean Howells had pioneered. But it is his vision of man's place in the universe, so much grimmer and more pessimistic than anything Howells could even begin to imagine, which has led literary historians to see him as composing, with Norris and Dreiser and some later writers, a school not of realism, but of naturalism, in American fiction. At this point, however, it is necessary to remind ourselves that, for

Norris himself, naturalism is as much a style, a mode of writing, as it is a subject or a way of perceiving the nature of reality.

*

Norris attempted to define literary naturalism by comparing it with the two other major literary modes available to the American novelist at this time: realism and romance. By realism Norris meant essentially Howellsian realism; that is, as we have seen, the faithful rendering of the surface details of ordinary life. Such a way of writing, Norris regarded as narrow, restrictive, and dull. 'Realism', he wrote, 'is minute; it is the drama of a broken tea-cup, the tragedy of a walk down the block . . . the adventure of an invitation to dinner.'[2] Or again, in similar vein, realism concerns itself with 'the smaller details of everyday life, things that are likely to happen between lunch and supper'.[3] Rather than Howellsian realism of this kind, Norris expresses a preference for romance, though he recognized that the rise to dominance of the school of realism in the 1890s had entailed the rejection of the romance mode by the serious novelist. 'Why should it be,' he asks, 'that so soon as the novelist addresses himself – seriously – to the consideration of contemporary life he must abandon Romance and take up that hard, loveless, colourless, blunt tool called Realism?'[4] Norris's distaste for realism is clear once again, but the crucial point is what he understands by romance. Clearly for him, romance is not to be preempted by the kind of sentimental, idealizing fiction against which Howells and his followers had so tirelessly inveighed. Interestingly, Norris goes behind this definition to see in romance, not a way of avoiding the realities of life, but rather a means of exploring its depths. Romance he defines as concerning itself with 'variations from the type of normal life'.[5] It looks beneath the surface of everyday life to discover some larger, profounder truth. Romance explores 'the unplumbed depths of the human heart, and the mystery of sex, and the problems of life, and the black, unsearched penetralia of the soul of man'.[6]

Ultimately, Norris believed that the novelist should aim at the bringing together of the modes of realism and romance, as he had defined these terms, thus creating a way of writing combining an accurate rendering of the surface details of life (realism) with an understanding of the underlying, general truths about man and nature (romance). But the version of this combination that Norris had in mind had already acquired a distinctive form. What it is, the work of Emile Zola, he believes, lets us see; 'This is not romanticism – this drama of the people, working itself out in blood and ordure. It is not realism. It is a school by itself, unique, somber, powerful beyond words. It is naturalism.'[7] For Norris it is naturalism which above all 'strives hard for accuracy and truth'.[8] The school of naturalism, it is, which combines the accuracy of realism with the truth of romance. This was the school to which he gave his allegiance, and this was the school to which his best novels – *McTeague* and *The Octopus* (1901) – belong.

What is most interesting in Norris's definition of naturalism is its emphasis on mode or manner of writing rather than on subject, message or meaning. Zolaesque naturalism had of course drawn heavily on philosophical notions of a broadly determinist kind: man is seen as the victim of environmental, hereditary, and biological factors over which he has almost no control. Norris's account of naturalism does not stress ideas of this kind; combining realism and romance, naturalism emerges as a way of writing rather than as a particular way of perceiving reality. None the less, the general truths that *McTeague* exhibits, through its exploration of the depths and mysteries and problems of human life, undoubtedly lie in the main within the materialist boundaries of philosophical naturalism.

McTeague does contain a substantial element of realism. The bustling life of the streets of San Francisco, McTeague's dental parlour, with a carefully itemized, quasi-scientific catalogue of the tools of his trade, the interiors of rooms, details of dress, meals, outings to the theatre or a park, all of these are evoked in meticulous and often vivid detail. Yet beneath the accurately documented surface of life the elemental passions in human nature are flowing. Early in the novel, in a crucial scene, as McTeague stands over the anaesthetized form of Trina, the girl he is to marry, in his dental chair, he finds himself violently assailed by crude, sexual desire:

> Suddenly the animal in the man stirred and woke; the evil instincts that in him were so close to the surface leaped to life, shouting and clamoring.
>
> It was a crisis – a crisis that had arisen all in an instant; a crisis for which he was totally unprepared. Blindly, and without knowing why, McTeague fought against it, moved by an unreasoned instinct of resistance. Within him, a certain second self, another better McTeague rose with the brute; both were strong, with the huge, crude strength of the man himself. . . . It was the old battle, old as

> the world, wide as the world – the sudden panther leap of the animal, lips drawn, fangs aflash, hideous, monstrous, not to be resisted, and the simultaneous arousing of the other man, the better self that cries, 'Down, down,' without knowing why; that grips the monster; that fights to strangle it, to thrust it down and back.
>
> (p. 22)

The battle here, even though expressed conceptually in terms of a conventional moral struggle between right and wrong, good and evil, in human nature, seems as primitive and primeval as that between mountain and mine in the original extract. And in both examples, the language used has left the world of Howellsian realism far behind. However crudely and insistently used, and with however great an admixture of what may seem mere hyperbole, repetition and melodramatic shrillness and intensity, the language here is the language appropriate to Norris's conception of romance. It was to be free to write like this that Norris was ready to abandon realism. To get at 'the black, unsearched penetralia of the soul of man' Norris believed (like D. H. Lawrence after him) that some such mode of linguistic freedom was required. The same need is served by the crude and insistent symbolism that Norris employs throughout the novel; image and symbol in the text are heavy with the general truths Norris wishes his fiction to illuminate. The final scene of the novel is a perfect illustration: McTeague trapped in the deadly heat of Death Valley, accidentally hand-cuffed to the body of the man he has just killed, alone now with the five thousand dollar treasure and a canary in its gilt cage which he had carried away with him in his flight.

Norris's natualism in *McTeague* does then involve a linguistic and symbolic freedom incompatible with the restraints imposed by a strictly defined realism. Like Stephen Crane and Harold Frederic, Norris needed to go beyond Howells and incorporate into his writing some of the poetic techniques of a romance writer like Nathaniel Hawthorne. But despite his own attempts at definition, Norris's naturalism in *McTeague* emerges, as has been suggested, as more than a new and distinctive literary mode. Norris's naturalism is also in the end a question of subject-matter, and a way of perceiving the nature of reality. The truth about man and reality, which the literary mode reveals, centrally involves a notion of conflict and violence at the heart of reality, and of man's liability to complicity in that conflict and violence. The dental chair scene thus ends with McTeague unable to prevent himself crudely kissing the helpless Trina. Once awakened, the brute within man cannot be wholly suppressed. 'What', asks Norris, 'was this perverse, vicious thing that lived within [McTeague], knitted to his flesh?' And he goes on to provide the answer: 'Below the fine fabric of all that was good in him ran the foul stream of hereditary evil, like a sewer. The vices and sins of his father and of his father's father, to the third and fourth and five hundredth generation, tainted him. The evil of an entire race flowed in his veins' (pp. 23–4). Possessed of such an inheritance, McTeague is fatally lacking in self-control; indeed everything about his subsequent behaviour confirms his helplessness before his own animal nature. Essentially he is a slow-witted, ponderous, easy-going man, but once aroused by anger or desire in any form, or inflamed by alcohol, his immense strength always erupts into acts of extreme violence and cruelty.

Nor, I believe, is it possible to regard McTeague as wholly a special case; in the novel he emerges as only the most extreme example of a general pattern of human behaviour, exhibiting man's vulnerability to internal and external forces, and undermining notions of individual freedom of action. The other characters in *McTeague* are no less the victim of impulses deep within their own natures which they are totally unable to control. Trina, who becomes McTeague's wife, wins a five thousand dollar prize in a lottery. But this stroke of apparent good fortune leads to her destruction. The gold takes possession of her life to such a degree that she cannot bear to part with it. Miserliness becomes second nature to her; there is nothing she can do but yield to it with ever-increasing abandon. Norris charts her degeneration with compelling power; and her final pathological state is revealed by the pleasure she takes in sleeping naked on top of her gold coins. Zerkow, a Jewish junk dealer, likewise grows increasingly obsessed by a service of gold plate which Maria, a simple-minded Mexican girl, believes her family once owned. He marries the girl in the blind hope that this will somehow give him possession of the plate. Subsequently he beats and threatens her in the insane belief that she is concealing the whereabouts of the non-existent gold. Finally, just as McTeague batters Trina to death, so Zerkow cuts Maria's throat. Marcus Schouler, at first McTeague's friend, is so driven by a sense of hurt and envy that he becomes the dentist's arch-enemy. Marcus had originally courted Trina but had given her up because of the dentist's interest; now he believes that McTeague owes him everything including the five thousand dollar lottery prize which he feels would have been his had he gone ahead and married Trina himself. Even the lives of the timid old couple who live in the rooms above McTeague's reveal the same pattern of the individual's inability to be master of his fate: the two are sentimentally drawn to each other, but are incapable of taking any kind of decisive action. Only accident can finally bring them together. In fact the lives of all the major characters in *McTeague* are dominated by the external force that is chance; just as their internal selves are the victim of uncontrollable impulses and desires, so their external lives are at the mercy of chance or fate. The lottery ticket that plays such a crucial part in the action of the novel is thus an appropriate symbol for a view of life that denies it any more significant structure of meaning.

*

McTeague's original publication owed a great deal to the support of William Dean Howells whom Norris had met in New York. Subsequently Norris repaid this debt, as it were, by persuading Doubleday, the publishing firm for whom he worked as a reader, to publish Theodore Dreiser's controversial first novel *Sister Carrie* (1900). Like Hamlin Garland, whom he also came to know in New York, Norris wrote of the American West, but, as we have seen, in imaginative terms he is more closely linked to Crane, whom he met as a fellow newspaper correspondent in Cuba, than to Garland or Howells. However, while it is not unhelpful to consider both Crane and Norris as 'naturalists', this in no way means that either writer set out consciously to expound a consistent and coherent philosophy of any kind. Despite the evidence of a powerful, naturalistic strain in *McTeague*, that is, Norris is not to be seen as wholly committed to a determinist stance which denies the individual any possible responsibility for his actions. The ordinariness of the characters in *McTeague* – like those in Zola – helps to explain their lack of self-consciousness, and so of more responsible self-control. But none of the characters is denied all possibility of choice; it is just that their better selves are unable to subdue or control the darker forces at work within their natures. As in the dental chair scene, Norris sees human nature essentially from a dualistic point of view. The struggle between good and evil may only be part of a larger pattern of conflict within reality, but at least some form of ethical conflict is allowed to occur. In the story of McTeague's decline and fall there is perhaps a hint of how Norris came to understand the precise nature of that conflict. The pattern of McTeague's life powerfully suggests an evolutionary process in reverse; there is a strong suggestion, that is, of atavism in the unfolding revelation of the brute strength and cunning lying within McTeague's nature. McTeague thus acts out in his individual life the same pattern of reversal to a more primitive, but more basic, level of human experience, which Crane sees as emerging when modern, civilized man is placed in the context of war. Both Crane and Norris seem to accept an evolutionary view of human development, but their analysis of human behaviour suggests that they regarded any human evolution away from primitive savagery towards more civilized existence as essentially fragile and precarious. At the very least one might argue that the realities of American social and economic life in the 1890s did little to dissuade them from such an essentially pessimistic point of view.

McTeague seems initially to have been modelled on an actual San Francisco murderer who attained considerable notoriety in 1893. The influence of the novels of Emile Zola, and in particular of the portrait of the murderer in *La Bête Humaine*, is also apparent. But Norris, in the creation of such a character, was also responding to contemporary ideas about the relationship of criminality to evolutionary theory. He had almost certainly read Max Nordeau's highly popular *Degeneration* (1895), a work which linked decadence and degeneracy in human beings to a failure to attain to the evolutionary level of the rest of the species: McTeague seems to be an example of such a human type. However, more generally, it was in the course of his studies at the University of California and at Harvard University (1890–5) that Norris came to see how his fairly traditional sense of the dualism within human nature could be understood as part of the process of evolution. Certainly his later novel, *The Octopus* (1901), makes it clear that he responded powerfully to the notion that the immense creative power he felt within nature – as, for example, in Placer County, California – could be identified with the evolutionary process itself.

The Octopus is an extraordinary book. The reader is rare who is not genuinely shocked when, about three quarters through, most of the main characters are wiped out in a decidedly unromantic and unheroic shoot-out. The subject of the novel is the struggle for power between the owners of the American railroads and the Californian wheat growers. But this great struggle between farmers and railroad tycoons, so close to the heart of the social, economic and political problems facing the western states of America in particular in the later nineteenth century, is ultimately not treated in political terms. Norris draws back from any radical political solution. Politics is replaced by mysticism.

The wheat which the land produces becomes a kind of absolute, transcendent reality, an objectification of natural energy or force which, we learn, will always prevail, no matter what particular human conflicts are caught up in it. This energy or force is now recognized as quasi-divine so that Norris seems finally to share the position, set out in works like James McCosh's *Christianity and Positivism* (1871) and especially John Fiske's *Outlines of Cosmic Philosophy* (1874), which maintained that traditional Christianity could be reconciled with Darwinism through a form of evolutionary theism: God not only set the evolutionary process in motion, but is immanent in the process itself. 'As far as one could look, uncounted multitudes of trees and manzanita bushes were quietly and motionlessly growing, growing, growing. A tremendous, immeasurable life pushed steadily heavenward without a sound, without a motion.' The movement from the life force defined here in the landscape around the Big Dipper mine to the divine force which is the wheat in *The Octopus* is not a very large one. Just as Norris's naturalism as a mode of writing combines romance and realism, so his naturalism as a way of perceiving reality moulds materialist determinism into evolutionary theism.

Notes

1 The text of this extract from Chapter 20 of *McTeague, a Story of San Francisco* is taken from the Holt, Rinehart and Winston edition, ed. Carvel Collins, New York, Chicago and San Francisco, 1950.
2 Frank Norris, *The Responsibilities of the Novelist*, New York, 1903.
3 'Zola as a Romantic Writer', *Wave*, 15, June 1896.
4 *The Responsibilities of the Novelist*, New York, 1903.
5 'A Plea for Romantic Fiction', *Boston Evening Transcript*, 19 December, 1901.
6 ibid.
7 'Zola as a Romantic Writer'.
8 'Frank Norris' Weekly Letter', *Chicago American Literary Review*, 3 August, 1901.

Further reading

Warren French, *Frank Norris*, New York, 1962.
Donald Pizer, *The Novels of Frank Norris*, Bloomington and London, 1966.

12

Kate Chopin (1850–1904)

Edna walked on down to the beach rather mechanically, not noticing anything special except that the sun was hot. She was not dwelling upon any particular train of thought. She had done all the thinking which was necessary after Robert went away, when she lay awake upon the sofa till morning.

She had said over and over to herself: 'Today it is Arobin; tomorrow it will be someone else. It makes no difference to me, it doesn't matter about Léonce Pontellier – but Raoul and Étienne!' She understood now clearly what she had meant long ago when she said to Adèle Ratignolle that she would give up the unessential, but she would never sacrifice herself for her children.

Despondency had come upon her there in the wakeful night, and had never lifted. There was no one thing in the world that she desired. There was no human being whom she wanted near her except Robert; and she even realized that the day would come when he, too, and the thought of him would melt out of her existence, leaving her alone. The children appeared before her like antagonists who had overcome her, who had overpowered and sought to drag her into the soul's slavery for the rest of her days. But she knew a way to elude them. She was not thinking of these things when she walked down to the beach.

The water of the Gulf stretched out before her, gleaming with the million lights of the sun. The voice of the sea is seductive, never ceasing, whispering, clamoring, murmuring, inviting the soul to wander in abysses of solitude. All along the white beach, up and down, there was no living thing in sight. A bird with a broken wing was beating the air above, reeling, fluttering, circling disabled down, down to the water.

Edna had found her old bathing suit still hanging, faded, upon its accustomed peg.

She put it on, leaving her clothing in the bath-house. But when she was there beside the sea, absolutely alone, she cast the unpleasant, pricking garments from her, and for the first time in her life she stood naked in the open air, at the mercy of the sun, the breeze that beat upon her, and the waves that invited her.

How strange and awful it seemed to stand naked under the sky! how delicious! She felt like some new-born creature, opening its eyes in a familiar world that it had never known.

The foamy wavelets curled up to her white feet, and coiled like serpents about her ankles. She walked out. The water was chill, but she walked on. The water was deep, but she lifted her white body and reached out with a long, sweeping stroke. The touch of the sea is sensuous, enfolding the body in its soft, close embrace.

She went on and on. She remembered the night she swam far out, and recalled the terror that seized her at the fear of being unable to regain the shore. She did not look back now, but went on and on, thinking of the bluegrass meadow that she had traversed when a little child, believing that it had no beginning and no end.

Her arms and legs were growing tired.

She thought of Léonce and the children. They were a part of her life. But they need not have thought that they could possess her, body and soul. How Mademoiselle Reisz would have laughed, perhaps sneered, if she knew! 'And you call yourself an artist! What pretensions, Madame! The artist must possess the courageous soul that dares and defies.'

Exhaustion was pressing upon and overpowering her.

'Good-by – because, I love you.' He did not know; he did not understand. He would never understand. Perhaps Doctor Mandelet would have understood if she had seen him – but it was too late; the shore was far behind her, and her strength was gone.

She looked into the distance, and the old terror flamed up for an instant, then sank again. Edna heard her father's voice and her sister Margaret's. She heard the barking of an old dog that was chained to the sycamore tree. The spurs of the cavalry officer clanged as he walked across the porch. There was the hum of bees, and the musky odor of pinks filled the air.

The Awakening (1899)[1]

* * *

Just as here, at the end of her life, crucial moments of awareness and recollection crowd into Edna Pontellier's consciousness, so this entire passage, in its language, imagery, and concerns, is crowded with insistent echoes of all that has gone before. As a result, passage and novel in this instance appear to form an exceptionally seamless whole. Edna, the novel's protagonist, has left New Orleans and returned to Grand Isle, on the edge of the Gulf of Mexico, where, in the previous summer, her 'awakening', her growth in self-awareness, and emergence as a woman in her own right, had begun. Her walk to the beach is described as 'mechanical' because she is acting automatically, instinctively; emotionally and intellectually she is in a state of shock which is almost trance-like. In the previous chapter she had been described as striving to overtake her thoughts which 'had gone ahead of her' (p. 183); now her thoughts exist only in the past. Thinking is over. As she walked to the beach, we are told, 'she was not dwelling upon any particular train of thought'. What has produced this condition, and destroyed Edna Pontellier's life, is, in an immediate sense, the departure of Robert, the young man whom she loves, and who is in love with her. She had learned of his going at the end of the previous chapter; and at the very moment when her expectations of the fulfilment of their love were at their intensest. Having read Robert's note of farewell, Edna's reaction was as follows:

> She went and sat on the sofa. Then she stretched herself out there, never uttering a sound. She did not sleep. She did not go to bed. The lamp sputtered and went out. She was still awake in the morning, when Celestine unlocked the kitchen door and came in to light the fire. (p. 185)

It is only now, in paragraphs two and three of the extract, that Kate Chopin lets us see what went on in Edna's consciousness as she lay awake the previous night. For these two paragraphs, that is, we are held back in the past, allowed to see why it is that Edna has returned to this beach at Grand Isle.

She has returned because she has realized that there is no other place in which she can be free. But the price of the freedom, which her awakening has brought her, she now accepts, is isolation and alienation. Arobin is the lover she has finally taken, but whom she does not love; Léonce Pontellier is the husband she has left; Raoul and Étienne are the children whom she loves; Adèle Ratignolle is the friend she respects. But Edna is no longer prepared to define her own identity, her own existence, merely through her relationship with any one of them. And now that he has gone, she is ready to acknowledge that even Robert would in the end have melted 'out of her existence, leaving her alone'. In the darkness and despondency of the wakeful night, she has been compelled to admit the absolute finality of her aloneness.

At an earlier stage in the novel, in Chapter 19, when Edna's sense of release and freedom and joy in living, arising from a growing understanding of her own independent existence, had temporarily faded, she had experienced days of confusion, of doubt and unhappiness. Then life had appeared to her 'like a grotesque pandemonium and humanity like worms struggling blindly toward inevitable annihilation' (p. 97). This darkly naturalistic, even nihilistic, vision – so characteristic of the 1890s – hovers around the sense of alienation she had experienced during the previous night: notice that it is not just Robert himself, but even 'the thought of him' that would finally melt out of her existence. Compared with Robert, Arobin, with whom she had experienced only sensual gratification, and Léonce, her partner in a loveless marriage, are as nothing. But Raoul and Étienne are a different matter; the children to whom she is mother haunt her consciousness, as paragraphs two and three of the extract make clear. In fact Kate Chopin's account of the movement of Edna's consciousness in the second paragraph is sufficiently elliptical to make the first reference to the children possibly misleading. A succession of lovers, Edna thinks, will not matter to her; and she is not concerned about her husband; but her children – they are something different. This might seem to mean that she is worrying over the effect scandal might have upon her children. In fact this is not so. No sooner do Raoul and Étienne enter her consciousness than her mind veers away to an earlier, intensely significant, conversation she had had with Adèle Ratignolle. This is the conversation that she claims she now fully understands.

Among the characters in the novel, Adèle Ratignolle is the one through whom, above all, Edna is able to begin to define the kind of woman she herself is. Adèle is physically splendid, a magnificent, matronly figure, possessed of charm and beauty; a descendant of the original French and Spanish settlers in New Orleans, she is a Creole, outgoing and communicative, where Edna, an American of Anglo-Saxon descent from Kentucky, is reserved and withdrawn. But in the dominant Creole society of *The Awakening*, Adèle is identified above all as an archetype of the 'mother woman' figure. For Adèle her role as mother is all that concerns her; her sewing constantly in her hand, she gives herself totally to her ever-growing family. Her life is her children. Adèle is the very model of the wife that Creole society demands, and therefore of what Léonce Pontellier expects from Edna. Significantly, it is a petty row over their children – whom Edna is accused of neglecting – that first hints at Edna's inner state of uneasiness and self-doubt. After an angry exchange with her husband, she had, near the beginning of the novel, sat outside in the dark feeling an 'indescribable oppression', a 'vague anguish', but unable to identify what is wrong with her (p. 14).

What in fact is wrong with Edna is that she is finding it increasingly difficult to accept her role as wife of Léonce Pontellier and mother of his children. Her own individual self, and her own womanhood, are struggling for recognition. As the story develops, she feels increasingly that the identity afforded her by marriage within Creole society is a false identity. Her inner being, the individual she really is, is more and more at odds with the public role to which a highly conventionalized society has consigned her. Just this complex of feelings had lain behind her exchange with Madame Ratignolle on the subject of children. What she had said to Mme Ratignolle was that 'she would never sacrifice herself for her children, or for any one'. Mme Ratignolle had been appalled by this idea, and Edna had tried to explain what she meant: 'I would give up the unessential; I would give my money, I would give my life for my children; but I wouldn't give myself. I can't make it more clear; it's only something which I am beginning to comprehend, which is revealing itself to me' (p. 80).

It takes time for Edna to get it clear. In the later stages of the novel she does in fact give up the security of her husband's house and money. But her children cannot be sacrificed so readily. Near the end of the story, her rebellion at the role forced upon her by motherhood is expressed with new intensity when she has to be present at the difficult birth of Adèle's latest child: 'With an inward agony, with a flaming, outspoken revolt against the ways of Nature, she witnessed the scene of torture.' Adèle's own exhausted whisper to her, however, is 'Think of the children, Edna. Oh think of the children! Remember them!' (p. 182). Afterwards to Doctor Mandelet, the one character in the novel who has any understanding of the transformation occurring within Edna, she explains '"I'm not going to be forced into doing things . . . I want to be let alone. Nobody has any right – except children, perhaps – and even then, it seems to me – or it did seem –" She felt that her speech was voicing the incoherency of her thoughts, and stopped abruptly. . . . "I don't want anything [she goes on] but my own way. That is wanting a good deal, of course, when you have to trample upon the lives, the hearts, the prejudices of others – but no matter – still,

I shouldn't want to trample upon the little lives" ' (pp. 183–4). Always it is the problem of the children to which she returns. At this point, however, she still believes that Robert is waiting for her, waiting for her return, and for the consummation of their love. As she imagines her lover's caresses, she remembers Adèle's words, 'Think of the children; think of them.' 'She meant to think of them,' Kate Chopin tells us, 'that determination had driven into her soul like a death wound' (p. 185). She tells herself that she will think of them tomorrow. But the implication of the imagery of wounding and death is that her new self will be destroyed. When she reaches home it is to find that Robert has gone. Edna's world is overturned once again. And she settles to the train of thought that is registered in these two early paragraphs in the extract.

As far as the children are concerned, the moment of decision has now arrived. In the space between sentences two and three of the second paragraph Edna is being asked – is asking herself – to sacrifice herself for her children. But the vision of Raoul and Étienne in her consciousness is matched by her memory of her earlier assertion to Madame Ratignolle. She will after all act out what she had said at a time when she had not fully grasped the import of what she was saying. In paragraph three, her children re-emerge, but now specifically as enemies, antagonists 'who had overpowered and sought to drag her into the soul's slavery for the rest of her days'. The imagery of capture and submission here is powerfully indicative of what a return to normal 'mother woman' life would mean for her. To permit herself to be forced to make that return would be to deny and thwart her awakened self. This is the sacrifice that it is now impossible for her to make; not even for her children will she sacrifice the individual being she has become.

Now, on the beach at Grand Isle, these thoughts belong to the past: 'She was not thinking of these things when she walked down to the beach.' With this sentence, the language and style of the passage alter dramatically. Ratiocination and debate are left behind. The language of the passage becomes lyrically poetic and evocatively sensuous. One of the great triumphs of *The Awakening* is the superb harmony Kate Chopin establishes between the vivid topography of land and sea-scape and the inner world of her main character. Edna's consciousness of her emerging self, and her awareness of the physical world around her, seem to flow into each other so that it is impossible to say which is cause and which effect. Edna's experience is expanded as much by her sensuous responsiveness to the natural world around her as it is by her slowly dawning recognition of the significance of her feelings for Robert. The result is that natural image and inner reality are scarcely distinguishable.

The sea, stretching here so brilliantly in the glare of the February sun, is in fact a dominant symbol in the novel. The sea is experience, opportunity, and danger; it is the world of adventure, and of sensual and sexual pleasure. The Gulf is all of these things, and from the first it has drawn Edna. At the end of Chapter 5, Robert invites Mrs Pontellier to the beach to swim. The idea appeals to Edna as at once attractive and wrong – the attraction is suggested by the 'sonorous murmur' of the sea and the breeze that was 'soft and warm' (p. 24) – and she is made aware of the contradictory impulses within her. 'A certain light', Kate Chopin writes, near the opening of Chapter 6, 'was beginning to dawn dimly within her – the light which, showing the way, forbids it' (p. 25). This light, however dim it may be, is the source of the anguished bewilderment she has begun to experience, and it is this which, on the night of the quarrel with her husband over the children, had driven her to sit outside, oppressed, in the darkness. At this point, in Chapter 6, the author glosses her protagonist's condition: 'Mrs Pontellier was beginning to realize her position in the universe as a human being, and to recognize her relations as an individual to the world within and about her' (p. 25).

The world about Edna includes Robert, but it also includes the sea and its appeal. And it is at this moment, when Edna is beginning for the first time to gain some understanding of the change occurring within her, that Kate Chopin describes the attraction of the sea in the terms that she repeats, exactly, here (in paragraph four of the extract) at the end of the novel. In Chapter 6, Edna is about to enter a new world, and of that world the 'whispering, clamoring, murmuring, inviting' sea is the symbol. What Edna does is accept the invitation of the sea. At this point, however, Edna cannot swim. All summer, we are told, she has been trying unsuccessfully to learn. Her fear is too great, she needs to feel there is a hand nearby to 'reach out and reassure her' (p. 47). But a few nights later, in Chapter 10, during a scene of immense, symbolic beauty, in which the evocation of the feel of the night, of the smells of earth and sea, of the soft motion of the water, is rendered with extraordinary lyrical power, Edna suddenly discovers that she can swim. She is a person reborn. She is likened to 'the little, tottering, stumbling, clutching child, who of a sudden realizes its powers, and walks for the first time alone. . .'. Edna is intoxicated, exulting. She shouts for joy. She feels 'as if some power of significant import had been given her to control the working of her body and her soul' (p. 47). Throughout the whole episode images of the sea, of swimming, and of the self's awakening, once again flow into each other. It was on this occasion that Edna had 'wanted to swim far out, where no woman had swum before', and, as she now recalls, had been suddenly terrified by thinking she could not regain the shore. As her sense of her own independence, of her rights as an individual, has grown, Edna has ventured further and further on the sea. But now, at the end, 'to wander in abysses of solitude' is what the sea's invitation has become: 'all along the white beach, up and down, there was no living thing in sight.' Only the bird with its broken wing, its descending spiral down to the water effectively caught in the participles and repetitions of the sentence.

The bird is no doubt an image of Edna herself: it too is an image that has occurred before. Mademoiselle Reisz, a pianist who has become Edna's friend and confidante, had said to her: 'The bird that would soar above the level plain of tradition and prejudice must have strong wings. It is a sad spectacle to see the weaklings bruised, exhausted, fluttering back to earth' (p. 138). Edna Pontellier has indeed soared above the level plain of tradition and prejudice. She has refused to conform; she has asserted her individuality and womanhood; she has gone so far as to move out of her husband's house and try to earn an independent living as a painter; she has taken a lover. But she has paid a price for her self-discovery, and with Robert's departure, bruised and exhausted is precisely what she is. But 'back to earth' – to a life of submissive conformity – that is the return she has refused to make. Like the bird with the broken wing, it is in the sea that she seeks refuge.

Last summer's bathing suit carries with it too strong an association of the accepted, conventional ritual of holiday sea-bathing. Through her nakedness, Edna is insisting on her own essential individuality; this is what she is. But such a boldness of assertion contains its own dangers: she is now 'at the mercy' of the sun, of the breeze 'that beat upon' her, and of the waves that invite her. Yet the passage seems to negate these hostile suggestions. Edna relishes her boldness, rejoices in her freedom. The image of awakening is present again with added urgency and intensity: Edna 'felt like some new-born creature, opening its eyes in a familiar world that it had never known'. The touch of wind and water upon her skin has an unrealized, transfiguring power. The waves coiling 'like serpents about her ankles' is yet another echo image: in Chapter 10, on the night Edna had learned to swim, the waves had broken 'in little foamy crests that coiled back like slow, white serpents' (p. 47).

That night Edna had exulted in her new-found power: as she had swum far out from land, the danger of the sea had seemed as nothing. Now again the sea seems to welcome her, accepting her body. The sentence concerning the touch of the sea, with its insistence on the sexual dimension of the swimmer's body's at-oneness with the sea, is yet another echo of Chapter 10. But the fear of swimming too far out, which she had finally experienced then, is now put aside. She has passed beyond fear. Instead she recalls an image from her childhood.

Among the first hints of the transformation occurring within Edna had been the breaking down, in Grand Isle, of her innate reserve. Under the influence of Adèle Ratignolle, in particular, she had begun to speak of herself and her past in a way that was itself an intoxication and a release. Early in the story, sitting with Adèle at the beach, looking out to sea, she had taken seriously a question about her thoughts. She had been admiring, she says, 'the sight of the water stretching so far away, those motionless sails against the blue sky', while the hot wind beating in her face had made her think of 'a summer day in Kentucky, of a meadow that seemed as big as the ocean' to the little girl walking through the tall grass. 'She threw out her arms as if swimming when she walked, beating the tall grass as one striking out in the water.' To her childhood vision, the grass had seemed to stretch on for ever; she couldn't remember whether such a limitless prospect had 'frightened or pleased' her. Finally, to Adèle she confesses that this summer in Grand Isle, she has sometimes felt as if she were 'walking through the green meadow again, idly, aimlessly, unthinking and unguided' (pp. 29–30). Here, at the last, she is indeed repeating that childhood experience of unlimited, unending freedom, but not in an idle or aimless or unthinking fashion. She is here because this is the path she has chosen. She has fought and struggled towards this freedom; but the price of its attainment is now being paid. She is growing tired; she is exhausted; the sea is overpowering her.

In the final, fleeting moments of her life, Edna reviews the attachments that might have kept her chained to the land. First her husband and children. They were undeniably part of her life, but had no claim upon all of it; Edna has come to understand that she cannot be a wife and mother at the expense of her own existence as an individual being. Mademoiselle Reisz is the artist figure whom Edna had admired and tried to emulate – it was as a working artist that she had hoped to survive economically after abandoning the security of her husband's money. In fact, Mademoiselle Reisz had neither laughed nor sneered at

Edna's artistic ambitions. All along she had seemed to understand Edna's situation, and if she had not actively urged her forward, she had done nothing to discourage the process of self-discovery. If Edna was not a true artist herself, Mademoiselle Reisz was sure that she was the audience for whom the artist willingly performed. And if it is the mark of the artist to possess 'the courageous soul that dares and defies', then Edna proves her title in the end. Yet there is an element of pessimism here too. Daring and defiance and courage do not add up to a guarantee of survival; tiredness and exhaustion may bring down the artist too.

Robert enters next into her consciousness. 'Good-by – because, I love you' had been his parting message. He had gone because his understanding had been too far determined by the conventions of his society; his departure was a gesture towards a notion of honour that Edna has come to see as without meaning. At Grand Isle, in the summer, it was perfectly acceptable for Robert to be 'in love' with other men's wives. That was a thoroughly conventional situation which he, and his society, knew and understood. When it begins to become clear to him – and to Edna – that his relationship with Léonce Pontellier's wife is no longer an elaborate, romantic game, he feels obliged to set off for Mexico. Edna loves him and waits for his return. But when he does return, the result is the same. He loves Edna, but cannot appreciate what has happened to her; for him she still 'belongs' to Léonce Pontellier. Edna tells Robert: 'I am no longer one of Mr. Pontellier's possessions to dispose of or not. I give myself where I choose' (p. 178). But it is precisely the revolution implied by this that Robert does not understand, and 'would never understand'. He remains trapped by the conventional norms and established assumptions of the highly traditional society from which Edna has broken free.

Doctor Mandelet is a minor character, but one who, as we have seen, like Mademoiselle Reisz, has at least some awareness of the awakening that Edna is experiencing. When Léonce Pontellier complains to him about the change he recognizes in his wife, the doctor advises a cautious approach. Léonce tells him that Edna 'seems quite well' but 'doesn't act well'. 'She's odd, she's not like herself.' And he goes on to explain that 'she's got some sort of notion in her head concerning the eternal rights of women; and – you understand – we meet in the morning at the breakfast table' (p. 109). At this stage, Doctor Mandelet suspects a conventional lover, but later he appreciates Edna's position at an altogether deeper level. The night before, after the difficult birth of Adèle's child which had so disturbed Edna, he had urged her to confide in him, assuring her he would understand, though warning her, significantly, that there were not many who would. It is this exchange that Edna, at the end of her strength, is recalling.

Finally, into Edna's failing consciousness float images from her childhood. She seems to sink into the sounds of the past; she hears the voices of her father and sister; the barking of a dog; the clang of the spurs of the cavalry officer with whom she had fallen childishly in love; the hum of the bees. The sensuous impact is strong, whatever these final images may seem to suggest. Is Edna seeking a return to the womb-like security of childhood? Or is she recognizing that it was in her childhood that the loss of the freedom of the bluegrass meadow had begun? Or is it simply that, having rejected the present, and being unable to conceive of any possible future, it is only the past, the innocent past before she was Edna Portellier, with which, realistically, she is left?

*

What Kate Chopin means by the ending of her novel is that the awakening of the title has been fully achieved. Edna has found her freedom and independence; her self, her individuality, have gained free, untrammelled existence; she is able to think, to act, and, most importantly, to feel, for herself. Alone and naked before the ocean, her self-hood has been given even stronger and purer definition. The bitter paradox, however, is that she has realized that she can preserve the purity and strength of her newly-discovered freedom only by destroying it. What this in turn implies is that, within the Creole social world of which Edna Pontellier is part, such freedom, such independence, on the part of a woman, cannot exist. Kate Chopin, that is, is unable to resolve the collision between individual and social values in the manner of earlier writers. Isabel Archer, in *The Portrait of a Lady*, seems to sacrifice her self-hood to a higher, but perhaps life-denying, duty; Stephen Crane's Henry Fleming in *The Red Badge of Courage*, rather like Theron Ware, in Harold Frederic's novel, accommodates himself to the new, corrupt, reality that he has come to recognize; Twain's Huckleberry Finn side-steps the issue by comically opting out of society. What Kate Chopin does is to face squarely the tragic implications of conflict with society for the individual for whom there is nowhere to escape to; nowhere, that is, except into a final at-oneness with that surrounding sensuous reality, in terms of which, as the account of her death shows, her awakening has so centrally defined itself. Edna is at last free to choose – but only as long as she chooses to die.

The Awakening is a superb and challenging novel. It challenges a whole tradition of novel-writing by and about women in nineteenth-century American literature. In the second half of the nineteenth century in particular, when writing was one of the few professions open to women, women writers played an extremely prominent part in America's literary culture. Many achieved immense popular success; but they succeeded largely by appealing to the simplest kinds of romantic idealism and sentimentalism, a conventional moral orthodoxy, and an equally conventional view of the domestic role of women in society. Rejecting all of these, *The Awakening* triumphs as a work of art. If not written on the scale of *Anna Karenina* or *Madame Bovary*, it is none the less worthy of comparison with such major novels. In its intensities of feeling, and the subtlety of its analysis of the position of the married woman in a highly conventional society, it is quite outstanding. Perhaps it is true that the forms in which Edna Pontellier's slowly discovered sense of independent existence are allowed to express themselves remain somewhat limited: personal fulfilment in love may seem too narrow an achievement for her to aim at. Yet it is difficult to see how, within the context of Creole society, any other form of self-fulfilment could have been available to her. Art is certainly present as another avenue of freedom; but the example of Mademoiselle Reisz, an isolated figure, hovering around the edges of an unappreciative society, hardly suggests that fulfilment in art necessarily means fulfilment in life.

What is entirely convincing in the novel is the picture of Edna's growth in understanding and self-awareness. Rendered in a fluent, flexible, and often lyrical prose, this development carries powerful psychological conviction. The novel is not long, but every response, observation, and perception falls into place in such a way that the sense of a gradual movement, a continuing process, is beautifully conveyed. Equally impressive is the vivid evocation of the natural landscapes and seascapes of the Gulf. The whole novel is shaped and formed to produce an impressive and satisfying unity of effect. One has to move forward to *The Great Gatsby* to find an American novel with a matching poetry.

Yet *The Awakening* is also very much a novel of the 1890s. It is a novel of pessimism, even of despair. It sees the individual as the victim of rigid patterns of social behaviour over which he or she has no control. It sees no real hope of change. And, in a sense, events proved that Kate Chopin's imaginative insights were all too accurate. Just as much as that meted out to Dreiser's *Sister Carrie* in the following year (1900), the reception of *The Awakening* demonstrates the continuing power and authority of the genteel tradition in American culture. However great the success of William Dean Howells and his followers had been in furthering the cause of realism in American writing, at the end of the nineteenth century American culture remained dominated by a conventional moral orthodoxy which literature was expected broadly to uphold. *The Awakening* openly defied that moral orthodoxy. As a result, it was universally dismissed as 'morbid', 'unwholesome', 'essentially vulgar', 'trite and sordid'. Kate Chopin was surprised and dismayed by these cries of horrified outrage. Mademoiselle Reisz had warned Edna Pontellier that the artist needed the 'courageous soul that dares and defies'. In writing *The Awakening*, Kate Chopin had shown herself to possess just such a soul. And given that the hostility displayed towards her novel more or less put an end to her writing career, her fate was not so very different from that suffered by the protagonist of *The Awakening*. Soon the novel itself was neglected and forgotten. After her death in 1905, such reputation as Kate Chopin retained identified her, on the basis of her two collections of short stories, *Bayou Folk* (1894) and *A Night in Acadie* (1897), as a minor contributor to the 'local color', regionalist movement in late nineteenth-century American fiction. It was essentially not until the 1960s, partly at least as a result of the emergence of the women's movement in America, that *The Awakening* began to receive its due. Kate Chopin might not have been wholly surprised.

Notes

1 The text of this extract from *The Awakening* is taken from the Women's Press edition, London, 1978.

2 *The Complete Works of Kate Chopin*, edited by Per Seyersted, was published by Louisiana State University Press, Baton Rouge, in 1969.

Further reading

Larzer Ziff, *The American 1890s*, New York, 1966.

Per Seyersted, *Kate Chopin, A Critical Biography*, Baton Rouge, 1969.

Judith Fryer, *The Faces of Eve, Women in the Nineteenth-Century American Novel*, New York, 1976.

13

Thorstein Veblen (1857-1929)

Cap and gown have been adopted as learned insignia by many colleges of this section within the last few years; and it is safe to say that this could scarcely have occurred at a much earlier date, or until there had grown up a leisure-class sentiment of sufficient volume in the community to support a strong movement of reversion towards an archaic view as to the legitimate end of education. This particular item of learned ritual, it may be noted, would not only commend itself to the leisure-class sense of the fitness of things, as appealing to the archaic propensity for spectacular effect and the predilection for antique symbolism; but it at the same time fits into the leisure-class scheme of life as involving a notable element of conspicuous waste. The precise date at which the reversion to cap and gown took place, as well as the fact that it affected so large a number of schools at about the same time, seems to have been due in some measure to a wave of atavistic sense of conformity and reputability that passed over the community at that period.

It may not be entirely beside the point to note that in point of time this curious reversion seems to coincide with the culmination of a certain vogue of atavistic sentiment and tradition in other directions also. The wave of reversion seems to have received its initial impulse in the psychologically disintegrating effects of the Civil War. Habituation to war entails a body of predatory habits of thought, whereby clannishness in some measure replaces the sense of solidarity, and a sense of invidious distinction supplants the impulse to equitable, everyday serviceability. As an outcome of the cumulative action of these factors, the generation which follows a season of war is apt to witness a rehabilitation of the element of status, both in its social life and in its scheme of devout observances and other symbolic or ceremonial forms. Throughout the eighties, and less plainly traceable through the seventies also, there was perceptible a gradually advancing wave of sentiment favouring quasi-predatory business habits, insistence on status, anthropomorphism, and conservatism generally. The more direct and unmediated of these expressions of the barbarian temperament, such as the recrudescence of outlawry and the spectacular quasi-predatory careers of fraud run by certain 'captains of industry', came to a head earlier and were appreciably on the decline by the close of the seventies. The recrudescence of anthropomorphic sentiment also seems to have passed its most acute stage before the close of the eighties. But the learned ritual and paraphernalia here spoken of are a still remoter and more recondite expression of the barbarian animistic sense; and these, therefore, gained vogue and elaboration more slowly and reached their most effective development at a still later date. There is reason to believe that the culmination is now already past. Except for the new impetus given by a new war experience, and except for the support which the growth of a wealthy class affords to all ritual, and especially to whatever ceremonial is wasteful and pointedly suggests gradations of status, it is probable that the late improvements and augmentation of scholastic insignia and ceremonial would gradually decline. But while it may be true that the cap and gown, and the more strenuous observance of scholastic proprieties which came with them, were floated in on this post-bellum tidal wave of reversion to barbarism, it is also no doubt true that such a ritualistic reversion could not have been effected in the college scheme of life until the accumulation of wealth in the hands of a propertied class had gone far enough to afford the requisite pecuniary ground for a movement which should bring the colleges of the country up to the leisure-class requirements in the higher learning. The adoption of the cap and gown is one of the striking atavistic features of modern college life, and at the same time it marks the fact that these colleges have definitely become leisure-class establishments, either in actual achievement or in aspiration.

The Theory of the Leisure Class (1899)[1]

* * *

Into this account of the growing taste in American colleges and universities for the use of formal academic dress and ceremonial, Veblen infiltrates a sketch of the movement of American history from the Civil War to the end of the nineteenth century. The apparent objectivity, the highly abstract and formal language, and the unemotional tone of the passage, are all potentially deceptive. They are largely devices to carry the reader along with Veblen's argument, compelling his assent. What he is assenting to, however, whether he realizes it or not, amounts to a devastating and comprehensive critique of American life and society in the period in question. Veblen's place in this volume is alongside Henry George and Edward Bellamy: all three are writers concerned to clarify the characteristic contradictions and limitations in America's economic and social arrangements. But the differences in tone between Veblen's writing and that of Bellamy and George are immense. Bellamy and George can both aspire to – and sometimes achieve – a prose of objective analysis and report; but their emotional commitments are so strong that their prose is frequently invaded by the intensity and fervour of their feelings. No such invasions occur in Veblen's prose. The whole of *The Theory of the Leisure Class* is written in the mode of dispassionate, scholarly, objective analysis and comment apparent here. Veblen's feelings about his subject are never allowed to emerge directly. Indeed there is some argument over whether they emerge at all and therefore over whether they even exist.

From the time of its original publication, *The Theory of the Leisure Class* has therefore inspired a continuing debate over just how much wit, irony and bitterness it actually contains. Is Veblen a writer of Swiftian ironic intensity, concealing his feelings beneath a mask of scholarly detachment and objectivity? Or is he really a neutral social scientist, content simply to describe and evaluate the data he has collected, setting it out in the somewhat cumbersome language and prose-style of the consciously unemotional, analytical observer? To arbitrate between these views is not a simple task, but careful study of the extract, and the language in which it is written, does seem to encourage us to lean more towards the first description than to the second. Is it really possible to regard the characteristic phraseology of this passage as wholly neutral and objective? An 'archaic view as to the legitimate end of education', 'the predilection for antique symbolism', an 'atavistic sense of conformity and reputability', 'a certain vogue of atavistic sentiment and tradition', 'a body of predatory habits of thought', 'quasi-predatory business habits', 'expressions of the barbarian temperament', 'the barbarian animistic sense', 'this post-bellum tidal wave of reversion to barbarism': is it possible to view such phrases as wholly devoid of critical implication? I suggest not. One would of course concede that lexical choices of this kind, because they have been used throughout the entire book, acquire a meaning that is more qualified than a first encounter with them in this passage might suggest. None the less, neither this admission, nor the fact that at various points in his book Veblen insists that the language he uses implies no kind of moral or critical judgment, provide anything like sufficient grounds for concluding that Veblen was in any way unaware of the implications of the language he chooses to employ here and elsewhere. That he occasionally goes to the trouble of disclaiming any critical intent merely shows his consciousness of the linguistic situation he is creating.

Significantly, *The Theory of the Leisure Class* closes with an onslaught on the canons of 'classic English', 'elegant diction', 'conventional spelling' and 'purity of speech'. What Veblen has mainly in mind, in making his attack, are the values and assumptions of orthodox American genteel culture with its characteristic rejection of any linguistic form or usage related to contemporary vernacular speech. For Veblen 'good writing' and 'good speaking' are typical activities of the monied, leisure class in American society, providing, as they do, evidence of years wasted in acquiring archaic and outmoded modes of communication whose value, he says, is purely honorific. *The Theory of the Leisure Class*, itself, however, is clearly not written in 'the slang of today', which Veblen suggests is the best vehicle for 'the ideas of today'; nor, as the extract indicates, is it written in the 'direct and forcible speech' which Veblen prefers to the cumbrous locutions of classic English. Whatever implications may be present in the discussion of language and style which brings *The Theory of the Leisure Class* to a close, one is that the book is hardly the work of a linguistically naive, innocent social scientist. Veblen has written in his chosen style and manner in a highly self-conscious way. Genteel fine writing does not provide the standard by which he wishes to be judged; elegance of diction and phrase does not concern him. What Veblen does admire and respect is the development of science and the industrial technology that has grown out of it. His language, with its frequent neologisms, and its aim at precision and accuracy of statement, reflects such respect and admiration. Science and genteel culture, Veblen implies, are not compatible. His own allegiance is clear, and if society dislikes the implications of the vocabulary and phraseology he uses to describe its essence as accurately as he can, he is perfectly prepared to go on using such language with at least the appearance of conventional scientific detachment and objectivity.

For the reader who is not wholly deceived by the apparent detachment and objectivity, the very absence of obvious emotional colouring enhances the impact of Veblen's work. Bellamy and George both write as outsiders, viewing the orthodoxies and conventions of established society from a new and hostile perspective. Veblen writes, as it were, from the inside, using the basic techniques of observation and analysis which the scientific method demands. Hence the growing prestige and authority of science itself, so frequently called upon by upholders of the economic and social *status quo* in America to bolster up their position, are used here to support a devastating analysis of that same *status quo*. The result is a book that bewildered its original readers. Just as the American universities and colleges in which Veblen studied and taught never knew quite what to make of him, intellectual America did not know what to make of his first book. And more than anything else it was its style that baffled; it seemed to give nothing away – certainly no indication of the author's own views or attitudes. For Veblen the mask of scientific objectivity worked extremely well, fundamentally because beneath it he could say what he liked.

*

In the opening sentences of the extract, Veblen insists on the recentness, particularly in the Middle West, of the fashion for requiring the use of the traditional cap and gown of academic dress in American colleges. In the paragraph preceding the extract, he had argued that there is a correlation between the wealth of a community and the formal structures of academic life within the institutions of higher learning it supports. Thus, while a community remains poor, the 'reminiscences of the medicine-man' play no part 'in the scheme of college life'. It is when a community grows rich, and acquires its own leisure class, that the insistence on academic ritual and ceremony grows. Why this 'regression' should occur, the second sentence of the extract explains: cap and gown exemplify both the 'antique symbolism' and, especially, the 'conspicuous waste' through which the leisure class is more than willing to demonstrate its conspicuous existence. Academic ceremonial and ritual, that is, are typical leisure-class activities because, in accordance with the general theory advanced by *The Theory of the Leisure Class*, they are conservative and backward-looking status symbols, and because they demonstrate the exemption of those who participate in them from the need to be engaged in productive work. But in this particular context, what Veblen goes on to argue is that the growing emphasis on the use of the traditional academic cap and gown is associated with a more general trend in American society towards the adoption of old-fashioned attitudes and habits of mind. This is the point of focusing on something as apparently trivial as academic apparel: it pinpoints with special clarity a phenomenon that has become widely diffused in American society.

The 'curious reversal' to traditional academic wear, Veblen explains, coincides with the culmination of a whole series of backward-looking trends in America whose origins he identifies with the Civil War. The trend itself Veblen describes three times as 'atavistic' – i.e. as a reversal to a more primitive stage of development. In other words, he is arguing that the whole period from 1865–1900 is characterized in America by progress in reverse: a civilization not developing, but regressing, returning to older, more primitive patterns of social conduct and behaviour. This 'wave of reversion' he identifies with the 'psychologically disintegrating' effects of the Civil War; he agrees, that is, with the view that the Civil War marked a decisive shift in the nature of American society and its characteristic behaviour.[2] In the two sentences that follow the reference to the Civil War, Veblen reverts to the mode of analysis characteristic of *The Theory of the Leisure Class* as a whole: he makes a series of observations of a broadly sociological kind in the form of general or abstract statements. These statements demand assent or dissent on intellectual grounds alone; the emotions are not involved. Here perhaps is the reason why *The Theory of the Leisure Class* was not received with the kind of outrage that greeted George's *Progress and Poverty*. Veblen's arguments appeared sufficiently theoretical and conceptual for readers to feel that they applied to no one in particular – or at least only to a particularly limited class of people among whom they would not count themselves. William Dean Howells, for example, thought very highly of the book, and wrote two successive leading articles in *Literature* in praise of it. Howells's support did much to ensure that the book would be widely read, but his account of it did encourage the view that its attack was directed only at an aristocratic social minority. Howells noted the 'passionless colour' of the book's style, and argued that it displayed 'no animus for or against a leisure class'.[3] Lester Ward, the leading American sociologist of the day, also wrote admiringly of the book, but he too tended to regard it as no more than a discussion of the way of life of an American aristrocracy.[4] These responses by favourable, well-disposed critics do suggest that Veblen succeeded almost too well in appearing to write in a purely abstract or theoretical vein: almost as though his thesis was detached from any particular environment or society.

Its demonstration that Veblen's views are not in fact as detached and theoretical as they often seem is what gives particular importance to this extract from the 'Higher Learning' section of *The Theory of the Leisure Class*. Here, for once, and to an extraordinary degree, Veblen chooses to tie his theory to the historical realities of the changing society of post-bellum America. There is an element of near casualness about his doing so. 'It may not be entirely beside the point . . .,' he writes, and goes on to make, not some minor observation, but an absolutely crucial linking of general theory to historical development. Of course the history in question is still conceived of in the most general terms, but it is the specific history of American society that is none the less described. The result is that the generalized abstractions acquire a new and more immediate burden of meaning. The 'predatory habits of thought', the 'clannishness' – by which Veblen means the selfish, self-seeking, characteristics of a limited group of people – and the 'sense of invidious distinction' induced by the experience of war are, Veblen argues, likely to be passed on to a post-war generation where they will take the form of an over-concern for personal status and its symbolic and ceremonial trappings. These are of course precisely the characteristics that *The Theory of the Leisure Class* has described and analysed in its previous chapters. In the sentence that follows in paragraph two, Veblen identifies the growth of 'quasi-predatory business habits', and an emphasis on 'status', 'anthropomorphism' (Veblen's code-word for conventional religious attitudes and beliefs) and 'conservatism' with the 1870s and 1880s in America. Hence the American leisure class is in fact characterized by its respect for violence and cunning (in economic life), its concern for prestige gained through an ostentatious display of wealth and possessions, its religiosity, and its reluctance to contemplate social change in any form. For Veblen, all these characteristics are atavistic; they signal a reversal to the attitudes and values of an older, more primitive world. Hence, in his terms, they are all reflections of 'the barbarian temperament'. However, Veblen agrees that there have been changes within the post-bellum period. The exploits of the more egregious 'robber-barons' of the Gilded Age – notice how Veblen links them with criminal outlaws – had occurred in the immediate post-war years; and Veblen believes that the revival of religious sentiment had peaked before the end of the 1880s. But the impulse towards ritual and ceremony, which Veblen sees as characteristic of primitive, less rational societies, took longer to establish itself in appropriate forms. Veblen suggests, however, that this impulse too is now in decline. Without the reinforcement provided by a new war, or the support of a leisure class which defines itself through the most obvious forms of conspicuously wasteful expenditure, and the status which such expenditure confers, these 'late improvements' in scholarly dress and ceremonial would fade away.

What Veblen has in mind here is the slow advance of the sciences within the curriculum of American colleges and universities. He insists repeatedly that American institutions of higher learning are essentially conservative in their attitudes, revealing the 'animus of the learned class towards the life process of an industrial community' (p. 377). Colleges and universities, he believes, are dominated by traditional religious attitudes, by a dislike of innovations of any kind, and by a hostility to industry and its technology. Science has developed, Veblen argues, in relation to the industrial process, and therefore has been slow to establish itself as a recognized branch of learning. However, although Veblen agrees (or pretends to) that 'a familiarity with the animistic superstitions and the exuberant truculence of the Homeric heroes, for instance, is, aesthetically considered, more legitimate than the corresponding results derived from a matter-of-fact knowledge of things and a contemplation of latter-day civic or workmanlike efficiency' (p. 392), he argues that 'an efficient collective life under modern industrial circumstances' (p. 393) is better served by the more scientific education which is slowly developing.

But the argument that the academic establishment's commitment to the rituals and symbols of an older, pre-industrial and pre-scientific society, should slowly fade, as the rationalism associated with the sciences gains ground, is balanced by Veblen's recognition that the power of the leisure class is directed towards the maintenance of just such conspicuously wasteful phenomena as formal academic dress. Here, for the fourth and last time in the passage, Veblen refers to the re-emergence in American society of 'barbarian' attitudes and habits of mind as a great wave engulfing the country in the post-bellum period. The wave image in fact provides the key to the central, underlying meaning of the entire extract. Reiterated four times, it embodies Veblen's vision of what happened to America in the post-bellum period. The transformation of American society is a sweeping, all-embracing, all-engulfing, process; it is the one, primary, dominant reality, irresistible and overwhelming. What it involves is above all a 'curious reversion', the retreat by American society into a more primitive way of life. Veblen's is a vision of civilized progress gone into reverse.

A consequence of the tidal wave of barbarism was the passing of the wealth of America into the control of a relatively small number of Americans, and the subsequent emergence of an American leisure class. That leisure class has provided and established the social and cultural norms and goals of American society, including its institutions of higher learning. The new demand in American colleges and universities for the employment of the ancient regalia of cap and gown is thus powerful evidence that higher education in America is defining itself as an essentially leisure class activity, wholly detached from the everyday realities of American collective industrial life. Veblen is in the end arguing that America is now wealthy enough to be able to afford the luxury of an out-dated, non-vocational, irrelevant system of higher learning. Like so many other aspects of American social life and behaviour, according to Veblen, education has become a leisure-class activity, its value increasing directly in proportion to its uselessness.

*

The extract, then, is untypical of *The Theory of the Leisure Class* only in the directness of its statement. The account it provides of the state of economic society in America in the post-bellum period is one that is sustained by the apparently objective analysis of earlier chapters. Veblen sees American society fundamentally divided by two contradictory impulses. The first is an 'instinct for workmanship' which is essentially productive, collective, progressive. Industrial and scientific development is its consequence and it is the ultimate source of the increasing wealth and power of America. Later in his life, Veblen would view the trained technocrats who embody this impulse as best fitted to run society. In the America he observed in 1899, however, Veblen saw the instinct for workmanship thwarted by the predatory impulse of the businessman whose only concern was pecuniary gain, the amassing of private wealth and property. The role of the leisure class was to provide a means of sustaining the predatory impulse by providing avenues through which the successes of that impulse could be made manifest through various forms of conspicuous waste and conspicuous consumption. Leisure activities of any kind defined themselves by the degree of their non-utility, the proof they offered of the participant's *exemption* from the need for industrial productiveness. It is in the light of such theories that *The Theory of the Leisure Class* examines a range of American social phenomena from the status of women, servants, clothes, domestic architecture and domestic goods, to religious observances, walking-sticks, sporting activities and higher education.

How Veblen came to develop his theories remains problematical. His parents were successful Norwegian immigrants in America. Their cultural allegiance seems to have remained divided between their old and new countries, and something of this division seems to have been passed on to their son. A kind of eccentricity characterized Thorstein Veblen throughout his entire life. He never found any social or intellectual context into which he comfortably fitted. He studied initially at Carleton College in Minnesota, where the courses he took largely exposed him to the kind of orthodox American philosophy and economic thinking which was designed to sustain and conserve the *status quo* in American society. Veblen, that is, was taught the moral and intellectual philosophy of an entrenched conservatism. Originating as far back as the period of the American Revolution when the Scottish philosophers James Beattie, Thomas Reid, and Dugald Stewart tried to defuse the threat to traditional moral and religious beliefs represented by David Hume's profound and radical scepticism, by appealing to the 'common sense' of all humanity, the naturalized American version of the Scottish common-sense philosophy had for about a hundred years proved an immensely flexible and adaptable weapon in the defence of a conservative moral, religious and social orthodoxy within America. In the post-bellum period, the philosophy had proved its continuing utility by its readiness to uphold property rights, competition, and all the other major components of the capitalist economic system. Only one of Veblen's teachers at Carleton, John Bates Clark, dissenting from the common sense tradition, was prepared to entertain the possibility of some evolutionary improvement in the prevailing economic order. Under Bates's influence, Veblen was soon reading David Hume, Herbert Spencer, T. H. Huxley, and other less orthodox philosophers.[5]

One result was, as *The Theory of the Leisure Class* makes clear, that Veblen came to accept Spencer's view of the nature of human society. At the beginning of Chapter 8, for example, he writes: 'The life of man in society, just like the life of other species, is a struggle for existence, and therefore it is a process of selective adaptation. The evolution of social structure has been a process of natural selection of institutions' (p. 188). But typically, Veblen's reading of Spencer and the others seems in no way to have determined his attitude towards the prevailing social and economic system. Further study at Johns Hopkins and Yale Universities, and his years as an instructor at the new University of

Chicago, seem rather to have encouraged his deeply-rooted scepticism. Again, his farming background had made him all too aware of the wheat producers' treatment at the hands of the railways' monopolistic power and the capitalist system in general, and of the struggle for a decent livelihood of workers of every kind. *Progress and Poverty* appeared while Veblen was still at Carleton; he 'did not hesitate to let it be known that he supported it'.[6] When, a few years later in 1886, *Looking Backward* was published, Veblen read it aloud with his wife. Subsequently she wrote of this reading: 'I believe that this was the turning-point in our lives, because it so affected me'; and she went on to assert that it was *Looking Backward* that persuaded Veblen to make economics the main subject of his studies.[7]

His reading of such works as *Progress and Poverty* and *Looking Backward* must at least have confirmed Veblen in the view, shared by so many of those critical of the current state of American society, that it was the spirit of competition, the competitive instinct, above all, that divided and disfigured American life. *The Theory of the Leisure Class* makes it clear that Veblen saw business competition as primarily an area in which ancient predatory habits were encouraged to flourish anew. But between the predatory impulse and the true interests of the industrial community as a whole there was a headlong collision. In his book Veblen argues that the collective interest is best served by 'honesty, diligence, peacefulness, good-will, an absence of self-seeking' and rational, agnostic attitudes of mind (p. 227). In the competitive situation, on the other hand, the interest of the individual is best served by 'shrewd trading and unscrupulous management'. The characteristics listed above as serving the interests of the community are 'disserviceable to the individual, rather than otherwise'. They act against 'a free and unfaltering career of sharp practice' (pp. 227–8).

The criticisms of capitalism implicit here could hardly be more devastating. In his later books, *The Theory of Business Enterprise* (1904) and *The Instinct of Workmanship* (1914), Veblen goes on developing such criticisms. Veblen came to believe that capitalism was bound to fail because its commitment to the maintenance of private property rights was becoming increasingly irreconcilable with advancing industrial technology. Property rights were preventing the proper utilization of resources for technological development. In other words, the business interest, with its commitment to profit-making, retained too much power over the basic industrial process, checking and hindering its progress. Capitalism tended towards the maintaining of inequalities between members of the community, and used the weapons of unemployment, monopolies, restricted production, and conspicuous waste, only to increase profits. In Veblen's view, capitalism would inevitably be succeeded by either socialism or a nationalistic militarism. He saw little hope in reform – change which tinkered with the capitalist system without radically altering it. In the view of many commentators, he underestimated the potential of a welfare state form of capitalism. But in the 1980s with what confidence may one argue that he was wholly wrong to do so?

In the end, of course, Veblen is important not as a prophet of the future of American society, but as an analyst of its present. Sometimes ponderous, sometimes witty, *The Theory of the Leisure Class* is a book of extraordinary and penetrating insight. Wielding language like a rough-toothed saw-blade, Veblen is able to cut through one assumption after another about American social attitudes and behaviour. The result is a book full of truths as uncomfortable today as they were in 1899. Beyond question, *The Theory of the Leisure Class* probes the economic, social, and cultural problems at the heart of American society in the period 1865–1900 more rigorously than any other single work. This it is that finally aligns Veblen with Henry George, Edward Bellamy, Henry Adams, Lester Ward, John Dewey and all those other intellectuals who saw in post-bellum America a major retreat from traditional human values, coupled with so great an intensifying of economic inequalities that even the principles of democracy themselves seemed to be under threat. The America that Veblen anatomized so corrosively is beautifully validated by a famous image: the figure of Henry Frick, an immensely rich steel magnate, seated within his splendid New York home on a superb Renaissance throne beneath a priceless Renaissance baldacchino, reading a copy of the *Saturday Evening Post*. Such a conjunction of financial power, leisure, conspicuous consumption, and tastelessness, is a perfect illustration of Veblen's *The Theory of the Leisure Class*.

Notes

1 This extract is taken from 'The Higher Learning as an Expression of the Pecuniary Culture', Chapter 14 of *The Theory of the Leisure Class, An Economic Study of Institutions*, London, 1924. All page references are to this edition.

2 Near the end of Chapter 5 in *Hawthorne* (1879), Henry James gives classic expression to this view. The Civil War, wrote James, produced 'a social

revolution as complete as any the world has seen'. It 'marks an era in the history of the American mind'. It 'introduced into the national consciousness a certain sense of proportion and relation, of the world being a more complicated place than it had hitherto seemed, the future more treacherous, success more difficult'. One might suggest that American literature in the period 1865–1900 is divided between writers who do or do not acknowledge and register this change.

3 See Joseph Dorfman, *Thorstein Veblen and His America*, London, 1935, p. 196.

4 Ward wrote that the style of Veblen's book was 'the farthest removed possible from either advocacy or vituperation and the language, to use the author's own words, is "morally colourless"'. See Dorfman, op. cit., p. 194.

5 For an excellent account of the conventional orthodoxy of the education to which Veblen was exposed at Carleton College – his experience would have been virtually the same at universities, colleges, or seminaries up and down the country – see Dorman, op. cit., pp. 17–29.

6 Dorfman, op. cit., p. 32.

7 ibid., p. 68.

Further reading

Joseph Dorfman, *Thorstein Veblen and His America*, London, 1935.

Carlton C. Qualey (ed.), *Thorstein Veblen, The Carleton College Veblen Seminar Essays*, New York and London, 1968.

14

Theodore Dreiser (1871–1945)

Mrs Hale loved to drive of an afternoon in the sun when it was fine and to satisfy her soul with a sight of those mansions and lawns which she could not afford. On the North Side had been erected a number of elegant mansions along what is now known as the North Shore Drive. The present lake wall of stone and granitoid was not then in place, but the road had been well laid out, the intermediate spaces of lawn were lovely to look upon and the houses were thoroughly new and imposing. When the winter season had passed and the first fine days of the early spring appeared, Mrs Hale secured a buggy for an afternoon and invited Carrie. They rode first through Lincoln Park and on far out toward Evanston, turning back at four and arriving at the north end of the Shore Drive at about five o'clock. At that time of year the days were still comparatively short and the shadows of the evening were beginning to settle down upon the great city. Lamps were beginning to burn with that mellow radiance which seems almost watery and translucent to the eye. There was a softness in the air which speaks with an infinite delicacy of feeling to the flesh as well as to the soul. Carrie felt that it was a lovely day. She was ripened by it in spirit for many suggestions. As they drove along the smooth pavement, an occasional carriage passed. She saw one stop and the footman dismount, opening the door for a gentleman who seemed to be leisurely returning from some afternoon pleasure. Across the broad lawns, now first freshening into green, she saw lamps faintly glowing upon rich interiors. Now it was but a chair, now a table, now an ornate corner which met her eye, but it appealed to her as almost nothing else could. Such childish fancies as she had had of fairy palaces and kingly quarters now came back. She imagined that across these richly carved entranceways where the globed and crystalled lamps shone upon paneled doors, set with stained and designed panes of glass, was neither care nor unsatisfied desire. She was perfectly certain that here was happiness. If she could but stroll up yon broad walk, cross that rich entranceway, which to her was of the beauty of a jewel, and sweep in grace and luxury to possession and command – oh! how quickly would sadness flee; how, of an instant, would the heart-aches end. She gazed and gazed, wondering, delighting, longing, and all the while the siren voice of the unrestful was whispering in her ear.

'If we could have such a home as that,' said Mrs Hale sadly, 'how delightful it would be.'

'And yet they do say,' said Carrie, 'that no one is ever happy.' She had heard so much of the canting philosophy of the grapeless fox.

'I notice,' said Mrs Hale, 'that they all try mighty hard, though, to take their misery in a mansion.'

When she came to her own rooms Carrie saw their comparative insignificance. She was not so dull but that she could perceive that they were but three small rooms in a moderately well-furnished boarding house. She was not contrasting it now with what she had had, but what she had so recently seen. The glow of the palatial doors was still in her eye, the roll of cushioned carriages still in her ears. What, after all, was Drouet? What was she? At her window she thought it over, rocking to and fro and gazing out across the lamplit park toward the lamplit houses on Warren Avenue and Ashland Boulevard. She was too wrought up to care to go down to eat, too pensive to do aught but rock and sing. Some old tunes crept to her lips and as she sang them her heart sank. She longed and longed and longed. It was now for the old cottage room in Columbia City, now the mansion up on the Shore Drive, now the fine dress of some lady, now the elegance of some scene. She was sad beyond measure and yet uncertain, wishing and fancying. Finally it seemed as if all her state was one of loneliness and foresakenness and she could scarce refrain from trembling at the lip. She hummed and hummed as the moments went by, sitting in the shadow by the window, and was therein as happy, though she could not perceive it, as ever she would be.

While Carrie was still in this frame of mind, the house servant brought up the intelligence that Mr Hurstwood was in the parlor asking to see Mr and Mrs Drouet.

Sister Carrie (1900)[1]

* * *

The most striking aspect of this extract is its emphasis upon things. The building-blocks of the passage are material objects: mansions, lawns, carriages, lamps, rooms, doors, furniture. The world evoked is an intensely and immediately tangible and physical one, which the allusions to the actual topography of Chicago enforce but in no way create. Yet, at the same time, Dreiser's prose lingers over the details of the scenes described in such a way that their solidity begins to fade, a 'mellow radiance' seems to invest the objects almost transmuting or dissolving their physicality into pure sentiment. The stable centre of Dreiser's fiction is always his sense of the immediate social realities of America, and of the material items, limited in range, but multifarious in form, which for him compose and define them. His approach, however, is rarely that of the social scientist; rather than remaining simply data, such items acquire meaning and value from the emotional needs they define or create in those who register them. In Dreiser's novels things become more than things; they become human needs or desires; they define hopes and aspirations; they measure existence and they are at the heart of the drama of life.

In this passage Dreiser himself, of course, is not directly present. The consciousness we are listening to is Sister Carrie's own; it is Carrie who is so responsive to the physical details of the world around her. What Dreiser is doing is offering us a sympathetic insight into Carrie's consciousness, letting us see the fundamental structures of feeling and impulse that make her the kind of person she is. Her discontent, her 'unrestfulness', her wistful longing and yearning, are the product of a particular vision of life: one that sees the ideal, the dream, always in terms of things which are just out of reach. To bring the ideal closer, to make the dream a reality, is the one over-riding motive that sustains the life that Dreiser charts for us in this novel. If the visionary ideal, as articulated here, strikes us as banal at best, meretricious at worst, that in no way necessarily undercuts the conviction or authority with which it is communicated to us through Dreiser's uncritical prose. The son of poor German immigrants, brought up in poverty, Dreiser is the first American writer to view the abundant materialism of late nineteenth-century America from within the perspective of the have-nots. His own early experience of unrelieved poverty and hardship thus made it impossible for him to be unsympathetic towards those whose aim in life was to rise above such conditions. *Sister Carrie* shocked its original readers (published in what was virtually a limited edition, it was effectively banned in 1900 and not reissued until 1907[2]) because it portrayed life in American society, directly and unambiguously, as a struggle or contest in which the individual might, or might not, chance to survive. As a result, almost without intending it – because he wrote of experience as he saw it rather than according to any kind of literary ideology – Dreiser exposed the enormous gulf between the conventions of orthodox morality and the realities of life as these were experienced by the urban masses in America. Realism, as a new literary mode, had been practised and defended by William Dean Howells and his supporters partly on the grounds that it provided a moral corrective to the absurd excesses of a morally idealizing, romantic fiction. In Dreiser's often clumsy hands, realism, by accident or design, became a tool for undermining the orthodox moral assumptions which still underpinned official, American culture.

*

Mrs Hale, Carrie's companion in this passage, is a minor character in the novel. She is a neighbour, the wife of a theatre manager and, like almost all the characters in the novel with whom Carrie establishes friendly relations, she embodies a way of life which Carrie regards as somehow finer and more fulfilling than her own. As the opening of the passage indicates, however, Mrs Hale, despite her own apparently comfortable way of life, is deeply drawn by images of wealth and power in American society that far transcend anything that she herself possesses. She loves to gaze appreciatively, we are told, at the newly-erected mansions on what will become North Shore Drive. Dreiser's own presence here, as omniscient author, is revealing in the sense that the comparison he draws between 'then' and 'now' clearly indicates his own complicity in Mrs Hale's admiration. That 'the present lake wall of stone and granitoid' (presumably some form of imitation granite) was 'not then in place' is made to sound like a drawback, though one compensated for by the 'well laid out' road, the 'lovely' lawns, and the houses which demand admiration simply because they are 'thoroughly new' and 'imposing'. The innocent eye that is present here, one must repeat, is as much Dreiser's as Mrs Hale's.

As the extract moves towards an evocation of Carrie's own response to the mansions on Shore Drive, Dreiser begins the process by which the physical objects gradually dissolve into the sentimental fancies that Carrie creates around them. It is early evening, the light is failing, the air is soft, the lamps cast a 'mellow radiance'; the appeal of the scene is to the 'flesh' as well as to the 'soul'. The natural world speaks insidiously to the material dimension of human nature. Carrie responds positively to the delicate seductiveness of the scene; she 'felt that it was a lovely day'. The banality of that feeling, however, should this time be ascribed to Carrie herself rather than to Dreiser; it is exactly what his character would feel. Carrie is uneducated, uncultured, sensitively aware of her own emotional needs and longings, but deprived of a language with which to articulate them. She could have said no more than that it was a lovely day. It is the author, of course, who tells us that she was 'ripened by it in spirit for many suggestions' – a description in which, despite the reference to the spirit, the concerns of the flesh seem to dominate over those of the soul. In any event, the rest of this paragraph defines the nature of what these 'suggestions' are. The objects in view are all infinitely appealing doorways into a world of richness and splendour: the gentleman, the lawns, the lamp, the chair, the table, the ornate corner, are all real enough, but for Carrie they speak of another, higher reality. Inevitably, into her naive consciousness come images of fairy-tale kings and palaces. The image of a doorway into another world emerges directly with the specific references to the 'richly carved entrance-ways', the 'panelled doors', the 'broad walk' and the 'rich entrance-way'. The essential characteristics of that other world are on the one hand a richly romantic materiality – the entrance-ways 'richly carved', the 'globed and crystalled lamps', the 'panelled doors', stained glass, and broad walks – and on the other, a freedom from care and the heartache of unsatisfied longings. Carrie imagines herself 'strolling' through this door, imitating the movement of the gentleman she has just seen 'leisurely returning' from some afternoon pleasure, and entering into possession of all the luxurious beauty; it is characteristic that she should liken the 'rich entrance-way' to a 'jewel', comparing one material possession to another. But it is here too that one can see Dreiser distancing himself somewhat from his heroine: it is only 'to her' that the door is like a jewel. And of course it is also only 'to her' that the world of riches and material splendours appears a world of carefree happiness. Yet the paragraph ends by underlining the fascination that the vision of this world of conspicuous consumption and luxury, with its promise of an end to sadness and yearning, exercises upon Carrie. She is reluctant to turn away; she seems to relish her absorption in the scene; she 'gazed and gazed, wondering, delighting, longing . . .', possessed by emotions that she cannot as yet satisfy.

In the brief exchange that follows, Dreiser's own sympathies are once again made abundantly clear. Carrie's allusion to a conventional piece of homely wisdom on the subject of happiness is dismissed as 'canting philosophy'. It is Mrs Hale here who voices what has clearly been Dreiser's own observation of the advantages brought by wealth.

The second half of the extract is concerned with Carrie's reactions to the contrast between the world she has been looking on at, and the world in which she actually lives. For Carrie the difference is defined by measuring house against house, room against room. The contrast is enough to spark off a train, not so much of rational thought, as of conscious feelings of dissatisfied longings. Seated in her rocking-chair, looking out at the lamps in the park and the houses, humming old tunes, her feelings, like her gaze, carry her away from the limitations of her house and room to more desirable, but unattainable goals. Out there, somewhere, is the object of her desires, which she can only visualize as something to possess: the mansion on Shore Drive, the 'fine dress', the 'elegance of some scene'. Because her dreams seem unattainable, she feels lonely, forsaken, isolated, in the gathering darkness of her room. Dreiser succeeds beautifully here in conveying a sense of Carrie's emotional state, of her unfulfilled desires and uncertain longings. The vision of wealth and luxury, displayed by the mansions of the Shore Drive, she has found simultaneously seductive and disturbing; she longs desperately, even obsessively, for the happiness, the end to care and anxiety, which she believes the world of wealth and ease represents; but she can see no way of gaining entry, of passing through the door into that world, which must therefore remain a dream, a lamp shining in the surrounding darkness.

*

Dreiser tells us that at this moment, sitting musing in her rocking-chair, Carrie is as happy 'as ever she would be'. What he means is that it is impossible that Carrie's hopes and dreams and yearnings should ever be fulfilled. In Dreiser's view that is what life is like. Carrie may advance towards her goal; but each advance simply reveals a further road to travel. In fact, in the story of her life that Dreiser is charting, Carrie Meeber has already made some progress. Aged eighteen, she has left a small mid-Western town and come to the great city of Chicago. In the extract, towards the end, she momentarily longs for 'the old cottage room in Columbia City': she longs for it because that room was home, and therefore provided her at least with the untroubled security she has not found in Chicago. She had left Columbia City dreaming, dreaming of a better life in Chicago. But the reality of the city quickly shattered that dream: life with her sister and her husband proves cramped, dull, and miserable, monotonous, devoid of pleasure. Carrie's search for a job in the city is a difficult and intimidating experience, which shatters her self-confidence. Work, when it is finally found, is constant, unremitting toil, which exhausts her physically and soon undermines her health. Too ill to work, and therefore no longer able to pay her way at her sister's, she is before long facing the prospect of returning, defeated, to Columbia City. Dreiser's wholly sympathetic account of these events, brilliant in its constant suggestion of the felt harshness of urban life for the weak and the poor, makes it entirely explicable that Carrie should instead find herself set up in rooms in a boarding-house, living with Drouet, the smart, well-dressed, knowledgeable salesman she had met originally on the train, during her journey to Chicago. In the extract, Dreiser emphasizes that the contrast which is disturbing Carrie is that between her 'three small rooms' and the mansions she has seen; it is not the contrast, that is, between her present rooms and 'what she had had'. The point is of course that after her sister's mean apartment, her soul- and body-destroying job, indeed her entire experience of city life, her three rooms, Drouet, and what he has to offer, represent a great advance. Restaurant meals, smart clothes, her own rooms: Drouet's ready money transforms the material circumstances of Carrie's life. Her dream seems attainable after all. As the passage we have been examining makes clear, however, Carrie's satisfaction in the life she has undertaken with Drouet is short-lived. 'What, after all, was Drouet?' The answer, as Carrie begins to realize, is that Drouet, for all his good-heartedness, his easy manners, his salesman's ready bonhomie, is essentially a lightweight, commonplace figure. Drouet's limitations become particularly evident when measured by the standard of the Mr Hurstwood who, the extract ends by telling us, is downstairs asking to see Mr and Mrs Drouet.

Hurstwood seems at first to represent the next stage in Carrie's material progress. He is an altogether more powerful and substantial figure than Drouet. The manager of a high-class city bar, he is a solidly respectable citizen, whose job brings him into contact with a wide range of Chicago's social élite. Married, with two grown-up children, he has all the weight and presence that Drouet lacks. That weight and presence also help to give depth and substance to *Sister Carrie* as a novel. Carrie herself is drawn with immense skill and sympathetic understanding; yet one may doubt whether, in isolation, she could have provided Dreiser with a sufficiently rich and rewarding focus for the kind of book about American society he certainly wished to write. The theme of the young and innocent country girl, driven by the harsh necessities of urban life to yield to the temptation represented by a man like Drouet, is effectively over by the end of the eighth chapter. For her to become the mistress of a different man is inherently a less interesting subject, and there is a further problem in that the sensibility and understanding allowed to Carrie – as the extract reveals – is not of a kind to permit very much in the way of further development.

What Dreiser does in this situation is to allow Carrie's half-understood sentiments of longing and desire to express themselves in aesthetic form: Carrie becomes a successful actress. What makes her a success, however, is no more than a capacity to communicate to an audience something of those hopes and yearnings that she herself has always experienced. Her face, we learn, expresses all the world's longing. 'The world is always struggling to express itself – to make clear its hopes and sorrows and give them voice,' she is told by Ames, who is Dreiser's version of a man of culture. 'That is why we have great musicians, great painters, great writers and actors. They have the ability to express the world's sorrows and longings, and the world gets up and shouts their names.' Carrie, Ames suggests, is no more than a medium, 'through which something is expressing itself' (p. 485). This then is the explanation of Carrie's success: by communicating in art precisely the kind of sentiments she experienced while gazing at the Shore Drive mansions, by encouraging an audience to equate their illusions with hers, Carrie can win through into the world of material comfort and luxury. Not of course that she finds happiness. Ames tells her that she must devote her talents now to the higher world of serious drama. And at the end of the novel Carrie is once again in her rocking-chair, still dreaming of a happiness she 'may never feel'.[3]

This account of Carrie's life, however, is less than fair to the undoubted power of *Sister Carrie*. The story of the protagonist's rise to fame and fortune gains immeasurably from the context in which it occurs: the story of the parallel fall – from security, public respectability, and esteem, to a nameless grave in Potter's Field – of the Mr Hurstwood who is waiting downstairs at the end of the extract. Dreiser's successful creation and communication of Carrie's restless longings and desires springs from the fact that he had experienced precisely these feelings himself. In the autobiographical *Book About Myself* (1922) he wrote:

> I doubt if any human being, however poetic or however material ever looked upon the scenes of this world, material or spiritual, so called,

> with a more covetous eye. My body was blazing with sex, as well as with a desire for material and social supremacy.

As a personal statement, this is more direct and explicit than anything in the novel, but its relevance is clear. Carrie acts out Dreiser's own psychic history. The story of Hurstwood's decline and fall, on the other hand, taps other, perhaps deeper, areas of Dreiser's inner being: his fear of failure, of going under, of finally sinking into the abyss of poverty and degradation. In the 1890s Dreiser read Herbert Spencer and the experience, as he said, blew him 'intellectually to bits'. Dreiser, that is, accepted the view that human society participated in exactly the same evolutionary struggle as occurred in the natural and animal worlds. Under the influence of Spencer and T. H. Huxley, he came to see, he wrote, that 'man was a mechanism, undevised and uncreated, and a badly and carelessly driven one at that'. What he saw day by day in his work as a journalist simply confirmed the vision of life he had discovered in the philosophy he was reading. What one finds in Dreiser, in other words, is the theory of Social Darwinism given authentic fictional life. Dreiser may stand for all those Americans who accepted a Social Darwinist point of view, not because they welcomed or approved of it, but because they felt it was true. It accurately described the world they saw around them. For Dreiser there were no alternative systems of belief, no past or traditional faith to which to turn. Literary causes or programmes did not concern him. To see man and society as engaged in a naturalistic struggle for survival was simply to see them as they were.

All such views crowd together in the picture of society offered by *Sister Carrie*. The individual is shown to be the more or less helpless victim of forces beyond his control. He is driven by passions within his own nature, or by events and circumstances in the outside world. What the individual is not capable of, is that independent, conscious moral choice, so crucial to orthodox and traditional beliefs. Carrie does not choose to give herself to Drouet; circumstances combine to bring her to that position. Hurstwood does not choose to become a thief; circumstances – and chance – combine to make it happen. In conventional moral terms, Carrie and Hurstwood are equally culpable, but Carrie's fortunes rise, while those of Hurstwood decline. For Dreiser, the one fate is no more deserved or understandable than the other. In the naturalistic universe, chance it is that reigns supreme. But most powerful and telling of all – and this is how the Hurstwood story immensely deepens and toughens the meaning of *Sister Carrie* – is Dreiser's evocation of an entire social world that is heartless, pitiless, and cruelly unconcerned about the fate of the unfortunate individual; a world in which the game is to the strong, the winner takes all, and the loser is left to his fate. If this, as Dreiser implies, is the true nature of reality, perhaps it is not surprising that the inner world of the individual consciousness should be given over to Carrie-like dreams and delusions.

It is then through Hurstwood's fate that Dreiser is able to explore the sinister and fearful nightmare created by the dark side of the same social realities that occasion Carrie's world of wistful longings. The kind of man that Hurstwood is, at the point when he calls on Mr and Mrs Drouet at the end of the extract, is best communicated by the subsequent, superb Chapter 18. Carrie's acting career is to be launched by her part in an amateur production put on in Chicago. Hurstwood, already pursuing her, is determined that a large and important audience will be there to watch. Thus, with the utmost social subtlety and skill, he manipulates all his friends, contacts and associates in Chicago's upper circles, so as to ensure a suitable audience. Unbeknown to all, he orchestrates the entire affair so that the evening becomes a spectacular success. It is Hurstwood's finest hour, and shows him as the kind of man who always fascinated Dreiser: successful, powerful, wholly in control. In later novels, such as *The Financier* (1912) and *The Titan* (1914), his admiration for such men leads him to make a hero out of the American businessman tycoon, however ruthless and morally corrupt he might seem. Here in *Sister Carrie*, perhaps more interestingly, it is the tragic disintegration of such a character that we witness and pity.

Hurstwood's desire for Carrie leads him into a disastrous breach with his wife and family, all of whom are devastatingly sketched by Dreiser as cocooned by their social position, unfeeling and totally selfish. Threatened with divorce proceedings and the certain loss of almost all his financial resources, Hurstwood finds himself tempted by ten thousand dollars in the safe in his office which has been accidentally left open. It is a remarkable scene. Hurstwood takes the money out of the safe, thinks about it, but decides that he cannot sacrifice his standing and reputation. He puts the dollar bills back. He then remembers that he has returned the money to the wrong boxes, so takes it out again to corrrect this mistake. This time the safe happens to click shut while he has the bills still in his hands. Chance has made up his mind for him. Dreiser found this scenario so appealing, so consonant with his vision of life, that he was to duplicate it in *An American Tragedy* (1925), often considered his most successful novel. The protagonist of the later novel decides to murder his pregnant mistress; he takes her boating on a lake; his nerve fails, but the boat overturns 'accidentally' and the girl is left to drown. In *Sister Carrie*, Hurstwood flees from Chicago to Canada with the money – and Carrie. From this point on his life slowly collapses around him. His prestige and reputation as a man of solid worth, his easy familiarity with the famous and powerful who patronized his establishment in Chicago, all these are lost to him. His life, as a result, is pitifully diminished. Even after he is no longer a fugitive from justice – he sends back most of the stolen money – and is able to begin a new life in New York, there is no real recovery. His name is gone (he becomes Mr Wheeler) and the spiral downwards continues. He uses most of his remaining capital in acquiring a partnership in a New York bar – but one entirely lacking the class of his establishment in Chicago – and for a year or two Carrie and he manage to survive in New York reasonably well. A piece of sharp business practice, however, leads to the loss of the bar, and Hurstwood is left with only a few hundred dollars. Out of a job, he tramps the streets of New York, gradually lowering his sights over the kind of job he will take on, and finally accepting employment of an increasingly degrading kind. As his money dwindles away, more and more it is Carrie, now slowly rising in the theatrical world, who provides the money on which they live. But, inevitably, as Carrie prospers, and Hurstwood becomes less and less recognizable as the confident figure of power and authority who had impressed her in Chicago, the two grow apart, until Carrie finally abandons him. Soon, homeless and penniless, Hurstwood becomes one of those social outcasts who haunt the shadows of New York City. He becomes the authentic inhabitant of that other, failed America, the America of poverty, not progress, which George, Bellamy, Howells, Garland, Norris and Crane all recognized, but could not create with imaginative fullness.

In his account of Hurstwood's decline, Dreiser's often prosaic prose is at its finest. As the materials of human life become more and more difficult to obtain – when the figure who once presided with such presence over a fashionable Chicago bar is reduced to begging in the streets or standing in the bread line with the rest of society's pitiful rejects – so Hurstwood becomes an increasingly powerful and haunting image of the cruelty and unconcern that lies at the centre of the struggle for survival which is what human existence becomes in an indifferent universe. Even more than Carrie herself, Hurstwood occupies the thematic centre of *Sister Carrie*. At the end of the novel, Carrie is able to retreat into her world of dreams and illusions. Hurstwood is destroyed by the reality she has escaped. Compared with the power and threat of that reality, the higher culture that Ames is meant to embody appears as more than a little threadbare.

Of all the writers we have looked at, Dreiser is the one most clearly the product of the times in which he grew up, the one for whom the notion of an American past has least meaning. Dreiser knows nothing of an older America with different traditions and values. For Whitman, freedom, democracy and the rights of man remained central to the meaning of America; for Dreiser such ideals have ceased to exist, swept away by the tide of an apparently scientific naturalism. For Whitman in 1865 the dream of America is still the dream of 1776; for Dreiser in 1900 the only dream is the dream of survival and success in the land of opportunity, the only reality, the bustling streets of Chicago and New York, the America that is the product of the rapid and ruthless economic expansion which, by the end of the nineteenth century, had indeed transformed the American world. As a result, Dreiser's fiction portrays and accepts the America against which all the other writers in this volume implicitly or explicitly speak out. But in recreating in massive and compelling detail this new, essentially urban, America, and delineating its overwhelming impact upon the individual struggling to live within it, Dreiser in 1900 was heralding a major dimension of twentieth-century American writing.

Notes

1 The text of the extract from Chapter 13 of *Sister Carrie* is taken from the Penguin reproduction of the so-called 'unexpurgated' University of Pennsylvania Press edition of 1981. This text is based on Dreiser's manuscript, which was considerably modified in the 1900, and subsequent editions. As it happens, however, the text of the extract itself hardly differs from the version appearing in all earlier editions.

2 Dreiser had submitted his novel to the firm of Doubleday, for which Frank Norris was a reader, because he was a great admirer of Norris's *McTeague* which Doubleday had published. Norris read Dreiser's manuscript, admired it enormously, and recommended its publication. Other members of the publishing house agreed, but Frank Doubleday himself was away when the decision to publish was taken. On his return, he decided that the book was 'immoral', and did everything in his power to ensure it should receive as little attention and publicity as possible. For a fuller account of the circumstances surrounding the publication of *Sister Carrie*, and the kind of changes made in Dreiser's manuscript, see Alfred Kazin's Introduction to the Penguin edition.

3 These are the closing words of the 1900 and subsequent editions. The Penguin/Pennsylvania edition, however, ends earlier with the suicide of Hurstwood. The latter ending rather reinforces the points I now go on to make about the significance of Hurstwood's role in the novel.

Further reading

Alfred Kazin and Charles Shapiro (eds), *The Stature of Theodore Dreiser*, Bloomington, 1955.

Donald Pizer, *The Novels of Theodore Dreiser: A Critical Study*, Minneapolis, 1976.

Index

NOTE: individual works are entered under their authors.

Adams, Henry, 189
agriculture, *see* farming
Aldrich, Thomas Bailey, 65
Amherst, Mass., 61–2, 64, 66, 67
anarchy, 97, 111, 118
Anderson, Sherwood, 124, 125
Appleton, D. & Company, 26, 31, 34
Astor, John Jacob, 3
Atlantic Monthly, 87, 112

Beattie, James, 187
Beecher, Henry Ward, 5
Bellamy, Edward, 6, 33, 100–14, 180, 181–2, 189, 201
  and brotherly love, 107–8
  on competition, 106, 112
  critics and, 110, 112–13
  and environment, 106–7
  and evolution, 107
  influence of, 110
  language, 104–5, 180
  Looking Backward, 36, 102–10, 112, 113, 188
  and new fiction, 108–9
  protest in, 105–6, 107
  utopian vision, 103, 106, 113
best-sellers, 6, 37, 86–7, 109–10
Boker, George, 65
Boswell, James, 96
Brönte family, 62
Browning, Elizabeth Barrett, 62
Browning, Robert, 62
Bryan, William Jennings, 105, 110
Bryant, William Cullen, 62
Burns, Robert, 146
Burroughs, John, 14
business world:
  monopolies in, 107
  values, 4–5, 91, 92–4

Cable, George Washington, 117
Calvinism, 80, 146
capitalism, 5, 33, 107, 112, 188–9
Carlyle, Thomas, 109
Carnegie, Andrew, 3
Century, The (Scribner's Monthly), 7
Chamberlain, Joseph, 35
change:
  inevitability of, 96
  social, 1–4, 6, 36, 96, 110–12, 152–3
Chase, Richard, 21
Chicago, anarchist attack, 97, 111, 119
Chopin, Kate, 165–77
  Awakening, The, 165–77
  evolution in, 176
  and freedom, 175, 176
  pessimism, 176

Chopin, Kate—*cont.*
sea in, 171–3
short stories, 177
Civil War, 22, 61
and atavism, 183
cause, 86
and change, 1
and glory, 136
idealism, 19, 20, 21
and realism, 7
Clark, John Bates, 187
competition, 106, 107, 112, 188
Conrad, Joseph, 139, 140, 145
conservatism, 2, 7
Conwell, Russell, 5
Crane, Stephen, 66, 74, 95, 129–42, 145, 162, 163, 201
art and life, 139
Maggie, A Girl of the Streets, 138, 139, 141
man as animal, 131
'Open Boat, The', 140, 141
poetry, 140
and realism, 140–1, 157, 160
Red Badge of Courage, The, 130–8, 139, 140, 141, 157, 175
short stories, 140
and sincerity, 139, 140
war imagery, 133, 134, 163
culture, American, 52–3, 54
and social change, 4–5, 6–7, 66–7

Darwin, Charles, 5, 31, 32, 96, 147, 164
Debs, Eugene, 110
determinism, 159, 162, 164
Dewey, John, 110, 189
Dickens, Charles, 6, 62
Dickinson, Emily, 56–68, 140
change in, 56, 57, 59
death in, 60
imagination, 64
interests, 61, 62, 63
isolation, 61–3, 64
modernism, 67
nature in, 66
quaintness, 66
reality, 63–4, 66–7
untitled poem 585, 63
untitled poem 1422, 59–60
untitled poem 1540, 56–9, 60–1
discontent, social, 28, 36, 110–12
Donne, John, 65
Donoghue, Denis, 64
Dos Passos, John, 1
Doubleday, publishers, 162
Dreiser, Theodore, 74, 191–203
American Tragedy, An, 200
Book About Myself, 198
and business world, 92–3, 200
cruelty in, 200
determinism, 199
and fulfillment, 196–7, 198–9
materialism, 193
and new America, 202
realism, 194
Sister Carrie, 162, 176, 191–202
Social Darwinism, 199

economic growth, 3–4
Edgeworth, Maria, 117
Eliot, George, 62
Emerson, Ralph Waldo, 7, 19, 62, 65, 113
employment, 2–3
entertainment, 88–9
Europe and America, 52–3
Evolutionism, 5, 32, 96–7, 107, 118, 163, 164

Farmers' Alliance, 106, 110
farming, 2, 3–4, 110–11, 117, 119, 125–6
Faulkner, William, 116
fiction, *see* romantic fiction
Fielding, Henry, 96

Fiske, John, 5, 96, 164
Fitzgerald, F. Scott, 153
Frederic, Harold, 95, 143–53
  Damnation of Theron Ware, The, 145–53, 175
  and the future, 152–3
  In the Valley, 151
  Market-Place, The, 151
  and realism, 145, 151, 152, 160
  and religion, 145, 148, 152
  Seth's Brother's Wife, 151
  symbolism in, 149–50
Frick, Henry, 189

Garland, Hamlin, 115–28, 162, 201
  and American Dream, 127, 201
  art and life, 120–1
  and author's role, 121–2
  and Crane, 139, 140–1
  Crumbling Idols, 122
  and evolution, 118, 127–8
  and George, 35, 127–8
  and local colour, 118, 119
  Main-Travelled Roads, 116–17, 119, 120–8
  and the novel, 120
  realism, 97, 117–18, 120, 121, 128
  'Up the Coulé', 115–16, 117, 122–7
  veritism, 121–2, 140
George, Henry, 6, 24–37, 180, 181–2, 189, 201
  and competition, 32–3
  economic theory, 30–2, 36, 128
  and heridity, 33
  influence of, 34–7
  and land, 27, 30
  and poverty, 29–30, 201
  Progress and Poverty, 26–9, 30, 31–3, 34–7, 110, 113, 127, 183, 188
  and social change, 28, 29
Gilded Age, 21, 184
Gissing, George, 145
Grange movement, 110
Grant, Ulysses S., 21

Hardie, Keir, 35
Hardy, Thomas, 6
Harper's Monthly, 6–7, 87, 88, 95, 110
Harris, Joel Chandler, 117
Harte, Bret, 117
Harvard poets, 65
Hawthorne, Nathaniel, 19, 49, 52, 62, 65, 150, 160
  House of the Seven Gables, 63
  Marble Faun, The, 42
Haymarket affair, 97, 111, 119
Hemingway, Ernest, 116
Herbert, George, 65
Herne, James A., 126
Higginson, T. W., 60, 61
Holland, J. G., 5
Holmes, Oliver Wendell, 7, 65
Homestead Act 1862, 125
Hopkins, Gerard Manley, 61, 66
Howe, Edgar Watson, 119–20, 145
Howells, William Dean, 84–99, 108, 118, 201
  Annie Kilburn, 118
  art and life, 86, 98, 120
  and Bellamy, 110, 113
  and business world, 92–4
  and Crane, 139, 140–1
  and critics, 88–9, 95
  and Garland, 118
  and George, 35, 113
  and Haymarket affair, 97, 111, 118
  Hazard of New Fortunes, A, 97–8, 113
  influence of, 95
  and James, 53–4
  and morality, 81, 86, 89, 93, 108
  and Norris, 162

Howells, William Dean—*cont.*
realism, 7–8, 53, 54, 81, 86, 90, 92, 94–7, 158, 160, 194
Rise of Silas Lapham, The, 85–95, 103
and romantic fiction, 85–90, 108, 120
and self-sacrifice, 86, 87, 89–90, 92, 93, 95
and Veblen, 183
Hume, David, 187
Huxley, T. H., 187, 199

idealism:
American, 20, 21, 31, 54
in romantic fiction, 89, 92, 95
idealization, *see* romantic fiction
immigration, 2, 3, 111
industrialization, 3
industrial unrest, 28, 36, 110–12

James, Henry, 38–55, 139, 145
Ambassadors, The, 48
American, The, 51
Americans in, 47, 50–1, 54
aristocratic life in, 46–7
and the artist, 52, 98
consciousness in, 40–1, 43, 47
Daisy Miller, 51
egotism in, 44, 45–6
in Europe, 9, 52–3
Europeans, The, 51
and freedom, 42–3, 44–5, 48, 50, 51, 52, 54, 82
Hawthorne, 52–3
internationalism, 50–1, 61
loss in, 52
Portrait of a Lady, The, 40–50, 51–2, 54, 175
realism, 40
Roderick Hudson, 50–1
and tradition, 43–4, 53
James, William, 40
Jefferson, Thomas, 22
Jewett, Sarah Orne, 117
Johnson, Samuel, 96
Johnson, Thomas H., 56

Keats, John, 12
Kegan Paul, publishers, 34

Labour Party, British, 34–5
Ladies' Home Journal, 109
land, 27, 30, 128
legislation, 125
Lawrence, D. H., 160
Lewis, R. W. B., 21
Lewis, Sinclair, 145
Lincoln, Abraham, 11, 12, 13–14, 15, 16–17, 21, 22
literary taste, 6–7, 87, 189
local colour movement, 117–18, 177
Lodge, George Cabot, 65
Longfellow, Henry Wadsworth, 7
Lowell, James Russell, 7, 62, 65

McCosh, James, 164
McKinley, President, 110
magazines, popular, 6–7
Malthus, Thomas, 32
Marx, Karl, 31, 33
materialism, 54
Matthiessen, F. L., 19
Melville, Herman, 12, 19
Methodism, 147, 148, 151
Mill, John Stuart, 27
Milton, John, 18
monopolies, 107
Moody, William Vaughn, 65
morality: and romantic fiction, 81, 86, 88, 108
and social change, 4–5
Morris, William, 35, 113

Nationalist movement, 110
naturalism, 36, 67, 106, 157–9, 160–1, 199, 202
New England, dominance, 7, 62, 64

New Nation, 110
New York school of poets, 65
Nordeau, Max, 163
Norris, Frank, 74, 95, 154–64, 201
  conflict and violence, 157, 162
  and evolution, 163
  freedom, 161–2
  McTeague, 154–7, 159–63
  naturalism, 157–9, 160, 162, 163
  Octopus, The, 159, 163–4
  and realism, 158, 159–60, 164
  and romance, 158–9, 164
  symbolism, 160
Norton, Charles Eliot, 7
novels, *see* romantic fiction

optimism, 106–7

Party of Hope, 21, 31
Peabody, Elizabeth, 35
Pellow, George, 97
People's Health Journal, 109
Perry, Thomas Sergeant, 97
pessimism, 83
philosophy:
  conservative, 187
  and novels, 87
  and social change, 4–6
Poe, Edgar Allan, 62
poetry, American, 19–20, 21–2, 61–2, 65–6
population explosion, 2–3
Populist party, 110
Pound, Ezra, 19
poverty, 28, 29–30, 201
protest, and social change, 4, 8, 97
Protestantism, 152
Puritanism, 64, 65, 80

realism, 7–9, 36, 96
  and critics, 177
  fluidity of, 67, 118
  and freedom, 106
  and inwardness, 54
  and local colour, 117–18
  optimistic, 106–7
  pessimistic, 83
  and romantic fiction, 88, 95
  see also individual writers
regionalism, literary, 117–18, 177
Reid, Thomas, 187
religion, 80, 145, 148, 152
  and social change, 4–5
revolution, 107, 109
Robinson, Edgar Arlington, 66
romantic fiction, 6, 7, 8
  falsity, 81, 86, 88, 108
  and realism, 158
rural life, 145, 151

Scott, Walter, 86, 117
Shaw, George Bernard, 34–5, 145
Shelley, P. B., 27
short stories, 116–17, 120
Sinclair, Upton, 110
small town life, 145, 151
Smith, Adam, 31
Snowden, Philip, 35
social change, 1–4, 6, 36, 96, 110–12, 152–3
Social Darwinism, 32, 33, 54, 199
Southworth, Mrs E. D. E. N., 7
Spencer, Herbert, 5–6, 31, 33, 34, 55
  influence of, 32, 96, 118, 127, 187, 199
Stedman, E. C., 65, 66
Stein, Gertrude, 3
Stevens, Wallace, 59
Stevenson, R. L., 74
Stewart, Dugald, 187
Stickney, Trumbull, 65
Stoddard, Richard, 65
Stowe, Harriet Beecher, 117
'stream of consciousness', 40
strikes, 28, 36, 110–12
Symonds, J. A., 74

Taft, Charles S., 14
Taft, Julia, 14
Taine, Hippolyte, 96
taste, literary, 6–7, 87, 189
Taylor, Bayard, 65
Tennyson, Alfred, Lord, 98, 113
Thomas, Norman, 110
Thoreau, Henry David, 63
Tolstoy, Leo, 6
traditionalism, 2, 6, 7
Transcendentalism, 5, 65, 87
Trollope, Anthony, 47
Twain, Mark, 6, 69–83, 117
  Adventures of Huckleberry Finn, The, 71–3, 74–83, 86, 175
  Connecticut Yankee at the Court of King Arthur, A, 82–3
  and conscience, 73, 74–7, 80
  contradictions of, 82
  and language, 80–1, 86, 98
  pessimism, 83
  Pudd'nhead Wilson, 74
  and reality, 80, 81, 82, 83
  satire, 82–3
  social environment, 73–4, 77, 81–2
  and Southern society, 77, 78–9, 80, 82, 86

unions, 111
urbanization, 3
utopian fiction, 109

values, and social change, 4, 7
Veblen, Thorstein, 178–90
  and atavistic trends, 178, 182–3, 184–6
  and Bellamy, 110, 180, 188, 189
  and capitalism, 188–9
  on competition, 188
  and critics, 183
  detachment, 180, 181, 182, 183–4
  and George, 35–6, 180, 188, 189
  irony, 180–1
  language, 181, 189
  philosophy, 187–8
  and the sciences, 181, 185
  and Spencer, 187
  Theory of the Leisure Class, The, 27, 178–89
veritism, 121–2, 140
Veron, Eugene, 122
violence, 28, 97, 110–12
Vonnegut, Kurt, 102

Walker, Francis A., 36, 112–13
Wallace, Lew, 86–7
Ward, Elizabeth, 7
Ward, Lester, 183, 189
Warner, Charles Dudley, 83
Warner, Susan, 7
wealth, 3, 5, 112, 186
Webb, Beatrice, 34
Webb, Sidney, 34
Wells, H. G., 139, 145
Whitman, Walt, 10–23, 62, 65, 118, 151
  Backward Glance O'er Travel'd Roads, A, 19
  Democratic Vistas, 21
  Drum-Taps, 12–13
  Leaves of Grass, 11–13, 19, 20, 21
  and Lincoln, 13–14, 16–17, 20
  and new America, 19–21, 22, 61, 64, 202
  'Out of the Cradle Endlessly Rocking', 14, 15
  poetry as process, 12
  private life, 62
  Specimen Days, 13
  'When Lilacs Last in the Dooryard Bloom'd', 11, 12, 13, 14–18, 21–2
Whittier, J. G., 7, 65
Winters, Yvor, 59, 63

women writers, 176
workers, social conditions, 28, 110–12

Youmans, E. L., 32

Zola, Emile, 158–9, 163